Case Studies in Knowledge Management Research

Edited by

Kenneth A. Grant

Case Studies in Knowledge Management Research
Volume One
Copyright 2011 © The authors

First published December 2011 by
Academic Publishing International Ltd, Reading, UK
http://www.academic-publishing.org
info@academic-publishing.org

ISBN: 978-1-908272-26-3

Note to readers.
Some papers have been written by authors who use the American form of spelling and some use the British. These two different approaches have been left unchanged.

Printed by in the UK.

List of Contributors

Pierre Barbaroux, Research Center of the French Air Force, Defense and Knowledge Management Department, France

Peter Balafas, HBOS (formerly of the Danwood Group), Edinburgh, UK

Zuraina Dato Mansor, University Putra Malaysia, Selangor, Malaysia

Ray Dawson, Loughborough University, Loughborough, UK

Monica De Carolis, University of Calabria, Rende, Italy

Cécile Godé-Sanchez, Research Center of the French Air Force, Defense and Knowledge Management Department, France

Kenneth A. Grant, Ryerson University, Toronto, Canada

Jie Gu, The Hong Kong Polytechnic University, HKSAR, China

Matt Hinton, The Open University Business School, Milton Keynes, UK

Manasa Kakulavarapu, Wipro Technologies, Bangalore, India

Dinar Kale, The Open University Business School, Milton Keynes, UK

Hans Koolmees, Zuyd University of Applied Sciences, Heerlen, The Netherlands

Rongbin W.B. Lee, The Hong Kong Polytechnic University, HKSAR, China

Stephen Little, The Open University Business School, Milton Keynes, UK

Cherie C.Y. Lui, The Hong Kong Polytechnic University, HKSAR, China

Jesús Martínez, Center for Legal Studies and Specialist Training, Generalitat, Government of Catalonia, Spain

Mario Pérez-Montoro, Department of Library and Information Science, University of Barcelona, Spain

Ved Prakash Wipro Technologies, Bangalore, India

Judi Sandrock, University of Pretoria, South Africa

Sylvia Schoenmakers, Zuyd University of Applied Sciences, Heerlen, The Netherlands

Henk Smeijsters, Zuyd University of Applied Sciences, Heerlen, The Netherlands

Peter Tobin, University of Pretoria, South Africa

Saverino Verteramo, University of Calabria, Rende, Italy

i

Contents

Contents

Case Studies in Knowledge Management Research

Introduction to Cases Studies in Knowledge Management Research

1. The Discipline of Knowledge Management

There is little doubt that Knowledge Management (KM) is regarded as an important issue. It is recognized in academe as a field of study of some considerable import and this is evidenced by the number of journals and conferences that focus on this subject. It is also an issue on which many organisations have invested considerable sums, with quite varied results.

To demonstrate the very high level of interest in KM, I recently carried out a bibliometric examination of KM-related publication from 1999 to 2009, using the ProQuest database. Over this 20 year period, I found almost 26,000 citations for "knowledge management", with a consistent level of interest at around 1,500 citations a year for the last five years and strong interest being shown in both trade and scholarly publications. To set these numbers in context, similar searches for two other popular management techniques -- "business process reengineering" and "quality circles" produced 9,336 and 2,361 citations respectively. (Some additional data from this bibliometric examination of the KM field are presented in my paper included in this book.)

Knowledge management (KM) exploded into prominence in the mid-1990s, with J-C Spender (2005) concluding that:

The most obvious news is that knowledge management (KM) has become big business, growing explosively since Drucker drew attention to it in 1988

(Drucker, 1988). We now see KM conferences all over the world, a huge number of KM trade journals, and battalions of KM consultants. The majority of organizations, both private and public, have KM projects of various types and their spending is enormous...There has been a parallel growth of academic discussion about knowledge. He then goes on to say,

As KM has risen in importance and managerial fashionability the hype and confusion has multiplied...

This is a common refrain within the IT literature. KM continues to attract widespread interest from researchers and industry. It is seen as a major area of concern by senior executives across the world (Rigby, 2010) Yet, no single widely accepted definition of KM exists. As Smith (2004) suggested, "knowledge management (KM) is a rapidly growing field that crosses diverse disciplines," from psychology to information systems, and can be "viewed as a conceptually complex broad umbrella of issue and viewpoints".

Despite this impression of the sudden emergence of KM, its roots can be traced back at least 50 years (Lambe, 2011). More specifically, it can be argued that the field considered to be knowledge management is actually the coalescence of at least four prior bodies of knowledge - the recognition of the importance of intellectual assets or capital; the concept of the learning organization; the existence of communities of practice and the evolution of IT applications beyond transaction processing to include interpersonal communications and unstructured data storage and sharing. My own bibliographic research (Grant, 2010) shows that these four prior bodies of knowledge still have a distinct visibility within the KM literature, along with a strong interest in the links between KM and business strategy. Thus, KM can be seen as an umbrella concept that continues to embrace a number of discrete themes, as is reflected in the cases presented in this book.

KM evolved as a business activity with strong input from industry practitioners and consultants, such as Sveiby and Risling (1986), Stewart (1991) and Drucker (1992). As the field developed, the visibility of practitioners in the literature diminished. Indeed, "by 2008, practitioners' contributions dropped to only ten percent of all KM/IC authors. Pragmatic field studies and experiments, which require an active cooperation of businesses and the involvement of practitioners, constitute only 0.33 percent of all inquiry methods. There has also been a decline in case studies." (Serenko et al., 2010). This is a significant concern, since case studies represent one of the best links between conceptual thinking and actual practice in the field.

Despite this reported decline, good case studies are still being written and this book presents some interesting examples.

2. Why a Book of KM Case Studies?

In the editorial to Leading Issues in Knowledge Management Research, a sister volume to this book, Charles Després described recent changes in both practitioner and academic journals that suggest a new period of interest in KM and identified a need for an increased focus on context as a key element of future research in the discipline (Després, 2011). Cases, by their nature, are inherently studies in context.

Indeed, case studies can be used in a variety of contexts. They can be used as a pedagogical device to promote a more active form of learning, they can be used as a framework to collect and document evidence about a phenomenon or the case can be a research objective in its own right (Remenyi et al., 2002). The use of case studies allows the researcher to handle the complexity that is often an inherent part of research in business.

From a research perspective,

- A case study is an empirical inquiry that investigates a contemporary phenomenon within its real-life context especially when the boundaries between phenomena and in context and not clearly evident. (Yin, 2003)
- Researchers usually learn by studying the innovations put in place by practitioners, rather than by providing the initial wisdom for these novel ideas"… "We believe that the case research strategy is well-suited to capturing the knowledge of practitioners and developing theories from it. (Benbasat et al., 1987)

- The case study produces the type of context-dependent knowledge that research on learning shows to be necessary to allow people to develop from rule-based beginners to virtuoso experts. (Flyvbjerg, 2006)

In other words, a case is not a controlled experiment; rather it is an examination of "real-life" and knowledge in context. Thus, case studies can be used to help develop practitioners, better researchers and the relevant body of knowledge (Eisenhardt, 1989, Eisenhardt and Graebner, 2007).

3. Selecting the Cases

In selecting cases for this book I considered four factors.

The first was that they provide an interesting story. Storytelling is one of the oldest forms of knowledge sharing that has also been recognized as one of the sub-disciplines within KM (Brown et al., 2005). Stories provide context, capture interest and allow the sharing of tacit knowledge. They tell us about good things and bad things. They allow the listener/reader to share vicariously in the storyteller's experience. As Yin comments, the "case study report can itself be a significant communication device. For many nonspecialists, the description and analysis of a single case often suggest implications about a general phenomenon." (Yin, 2003) While teaching cases are most obvious examples of this form of narrative case study, I would suggest that a good storyline is surely important to most case uses.

The second factor I considered was that the case makes a good contribution to the field. The case should be relatively timeless (i.e. it still has applicability), it should offer some potential for generalization or at least the use of its findings and approach in future studies.

The third factor was that the case write-up be fairly comprehensive. That is, within the length limitations of the paper, it demonstrates the relevance of the issue being studied, the appropriateness of the case study method for the study, provides some guidance on the methodology used, a good description of the case setting and findings and, most importantly, a discussion of the contribution of the study to the field. As Eisenhardt (1991) suggests, "Research that must fit into the page limit of a journal article is necessarily limited in scope and story detail", however the cases chosen have made good efforts in most of these areas.

Finally, I looked for a broad range of cases so that, when taken together, they addressed the key areas of interest within the KM community and a broad range of organizational contexts.

4. The Cases Selected

Table 1 summarizes the 12 cases chosen. They come from 10 different countries on four continents. While most are single case studies, the unit of analysis includes both individual organisations, public and private sector, and industries. The cases demonstrate the wide-ranging reach of KM thought, including: addressing fighter pilot competencies; the need for knowledge creation in the Indian pharmaceutical industry; organisational learning in Malaysian strategic alliances; knowledge communities in the Catalonian justice system; and the importance of intellectual capital management in European automotive manufacturing.

The focus of the cases demonstrates a range of innovative approaches to knowledge management. Most have links to the business strategies of the organization studied. Three examine Intellectual Capital/Asset practices, four take an Organisational Learning perspective, four look at Communities of Practice and four study the implementation of KM IT systems.

The cases also demonstrate the wide variety of approaches available to researchers using the case method. While most examine a single case, two present multiple case studies that demonstrate multiple levels of analysis (#3 & #6).

As might be expected, the most frequent methods of data collection are interviews and examination of available documentation. Two of them (#5 & #9) use surveys as the primary data collection method and some combine focus groups, interviews and surveys. One is a form of action research

(#2), where one of the researchers worked within the company being studied.

The majority of the cases reported on successful projects although, in some cases (#3, #5 & #11), they also identified areas of concern and potential improvement. Case #2 is worthy of particular examination as it discusses the failure of a project originally reported as a success. Dawson and Balafas revisit a case study from several years earlier to discover that, while the original research suggested a successful KM project, the company had not followed through to implement what had been planned. They highlight that, while the planned KM project had strong support within the company, it also lacked a clear identification of the benefits and, in hindsight, this proved to be critical. This is a challenge that seems to be faced by many KM projects, where, while knowledge management is seen to be a "good thing" this is not enough to ensure adoption of KM.

In conclusion, the cases in this book demonstrate that KM is alive and well across the world and that researchers continue to find the case method a useful tool to use in their work. They also demonstrate that KM is, perhaps, best considered as a meta-discipline, within which a variety of themes can be pursued.

Just as Michael Polanyi asserts that all knowledge is, to some degree, personal, the choice of papers for a book such as this reflects the personal biases of the editor. I hope that you will find the cases chosen as interesting as I did, and a useful contribution to case study research in KM. My thanks goes to all the authors who have allowed their work to be reproduced in this book.

Kenneth A. Grant
Professor
Ted Rogers School of Management
Ryerson University
Toronto, Canada

	Authors	Subject	Case Focus					Methodology Notes
			KM Strategy	IC/IP	Org. Learning	CoP	KM Systems	
1	Barbaroux, P & Gode-Sanchez, C. 2008	French fighter squadron competences	X		X			Single Case, exploratory study, interviews
2	Dawson, R.J. & Balafas, P.J., 2008	KM Failure in UK company					X	Single Case, Action Research, interviews
3	Grant, K.A. 2010	KM in Professional Services Firms	X	X	X	X	X	Management Fashion Theory, Multiple Case, 5 firms, interviews
4	Gui, J., et al. 2010	IC Performance in Fund Service in a Bank		X				Single Case, focus groups, interviews & survey, Mix of qual. and quant.
5	Kakubavarapu, M & Prakash, V., 2007	Knowledge sharing in an Indian IT services firm	X				X	Single Case, interviews and survey
6	Kale D. et al. 2003	Innovation in Indian pharmaceutical industry	X					Multiple Case, 5 firms, Mix of qual. and quant.
7	Mansor, Z.D. 2010	Malaysian strategic alliances	X		X			Single Case, interviews
8	Perez-Montoro, M. & Martinez, J., 2007	Knowledge creation in Spanish justice system				X	X	Single Case, Pilot & rollout
9	Sandrock, J. & Tobin, P., 2007	Knowledge sharing in a global mining company				X		Single Case, survey and focus group Mix of qual. and quant.
10	Smeijsters H, et al. 2008	Patient-centred learning			X			Single Case Action Learning
11	Tull, J.A. & Dumay, J.C., 2007	IC Management in European automotive manufacturer	X	X				Structuration Theory, Single Case, Interviews
12	Venteramo, S. & De Carolis, M. 2009	Practice groups in Italian consulting firm	X			X		Single Case, interviews

Table 1: The Cases in this Book

References

Benbasat, I., Goldstein, K. & Mead, M. (1987) The Case Study Research Strategy in Studies of Information Systems. MIS Quarterly.

Brown, J. S., Denning, S., Grok, K. & Prusak, L. (2005) Storytelling in Organizations: Why Storytelling Is Transforming 21st Century Organizations and Management, Oxford, Elsevier Butterworth-Heinemann.

Després, C. (2011) Editorial. IN DESPRÉS, C. (Ed.) Leading Issues in Knowledge Management Research. Reading, UK, Academic Publishing International Ltd.

Drucker, P. (1992) Managing for the Future, Oxford, Butterworth Heinemann.

Eisenhardt, K. M. (1989) Building Theories from Case Study Reseach. Academy of Management Review, Vol. 14, 532-550.

Eisenhardt, K. M. (1991) Better stories and better constructs: The case for rigor and comparative logic. The Academy of Management Review, 16.

Eisenhardt, K. M. & Graebner, M. E. (2007) Theory Building from Cases: Opportunities and Challenges. Academy of Management Journal, 50.

Flyvbjerg, B. (2006) Five Misunderstandings About Case-Study Research. Qualitative Inquiry, 12.

Grant, K. A. (2010) Knowledge Management, an Enduring Fashion. 7th International Conference on Intellectual Capital, Knowledge Management & Organisational Learning. The Hong Kong Polytechnic University, Hong Kong, China.

Lambe, P. (2011) The unacknowledged parentage of knowledge management. Journal of Knowledge Management 15.

Remenyi, D., Money, R., Price, D. & Bannister, F. (2002) The Creation of Knowledge Through Case Study Research. The Henley Working Paper Series, HP 0218.

Rigby, D. (2010) Management tools: knowledge management. Boston, Bain & Company.

Serenko, A., Bontis, N., Booker, L., Sadeddin, K. & Hardie, T. (2010) A scientometric analysis of knowledge management and intellectual capital academic literature (1994-2008). Journal of Knowledge Management, 14.

Smith, A. D. (2004) Knowledge Management Strategies: a multi-case study. Journal of Knowledge Management, 8.

Spender, J. C. (2005) An overview: what's new and important about knowledge management? Building new bridges between managers and academics. IN LITTLE, S. & RAY, T. (Eds.) Managing Knowledge: An Essential Reader. London, Sage.

Stewart, T. A. (1991) Brainpower. Fortune, 123, 44-50.

Svieby, K.-E. & Risling, A. (1986) öretagetKunskapsf ("The Knowhow Company") Sweden.

Yin, R. K. (2003) Case Study Research: Design and Methods., Third Edition, Thousand Oaks, California, Sage Publications.

How Organizations Learn to Develop Capabilities: The Case of French Fighter Squadrons

Pierre Barbaroux, and Cécile Godé-Sanchez
Research Center of the French Air Force, Defense and Knowledge Management Department, France

Editorial commentary

In this paper, Barbaroux & Godé-Sanchez examine the contribution that organisational learning makes to the development of capabilities, both for the individual and for the organization. They present an interesting model for organizational learning, with two key components -- modes of learning and context of learning. The model is tested in an exploratory case study of the post-flight reviews in three French fighter squadrons. The primary data collection method was individual interviews with flight crew.

The relatively detailed case narrative presents a refreshing perspective on knowledge sharing and transfer, demonstrating a variety of techniques that can make tacit knowledge more explicit and also allow tacit knowledge exchange in a semi-structured environment. The approaches used by the squadrons could be well adapted to other professional environments. The model is a useful descriptive tool for examining organisational learning.

Abstract: This paper investigates how organizational learning provides the organization with effective means to develop capabilities. Building on the distinction between *modes* and *contexts* of learning, we introduce a model of organizational learning to study how knowledge is shaped and made explicit, how it is created and

1

shared, and how it is disseminated within the organization. We elaborate on an explorative case study focusing on three French Air Force fighter squadrons. Our main findings can be summarized as follows. First, organizational learning involves a variety of modes and contexts to be aligned and coordinated in order to improve organizational performance. Second, post-flight review enables squadrons to harness critical thinking and open mind attitudes and develop reflective capabilities.

Key words: Organizational learning, learning strategy, capabilities, knowledge management, after-action reviews

1. Introduction

The literature on organization theory and strategic management acknowledges the critical role played by the acquisition of capabilities in organizational life (Teece and Pisano 1994). The central issue is to understand how organizations acquire, exploit and adjust their capability portfolio in adapting to high-velocity environments (Wirtz et al. 2007). We contend that organizational learning provides organizations with effective means to develop new capabilities. Scholars consider learning as a process that fosters the creation, storage, dissemination and exploitation of tangible and intangible resources within the firm (Teece et al. 1997). As the foregoing implies, learning drives most organizational change that comes along with the acquisition and exploitation of new knowledge.

This paper investigates how organizations implement appropriate learning strategy to develop capabilities. We build on the distinction between *modes* and *contexts* of learning to offer a conceptual model of learning in organizations. A mode of learning refers to the combination of specific types and levels of learning. A type of learning refers to the mechanism through which individuals as well as organizations learn. (e.g., learning by doing, learning by using, learning from others, and learning from imitation). In addition, each type can generate different levels of feedback and change (e.g., single-loop and double-loop, incremental, radical, and architectural change). A context of learning reflects a particular architecture for creating, absorbing and disseminating specific knowledge (e.g., communities of interest, functional teams, and communities of practice). Within this conceptual framework, organizational learning is supported by the combination of distinctive modes and contexts of learning that yields to the production of new knowledge and capabilities.

To study the addressed research question, we conducted an explorative case study (Yin 2003) which focuses on three French Air Force fighter squadrons. This case study is based on a research contract funded by the French ministry of Defense, which especially questioned the acquisition of new capabilities related to the introduction of the multi role fighter aircraft. We used mixture data collection methods to achieve triangulation and enhance confidence in our findings (Eisenhardt 1989). We begin by developing a conceptual model to study organizational learning. Then, we present our explorative case study which focuses on how French Air Force fighter squadrons learn from post-flight reviews. Finally, we draw on the main implications of our model and findings for the study of organizational learning and future research.

5. Organizational capabilities and organizational learning: A conceptual framework

We consider the organization as a knowledge-based system (Daft and Weick 1984) which is made up with different units (e.g., employees, functional teams, communities, divisions, departments, suppliers, and customers) that create, disseminate and share a variety of knowledge types (Lundvall and Johnson 1994; Jensen et al. 2007). The processes through which the organization manages its knowledge assets (Boisot 1998) are therefore critical, in particular because knowledge-based activities support the development and refinement of a variety of capabilities (Penrose 1959; Teece and Pisano 1994). This cognitive view of the organization has two main implications. First, it assumes that the organization is a knowledgeable entity capable to develop adapted responses to changing circumstances (Daft and Lewin 1993). Second, it provides operational concepts and metaphors for building and refining models and visions of the organization as a learning, innovative and adaptive system (McKelvey 1997; Lewin et al. 1999).

5.1. Organizational learning and organizational capabilities

Conceptions of organizational learning are very diverse (Wang and Ahmed 2007). Pawlowsky (2001) reported twenty different views of organizational knowledge, and classified the concept of organizational learning into five different perspectives. Dodgson (1993) also discriminated multiple and often conflicting approaches of learning in organizations. The author focused on three main areas (the goals of learning, the learning processes *per se*, and the factors which might impede or facilitate learning in organizations) and explained how different methodologies and disciplines lead to divergent conceptions of organizational learning. Specifically, scholars are keen to distinguish various types and levels of learning in order to grapple with the diversity of organizational learning (e.g., from simple adaptive learning to higher-orders reflective learning modes). Bateson (1972) and Argyris and Schön (1978) distinguished three levels of learning, each level reflecting distinctive feedback effects on the organization's routines and capabilities (e.g., single-loop or Learning type I, double loop or Learning type II, and deutero learning or Learning type III). Zollo and Winter (2002) also separated three types of learning (namely accumulation, articulation, and codification) that differ according to the degrees of cognitive effort and deliberation attached to them. Nonaka (1994) considered organizational learning as made up with four distinctive individual and collective sub-processes that foster knowledge creation and dissemination within the organization (e.g., socialization, externalisation, combination and internalisation). In spite of strong dissimilarities, all approaches of organizational learning confront the problem of connecting the individual level to the organizational level of learning. While this connection is the source of debates between individualistic and holistic perspectives of organizational phenomena, a consensus has emerged within the academic community. This consensus revolves around the contention that organizational learning (i) does not reduce to the sum of individual learning outcomes and (ii) provides the organization with effective means for capability-development and enhancement.

In line with the foregoing, we suggest that organizational learning is tightly connected to the creation, integration, and dissemination of individual as well as collective capabilities. Following Teece et al. (1997, p. 515), the concept of capability "emphasizes the key role of strategic management in appropriately adapting, integrating, and reconfiguring internal and external organizational skills, resources, and functional competences to match the requirement of a changing environment". The previous definition insists on the role played by managers in identifying, exploiting and renewing strategic knowledge assets within the firm, and on the managerial mechanisms by which intangible resources generate sustainable competitive advantage (Prahalad and Hamel 1990). In her study of a series of development projects, Leonard-Barton (1992) distinguished four types of capabilities that must be continuously aligned and combined by the organization to deliver strategic value: technical skills, technical systems, managerial systems and values and norms. Complementing the competence-based view of the firm, we contend that the creation, integration and dissemination of several types of capabilities depend upon organizational learning. In seeking to adapt to high velocity environments, the organization must constantly adapt, renew, reconfigure and re-create its organizational boundaries and capability portfolio, either by focusing on in-house assets or absorbing external knowledge (Chesbrough 2003). In this context, scholars and practitioners should place their attention to organizational learning as it represents the main engine for innovation and change within the organization. However, the variety of conceptions of organizational learning yields only partial views of this phenomenon. Indeed, each conception focuses on separated facets without considering organizational learning as a consistent whole. Such proliferation of alternative views tends to impede the operationalization of organizational learning as a global and reliable process aligned with the organization's strategy. Next section introduces a conceptual model of organizational learning which does not separate its various facets (e.g., types and levels of learning) but links them together.

5.2. Combining modes and contexts of learning to develop capabilities: A model

There is a need to cope with organizational learning as a global process made up with distinctive mechanism involving frequent interactions among knowledgeable individuals, groups, teams and communities within and across the boundaries of the organization.

To study such complex dynamics, we suggest that organizational learning depends on distinctive modes of learning, each mode being defined by the combination of particular types and levels of learning. In addition, we suppose that organizations should also provide individuals with appropriate contexts in order to fully grasp the benefit of a particular mode of learning. Our main contention, therefore, is that organizational learning is made up with two major components that must be combined, aligned and integrated to provide the organization with effective means to develop capabilities.

The two components are defined as follows (Table 1):

1. The mode of learning is defined by combining a type and a level of learning. The type refers to the individual and collective mechanisms through which knowledge and capabilities are developed, shared and incorporated into practices. Examples of types are widespread in the literature and encompass socialization, adaptive learning, learning by imitation, learning by doing, learning from failures, and learning by using (Boerner et al. 2001). The level of learning refers to the nature of the feedback effect attached to a particular type of learning which affects the organization's capabilities. Examples of levels include Argyris and Schön's (1978) concepts of single-loop, double-loop and deutero-learning. The level of learning can also be used to discriminate innovation strategies according to their degree of "radicalism". Examples of distinctive levels of change in innovation include March's (1991) concepts of exploitation and exploration, and Henderson and Clark's (1990) distinctions between incremental, radical, modular and architectural innovation and change (see also Sanchez and Mahoney 1996).

2. The context of learning refers to the architecture of interactions between individuals (e.g., hierarchical relationships, formal and informal ties, trust relationships, decentralized interactions). Contexts also rely on the quality of the knowledge created and exchanged by people (e.g., tacit knowledge, explicit knowledge, strategic knowledge) and on the artifacts used by the organization and its employees to create, store and disseminate knowledge (e.g., communication technologies, documentations, technical systems). Examples of contexts of learning include the community of practice and the functional team (Wenger et al. 2002), the corporate division (Galunic and Eisenhardt 2001), and the inter-organizational network (Chesbrough 2003).

By focusing on organizational learning as the combination of particular modes and contexts, we seek to explore the process by which organizations learn to adapt and develop appropriate capabilities. This view of organizational learning, therefore, focuses on the process of how knowledge is shaped and made explicit, how it is created and shared, and how it is disseminated through a variety of learning modes and contexts.

Table 1: A model of organizational learning

COMPONENTS		EXAMPLES
MODES Combination of types and levels of learning	**TYPES** Individual and collective learning mechanisms	Learning by doing Learning from imitation Socialization, Learning from others
	LEVELS Nature of the feedback effect	Single-loop Double-loop Deutero-learning
CONTEXTS Made up with a variety of architecture, artifacts and knowledge	**ARCHITECTURE** Nature of the interactions between individuals	Hierarchical relationships Informal dialogues Formal ties Trust
	ARTIFACTS Communication and knowledge sharing technologies	Documentations Intranet Instant communication Language
	KNOWLEDGE Quality of the knowledge exchanged	Tacit knowledge Codified knowledge Data/Information Culture

6. How French fighter squadrons learn from training flights?

To examine the above question, we conducted an explorative case study within French combat squadrons, focusing on post-flight reviews (Ron et al. 2006). Such after-action reviews are highly regarded by the French Air Force since they represent a critical learning process to improve performance level of squadrons. We interviewed pilots and navigators from three fighter squadrons (bombers, Air Defense, and multi-operations) and skilled on different aircrafts (Mirage 2000D, Mirage 2000 RDI and the all-purpose aircraft Rafale). In this paper, we focus on training missions achieved by one or two patrols, each patrol consisting of two aircrafts.

6.1.   The post-flight review

Working days in a French squadron begin with a 30-minutes general briefing for the pilots and/or the aircrews scheduled to fly. The briefing includes weather situation, landing runway condition, and engine failure considerations (the "question of the day"). Right after such formal and codified presentations, the formation leaders brief the squadron concerning training schedules. This time represents the first step of the squadron learning process since it provides opportunities for pilots to review some lessons learned from similar training missions. They describe a number of problems they faced during course of action through informal discussions. In attending such debates, junior pilots learn from the seniors' experiments. Moreover, formation leaders encourage them to participate in discussion, in sharing their own experiment or questioning senior pilots. Viewed broadly, every pilot has the opportunity to learn from each other in honestly reporting their actions and reasoning. Finally, pilots or aircrews split into patrols to attend dedicated briefing before the sortie.

Immediately after the flight, pilots and aircrews formally debrief the mission with a 40/45-minutes post-flight review. We call such a review "formal" since it follows a structured process provided by the NATO Air Forces manual. More precisely, patrols use the NATO briefing guide, but follow the checklist backwards. In that way, the course of post-flight review is standardized, codified, and collectively known by pilots. In addition, squadrons are equipped with a dedicated mission restitution system to achieve a rigorous analysis of the flight. Reviewing flight films recorded by the cockpit-mounted system enable pilots to understand what happened during the flight. They can construct an accurate representation of the patrol formation and evaluate the collective performance of the sortie. In that way, post flight reviews enable participants to broadly focus on mission accomplishment and to assess the functioning of formations as a whole. Such collective task assessment is facilitated by the shared assumption that critical examination of one's own experiment is the key to improvement.

8

Each pilot's video record is scrutinized during the debriefing, with particular attention paid to inappropriate actions (errors), cause of errors, and potential remedies. Critical stages concern targeting point (especially for bombers' squadrons) and the way each pilot flew his plane in combat (especially for air defense squadrons). The atmosphere is safe but tense since each pilot's mistake and ways of correcting it are criticized by others. However, participants acknowledge that detection and correction of errors is the better way to learn. First, observing the errors of others help to correct one's own. Second, having colleagues present to the debriefing improve the opportunities to catch the errors and to find appropriate remedies. Third, to be accountable for one's own mistakes is the better way to avoid reproducing them the next time around. If junior pilots are especially involved in this critical examination process, seniors and formation leaders are also concerned. Moreover, they have to give the example in publicly sharing their successful but also their less successful experiments. Even the most skilled pilot makes errors and learns from his own failures and others' criticizes and comments. The later help him to stand back in order to assess the mission accomplishment.

In fact, post-flight review must be viewed as a structured and democratic social system. In operating in the way of critical examination, each pilot and/or navigator recognizes the core values of the debriefing culture, alike honest reporting and public accountability. In that way, post flight review represents opportunity to socialize for the seniors and to be recognized as a member of the community for the youngest. It is a multi-layered learning process which enables participants to improve their individual as well as their collective performance.

6.2. Aligning distinctive types of learning in the post-flight review

The dominant mode of learning in post-flight review consists in liking together individual experiences, collective practices and organizational performance. Post-flight review relies on the integration of three types of learning:

1. Learning from experimentations. This type of learning is merely individualistic. It involves the active participation of pilots and air-

crews ready to learn from the corrections of personal trials and errors.

2. Learning from others. This type of learning introduces a social facet through the connection of distinctive individual experiences (e.g., learning from imitation). By facilitating the sharing of expertise and articulating contingent judgments and opinions on peculiar behaviors, actions and attitudes, learning from others fosters the dissemination of best practices, know-how and other critical knowledge among patrols and squadrons.

3. Learning from failures. This type of learning puts particular emphasis on the analysis of observed deviations from expected, planned or desired outcomes (Cannon and Edmondson 2005). The deviations that the squadrons and/or the individuals experiment are not necessarily large: small failures can also generate essential lessons and trigger vital organizational adaptations.

The integration of the previous types within a single post-flight review mode of learning is facilitated because each type is based on the following identical three-step process: (i) detection of errors, (ii) analysis of their causes and (iii) correction of the resulting deviations through individual and collective experimentations (Cannon and Edmondson 2005). The ensuing integrity of the foregoing process is reinforced since the level attached to it as a mode of learning is principally incremental or single loop (Argyris and Schön 1978). Therefore, the alignment of the three types of learning and their integration in a reliable learning mode, are not likely to be altered in response to corrective actions undertaken to eliminate detected and potential errors. However, post-flight review can generate cumulative adaptations that undermine the rules, procedures, models and values which have generated the trial and error sequence under evaluation. Double-loop and radical changes can therefore characterize the nature of the feedback effects of post flight review on the organization's routines, tactics and procedures. Eventually, post-flight review might induce deeper modifications of the dominant logics and methods employed by the organization to enable its employees to train, learn and educate. In this way, post-flight review can lead to the alteration of the learning modes (deuteron-learning).

6.3.   Designing and coordinating a variety of contexts in the post-flight review

As an integrated mode of learning, post-flight review requires appropriate architecture and artifacts in order to encourage experimentations and interactions among aircrews. For example, to state the weather situation of the current training geographical zone often involves exchanging data and tacit knowledge on how to behave in such and such situation. Therefore, pilots and navigators need a variety of artifacts and modes of communication to acquire, share and disseminate knowledge about the weather situation. We assume that exchanging personal knowledge could be facilitated by allowing individuals to establish spontaneous and informal dialogues within the limits of formalized courses of action. In addition, we have found that participants in the post-flight review utilized specific communication artifacts aligned with the type of knowledge exchanged and shared. Hence, post-flight review relies upon a variety of contexts attached to and aligned with the various types of learning embedded in the global mode of learning.

Specifically, we identified two features of the post-flight review's context of learning. These features can be summarized as follows. First, post-flight review is based on a dual architecture which combines informal dialogues with hierarchical interactions among individuals. This leads to the implementation of a formalized but safe communicational atmosphere that improves individuals' willingness to share knowledge and experiment with novelty (Brown and Duguid 1991). Subsequently, we suggest that designing effective modes of learning within high-velocity environments requires aligning formal groups (e.g., hierarchical communities and functional teams) and informal communities (e.g., occupational communities) within a single integrated mode of learning. In that view, each type of formal and informal communication architecture involves dedicated technologies. The second feature, therefore, is concerned with the diversity of artifacts deployed and promoted within distinctive squadrons. In seeking to develop learning from experimentations, learning from others and learning from failures, the squadron leaders must promote the use of a variety of digitized and non digitized technical systems and documentations. The latter improve the capitalization and dissemination of personal expertise as well as collective experiences. Therefore, organizational learning entails the deployment of a mixture of communication technology and artifacts, each being dedicated to the management of specific types of knowledge (e.g., articulation, storage and dissemination of tacit and explicit knowledge). Finally, the artifacts employed by individuals and the communicational atmosphere must be aligned to enable fruitful interactions and foster the development of organizational capabilities.

Table 2: Post-flight review modes and contexts of learning

MODES	TYPES	Learning from experimentation
	Individual and collective	Learning from failures
		Learning from others
	LEVELS	Single-loop (Short Term)
	Incremental and radical	Double-loop (Medium and Long Term)
CONTEXTS	**ARCHITECTURE**	Hierarchical relationships and Informal
	Duality	dialogues
		Formal interactions and trust relationships
	ARTIFACTS	Documentations (NATO briefing guide)
	Heterogeneity	Mission restitution system
		Language and face-to-face interactions
	KNOWLEDGE	Tacit knowledge and personal experience
	Variety	
		Data and information

7. Discussion

We consider post-flight review as a learning strategy (Beer et al. 2005) the organization implements to survive and thrive within high-velocity environments. Such strategy is highly formalized to ensure organizational reliability and, by the same time, flexible enough to enable individuals' efforts and experimentations (Adler and Borys 1996). Therefore, post-flight review can be construed as a dual organizational process which enables the organization to develop capabilities by mixing individual and collective *modes* of learning with formal and informal *contexts* of learning.

7.1. Developing reflexive capabilities through organizational learning

Beyond the acquisition of technical skills related to the use of technological artifacts (e.g., the mission restitution system) and aircraft maneuvering, post-flight review entails a collective process which challenges the intricacy of articulating and sharing personal knowledge. Considering capability-enhancement through organizational learning leads us to acknowledge the "ineffability of tacit knowledge" (Tsoukas 2003, p. 410). While organizational learning enables individuals to reduce the costs and efforts attached to the articulation of personal expertise, the dominant logics supporting the post-flight review mode of learning does not focus on codified knowledge only. Instead, it insists on the role played by tacit knowledge embedded in daily work practices. By offering appropriate contexts to interact with others and build collective practices through various types of learning, the three-step process on which post-flight review relies involves additional capabilities. As Tsoukas argued, operationalizing tacit knowledge requires "instructive forms of talk [by which] practitioners are moved to *review* the situation they are in, to relate to their circumstances in a different way" (Tsoukas 2003, p. 424).

The detection, analysis and correction of errors come along with the development of new ways of interacting and disseminating knowledge. Pilots and aircrews not only convert tacit knowledge into explicit but come to connect skilled performance in new ways through social interactions. In developing new ways of communicating and sharing knowledge, individuals seize many opportunities to put their critical thinking and open minded attitudes into practice and improve collective performance. Such behavior leads pilots and aircrews to reflect on their own experience, expertise and role within the organization, and triggers the development of a reflective capability.

7.2. Towards a multidimensional model of organizational learning

Our case study has several implications both for scholars and practitioners involved in organizational learning initiatives. First, designing appropriate contexts of learning is critical to ensure personal engagement and create conditions for synergies to emerge between individual and collective types of learning. In this respect, managers play an essential role since they provide individuals and collectives with several incentives and artifacts to communicate and share knowledge. Such behavior diverges from conventional authority-based modes of management which are commonplace in today large corporations. Organizational learning instead requires blending coercive leadership with enabling governance mechanisms. Hence, managers ought to encourage individual participations within formal functional teams and informal communities, while avoiding communication failures and conflicts to occur.

In addition, this view argues for a conception of capability that differs from the deterministic approach of organizational capability as the final outcome of a single knowledge creation and/or absorption process. While technical skills emerge from the combination of individual and collective types of learning, the artifacts, governance and values attached to the post-flight review do not result from, but are elements of the contexts embedded in it. Hence, the use of documentations and mission system restitution (artifacts), the mixing of hierarchical relationships with informal dialogues (dual architecture), and the promotion of professional expertise and critical thinking, and open minded values (reflective capability) are component capabilities of the contexts embedded in the post-flight review mode of learning.

Finally, our findings argue for a pluralistic, multidimensional approach of organizational learning. When strategic adaptations are at stake, the organization ought to take into account a variety of variables regarding its own capabilities and the nature of the external environment. By implementing and aligning several individual and collective modes along with formal and informal contexts of learning, the organization expands the scope of its current and future responses to unpredictable demands for adaptation. A multidimensional approach of learning, therefore, enables the organization to gain additional flexibility within hyper competitive environments.

8. Conclusion

In this paper we proposed a model for studying organizational learning. This model assumes that the latter requires a variety of modes and contexts of learning to be integrated and aligned. The foregoing is in line with the resource-based view of the firm. It contends that organizational learning should be considered as a critical process which enables the organization to create, integrate and disseminate a variety of individual as well as collective knowledge and capabilities. Building on an explorative case study, we focused on three French combat squadrons involved in training missions. These squadrons learned to improve performance by organizing day-to-day post-flight reviews. We found that the integration and alignment of a variety of types and contexts within a single mode of learning provide the organization with operational means to create, capitalize and disseminate knowledge, and improve organizational performance. In addition, we considered that the post-flight review learning process offers both contexts and opportunities to develop a variety of technical, managerial and reflective capabilities.

References

Adler P.S., and Borys B. (1996) "Two Types of Bureaucracy: Enabling and Coercive", Administrative Science Quarterly, Vol. 41, pp. 61-89.

Argyris, C. and Schön, D. (1978) Organizational Learning, Reading, MA: Addison-Wesley.

Bateson, G. (1972) Steps to an Ecology of Mind: A Revolutionary Approach to Man's Understanding of Himself, San Francisco: Chandler Press.

Beer, M., Voelpel, S.C., Leibold, M. and Tekie E.B. (2005) "Strategic Management as Organizational Learning: Developing Fit and Alignment Through a Disciplined Process", Long Range Planning, Vol. 38, pp. 445-465.

Boerner, C.S., Macher, J.T. and Teece, D.J. (2001) "A Review and Assessment of Organizational Learning in Economic Theories", In M. Dierkes, A. Berthion Antal, J. Child and I. Nonaka (Eds), Handbook of Organizational Learning and Knowledge (pp. 89-117). Oxford: Oxford University Press.

Boisot, M.H. (1998) Knowledge assets: Securing Competitive Advantage in the Information Economy, Oxford: Oxford University Press.

Brown, J.S. and Duguid, P. (1991) "Knowledge and Organization: A Social-Practice Perspective", Organization Science, Vol. 12, No. 2, pp. 198-213.

Cannon, M.D. and Edmondson, A.C. (2005) "Failing to Learn and Learning to Fail (Intelligently): How Great Organizations Put Failure to Work, to Innovate and Improve", Long Range Planning, Vol. 38, pp. 299-319.

Chesbrough, H. (2003) Open Innovation: The New Imperative for Creating and Profiting from Technology, Boston Massachusetts: Harvard business School Press.

Daft R.L. and K. Weick (1984) "Organizations as Interpretative Systems", Academy of Management Review, Vol. 9, No. 2, pp. 284-295.

Daft R.L. and A.Y. Lewin (1993) "Where are the Theories for the "new" Organizational Forms? An editorial essay", Organization Science, Vol. 4, No. 4, pp. i-vi.

Dodgson, M. (1993) "Organizational Learning: A Review of some Literatures", Organization Studies, Vol 14, pp. 375-394.

Eisenhardt, K. (1989) "Building Theories from Case Study Research", Academy of Management Review, Vol 14, No. 4, pp. 532-550.

Galunic D.C. and Eisenhardt, K.M. (2001) "Architectural Innovation and Modular Corporate Forms", Academy of Management Journal, Vol. 44, No. 6, pp. 1229-1249.

Henderson, R.M. and Clark, K.B. (1990), "Architectural Innovation: The Reconfiguration of Existing Product Technologies and the Failure of Established Firms", Administrative Science Quarterly, Vol. 35, No. 1, pp. 9-30.

Jensen, M. B., Johnson, B., Lorenz, E. and Lundvall, B.A. (2007) "Forms of Knowledge and Modes of Innovation", Research Policy, Vol 36, No. 5, pp. 680-693.

Lundvall, B-A. and Johnson, B. (1994) "The Learning Economy, Journal of Industry Studies, Vol 1, No. 2, pp. 23-42.

Leonard-Barton, D. (1992) "Core Capabilities and Core Rigidities: A Paradox in Managing New Product Development", Strategic Management Journal, Vol 13, pp. 111-125.

Lewin, A.Y., Long, C.P. and Carroll, T.N. (1999), "The Co-Evolution of new Organizational Forms", Organization Science, Vol. 10, No. 5, pp. 535-550.

McKelvey, B. (1997) "Quasi Natural Organization Science", Organization Science, Vol 8, No. 4, pp. 352-380.

Nonaka, I. (1994) "A Dynamic Theory of Organizational Knowledge Creation", Organization Science, Vol 5, No. 1, pp. 14-34.

Pawlowsky, P. (2001) "The Treatment of Organizational Learning in Management Science", In M. Dierkes, A. Berthion Antal, J. Child and I. Nonaka (Eds), Handbook of Organizational Learning and Knowledge (pp. 61-88). Oxford: Oxford University Press.

Penrose, E.T. (1959) The Theory of the Growth of the Firm, Oxford: Basil Blackwell.

Prahalad, C. K. and Hamel, G. (1990) "The Core Competence of the Corporation", Harvard Business Review, May-June, pp. 79-91.

Ron, L., Lipshitz, R. and Popper, M. (2006) "How Organizations Learn: Post-flight Reviews in an F-16 Fighter Squadron", Organization Studies, Vol. 27, No. 8, pp. 1069-1089.

Sanchez, R. and Mahoney (1996) "Modularity, Flexibility, and Knowledge Management in Product and Organization Design", Strategic Management Journal, Vol. 17, pp. 63-76.

Teece, D. and Pisano, G. (1994) "The Dynamic Capabilities of Firms: An Introduction", Industrial and Corporate Change, Vol 3, pp. 537-356.

Teece, D., Pisano, G. and Shuen, A. (1997) "Dynamic Capabilities and Strategic Management", Strategic Management Journal. Vol. 18, pp. 509-533.

Tsoukas, H. (2003) "Do we Really Understand Tacit Knowledge?", In Easterby-Smith, M. and Lyles, M.A. (Eds), Handbook of Organizational Learning and Knowledge Management, pp. 410-427, Blackwell Publishing.

Wang, C. and Ahmed, P. (2007) "Dynamic Capabilities: A Review and Research Agenda", International Journal of Management Reviews, Vol 9, No. 1, pp. 31-51.

Wenger, E., McDermott, R. and Snyder, W (2002) A Guide to Manage Knowledge. Cultivating Communities of Practice, Harvard Business School Press: Harvard.

Wirtz, B.W., Mathieu, A. and Schilke, O. (2007) "Strategy in High-Velocity Environments", Long Range Planning, Vol. 40, pp. 295-313.

Yin, R. (2003) Case Study Research: Design and Methods, 3rd edition, Sage Publication, Beverly Hills.

Zollo, M. and Winter, S. (2002) "Deliberate Learning and the Evolution of Dynamic Capabilities", Organization Science, Vol 13, No. 3, pp. 339-351.

What Problem Are We Trying to Solve? - A Case Study of a Failed Knowledge Management Initiative

Ray Dawson[1] and Peter Balafas[2]
1Loughborough University, Loughborough, UK
2Peter Balafas, HBOS (formerly of the Danwood Group), Edinburgh, UK

Editorial Commentary

This paper demonstrates the importance of longitudinal analysis and the challenges of doing action research in case study work. While many case studies are one-time "snapshots," this is a post-implementation study of a project within a UK business, whose first stage had been reported in an earlier paper. Contradicting the findings of the first paper (which was very positive re the methodology adopted to design and implement an IT-based KM system), Dawson & Balafas deserve much credit for their self-critical reflective approach to the project and their identification of the reasons for the post-implementation failure. Despite following a well-supported study approach and gaining top executive commitment to the planned implementation, the project failed.

The detailed failure analysis is a good contribution to KM project literature, questioning the role of knowledge audits and suggesting the value of a more problem-focused approach. Data were collected from interviews, attendance at meetings and document analysis. Readers may wish to consider how the lessons learned are similar or different from those discussed in the literature on successes and failures in other types of IT projects.

Abstract: This paper concerns action research to establish knowledge management implementation methodology as part of an overall process improvement initiative at the Danwood Group. As a first step, a knowledge audit was carried out of the existing working systems, including a review of computerised information systems used by the company. This audit revealed that two independent systems had a significant overlap of functionality and data stored. A detailed examination of these systems showed that there were potential savings to be made by combining the systems so that they could share the data and some of the functionality. A design proposal was then put to the company to merge the two systems.

The company accepted the proposal in principle, but it never approved the funding to carry out the necessary changes. This led the research team to carry out an in-depth review of their knowledge management implementation approach to discover where it had gone wrong. It was found that while the company management had recognised the inefficiency in their systems and they had accepted the suggested improvement, the initiative had failed as the company had not perceived they had any significant problem with the systems concerned and, therefore, the improvement was given the lowest priority. These systems performed adequately in that they delivered what they were required to do, even if it was not in the most efficient manner, whereas there were other areas of their business where there were problems that required more immediate attention. This meant that there was a lack of enthusiasm to even start the system merger project.

This resulted in a revised methodology for knowledge management initiatives based on an initial problem audit rather than a first step of a knowledge audit. Having a clear idea of "what problem are we trying to solve" has since been shown to produce more enthusiasm by both users and management to drive through the necessary changes and this subsequently leads to knowledge management system implementations that are far more likely to be considered successful.

Keywords: Knowledge audit, systems analysis, systems implementation, return on investment, project failure

1. Introduction

This paper covers the experiences of research at The Danwood Group, a medium sized company based in the UK East Midlands. The project reported in this paper was part of a wider research project on process improvement at the company. The research undertaken used an action research approach as one of the authors was employed by the company to carry out various project management tasks while actively taking part in the research project. This enabled the researchers to examine all aspects of the company data and processes from an internal perspective and eventually gave the opportunity to try new initiatives in the working environment.

It is commonly advocated that a first step to gauge the effectiveness of an organisations information and knowledge strategy is to carry out a knowledge audit (Liebowitz et al. 2000). This should enable inefficient and ineffective knowledge and information mechanisms and processes to be identified and any shortfalls determined. A knowledge audit was therefore carried out at the Danwood Group. The result was that an area of inefficiency was indeed identified where two systems overlapped in their functionality. A proposal was put forward to the company to merge the two systems to create greater efficiency. This proposal was considered by the company board and it was accepted in principle.

At first sight this had been a competent, systematic analysis of the knowledge supporting systems within the company, where a logical step by step methodology had produced a significant business improvement, and the researchers felt able to congratulate themselves and publicise their achievement (Balafas & Jackson 2003). Unfortunately, the reality of the situation was not as expected. A follow up investigation showed that the change had never been funded and no employee or contractor had been assigned to carry out the software development necessary. The initiative had effectively been abandoned.

This disappointing result for an initiative which had followed standard knowledge management methods led to the researchers reassessing their approach in an effort to understand the problem and ensure their failure would not be repeated. This paper describes the case study at the Danwood Group and the subsequent evaluation of the methods used.

2. What is knowledge and what is a knowledge audit?

It is recognised that the definitions of knowledge and information can be a problem for knowledge managers, and some authors, such as Wilson (2002), suspect that knowledge management is simply information management with a new name. There are many definitions of knowledge but for the purposes of this paper the simple definition given by Gunnlaugsdottir (2003) is adopted, that knowledge within an organisation is *"information with a contextual element"*. Expanding this, knowledge enables the implications of any information to be understood in different contexts and appropriate judgement to be made concerning that information in any particular context.

On the basis of this definition, knowledge management must also encompass information management (Marwick 2001) as it is information that provides the foundation for the application of knowledge in any context. The authors of this paper do not wish to become burdened with the definitions of knowledge and information, or knowledge management and information management, so these issues are side stepped with the assertion that whether the systems examined in the case study in this paper are considered to be knowledge systems or information systems does not matter as both will be the tools of a knowledge worker. A knowledge audit will therefore involve examining what explicit knowledge and information is held in documents and electronic systems and also the tacit knowledge and information held in the heads of employees (Burnett 2004). The audit also concerns the identification of the capabilities of these systems and employees, and where and how the knowledge and information are used. Other aspects could concern the communication channels and flows of information and knowledge in an organisation.

In this case study, however, it was not necessary to cover every possible aspect of a knowledge audit at the Danwood Group as a straight forward examination of the capabilities and information held in the main electronic systems used by the company was enough to highlight the potential overlap between two of the systems used.

3. The electronic systems in the case study

In this case study two systems were reviewed as part of the overall knowledge audit. These were the Customer Relationship Management (CRM) system and the Customer Query Logging (CQL) system.

The CRM system at the Danwood Group, as with all CRM systems, served the purpose of keeping records of customer details and contacts to support the building of strong relationships with new and existing customers. The system was relatively new and functioned reasonably well in giving the functionality expected of it by the company agents using it.

The CQL system supported existing customers by logging and tracking any problems and queries customers had with the products they had purchased. Because the resolving of a problem involved identifying a suitable specialist in the problem area who then had to liaise with the customer, problems, on average, took two to five days to resolve. However, some of the more difficult problems could take a number of weeks to resolve. There were a number of immediate problems identified with this system as its use was confined to mainly logging the process. As the delays in responding to customers were often caused by the slow communications between staff in the company, it would have been useful if the system could have played its part in speeding up communications perhaps by highlighting where communication problems occurred and sending reminders where necessary. However, the system lacked any such proactive abilities.

The two systems clearly had an overlap in their data and functionality. Both had to record customer data and both recorded interaction with the customer, though the type of interaction was not the same. It was immediately obvious that the systems had enough in common to warrant an in depth analysis so this was carried out over a period of three months by the author employed by the Danwood Group.

4. Research methodology

The key method of capturing data was through interviewing members of staff within the Customer Services department. As the author based at the company was working within this department, interviews could be carried out using both informal as well as formal methods with some interviews being unstructured and some that were structured. The first method employed was the use of unstructured, informal interviews. As he was working alongside the users of these systems the author could take the opportunity to ask his colleagues about how they carried out their work and the how the systems supported their role. This built a general appreciation and understanding of the functionality and use of the systems that could then be used to design a more structured question set to carry out more detailed investigation through more formal interviews. The initial informal interviews also identified the principle customer liaison experts in the department that were later approached for the more formal structured data gathering. The informal approach continued to be used throughout the research period, however, as it was often useful to seek clarification or seek expansion of points raised in earlier interviews. The informal approach also proved useful for the author to convey his motives and to try and solicit cooperation from his colleagues by explaining how the research could lead to benefits for all employees working in the Customer Services area.

A second major source of useful information was through attending strategic meetings within both the IT and customer services departments. The Danwood Group provided the author with "open access" to any meeting or seminar deemed beneficial for the research. It was discovered that networking with people from many areas of the business played a very important role, as it provided a multi-angle view to shared problems and it gave a better insight into how a total solution could be effectively designed.

A third source of data was the company documentation relating to the systems under investigation. System documents such as user manuals helped identify all the functionality of the systems and were particularly useful for less used facilities. Other documents gave reports of specific data held which helped identify how the systems were being used.

As diagrammatic representations of concepts normally form the basis for a better understanding of a system, diagrams of the current systems were produced. The diagrams were then presented to the users and amended accordingly in order to capture a realistic snapshot of the current systems.

The full functionality of both systems was elicited from the interviews and documentation for analysis. A table was drawn up listing all the functions available for each system. From the structured interviews with key members of staff who were known to be experts in the customer relationship domain, it was also possible to create a list of business objectives that the systems should be supporting. This progressed to the creation of a second table for each of the two systems which, this time, listed the desired functionalities to achieve the business objectives.

A comparison between the tables that listed current and those that listed desired functionality was then performed in order to identify the missing links. The result of this "gap analysis" confirmed that there was a certain commonality in the functionality of these two systems and there were also several business objectives that were not currently being adequately supported. The functionality analysis that took place pinpointed several weaknesses in the systems, especially in the case of the CQL system. It was therefore determined that the CQL system would need to be improved regardless of any optimisation through any subsequent merger with the CRM system.

5. The proposed solution

The analysis undertaken enabled the specification of improved systems for the company. Two phases of improvement were suggested. The first, short term improvement, involved the specification of a new, enhanced version of the CQL system which, due to its revitalised functionality, was renamed to IQLS (Intelligent Query Logging System). The IQLS specification was informally presented to the Danwood IT manager, as well as to the development team, all of which added their own input into how the system could be best implemented. Again diagrams were used to help convey the ideas, an example of which is given in Figure 1. The specification was then added to a report, which was formally approved by the Danwood Group's Managing Director.

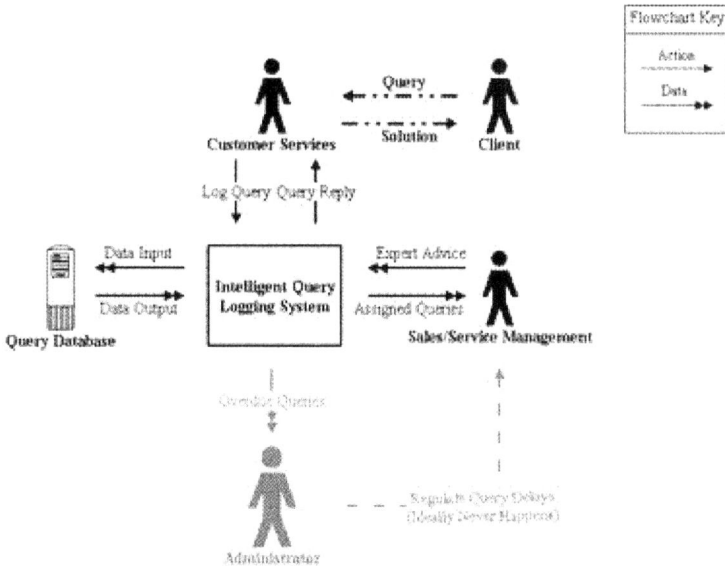

Figure 1: Concept diagram for the new Intelligent Query Logging System

The second improvement was the more significant enhancement involving merging the CRM and CQL systems. After performing the analysis on the two systems it was determined that by connecting them together, the resultant "hybrid" system would form the total solution that the Danwood Group required, as all the functionality and essential customer information would be available through a single, centralised system.

The merging together of the two systems in use would require a major investment of effort to develop the new systems and to implement the new system in a smooth switchover that did not have any negative impact on the users in the Customer Services department. This required a justification for the investment.

Ideally, to show any return on investment, quantitative metrics that demonstrate the effect of improved systems on an organisation's business success should be used. However, these metrics would need to focus on defining values for the intangible as well as the tangible benefits that can result from the implementation. In this case study, tangible benefits, such as increase in revenue and profit levels, and cost cutting in man-hours and product costs, were not available, as the values after improvement could not be available to compare with the values before. The intangible benefits, such as improved customer satisfaction, staff job satisfaction, quality improvement, enhanced confidence, future business, teamwork and intellectual capital, that organisations need to maintain competitive advantage were also not available for the same reason. To overcome this problem, benchmark figures were identified for the tangible benefits, such as revenue and man-hours used, and surveys were designed to attempt to give some quantitative value to many of the intangible benefits based on the users ratings of aspects such as customer satisfaction. These metrics could then be collected both before and after the systems improvements were implemented to enable a full evaluation of the return on investment to be determined. Unfortunately, this evaluation could only take place after the improvement implementation, so the business case for the improvements put to the company board had to rely on rather speculative projections for the return on investment.

Despite the lack of concrete figures to show a return on investment, the logic of the proposals put forward was clear, with the identified duplication of data and the overlap in functionality between the systems being clearly an undesirable feature of the current systems. Indeed, the Danwood Group Board had no problem in seeing this logic and they accepted the changes suggested in principle. The researchers were obviously pleased that their efforts in the overall process improvement project had yielded such an early success and turned to other aspects of the research at the company with enthusiasm.

6. The problem

The fact that the researchers continued to work with the company was, perhaps, fortunate as it was possible to observe the longer term effects of the proposals. The problem was that the effects were non-existent. As time progressed it became clear that the success of this initial research was not as it first seemed. Although the company had accepted the proposals in principle, it never approved the funding to carry out the changes required and no employee or contractor was ever assigned the task of implementing the changes. Eventually it became clear that the proposals had, in effect, been abandoned.

This outcome was a surprise and indeed an important reality check for the research team. For the proposals to be abandoned amounted to a failure for this initial research. What had gone wrong? If the company had accepted the value of the proposals, why did the company not follow through with the implementation? This problem led to a re-evaluation of the whole project approach and an investigation into why an apparent project success had turned into such a clear failure.

The first aspect examined was the researchers' own role in working with the company. Had the company simply lost faith in the research team and had become no longer interested in their ideas? Fortunately the continued work carried out at the company showed that this was not the case. Indeed, the company continued to be very supportive of the work undertaken by the author employed by the company, showing interest in his work and his ideas. Therefore, this was not the reason for the problem.

The fact that one of the authors continued to be employed by the Danwood Group proved to be invaluable in getting to the bottom of the problem encountered. The author was able to chat informally with colleagues at all levels from the lowest level employee up to the directors and could observe their reactions on these and other occasions, such as in meetings, when the project proposals were discussed. This close contact with the company meant the information could be acquired without the problem becoming a major issue. This method of gathering information proved to be very successful and before long a full picture began to emerge showing why the proposed changes had come to nothing.

7. Reasons for the failure

There were a number of reasons discovered for the lack of implementation of the proposed changes:

- The Danwood Group is not adverse to change. On the contrary, it is a dynamic, forward looking company and hence its involvement with the University to carry out research on process improvement. However, this does present problems as, at the time the proposals were made, there was a backlog of over 100 IT change requests waiting for action at the company. While this would account for some delay, it would not cause the change to be abandoned completely. Further enquiries showed that the proposals put forward by the research team were designated the lowest priority. This has the effect that, in a dynamic company where improvements are continually being requested, the proposal would be unlikely to ever rise up the list of outstanding tasks far enough for action to be taken. There would always be a task deemed more important. This does explain why the proposals were never implemented, but it does not explain why they were not considered important enough to be designated a higher priority.
- There appeared to be a negative attitude towards knowledge management. Some of the senior management team regarded knowledge management to be little more than a fad. The problem is that the term "Knowledge Management" is often surrounded by hype (Malhotra 1998) and can be the subject of sometimes exaggerated claims that it is "essential for survival", the "key to prosperity" or that it will "revolutionise a business". Such claims have been heard by managers before. An example would be the hype that once surrounded total quality management (Kemp 2006). In reality, total quality management hasn't gone away, but rather, many of its ideas and principles are now incorporated into most companies' standard procedures. This means that, despite the common use of its philosophy, the term "Total Quality Management" isn't used as often today and certainly the hype that surrounded it has faded away. The same could well happen to knowledge management as its ideas are accepted and internalised, the term could eventually become less prominent. Despite the reality, therefore, it is very possible for managers to mistakenly view these initiatives as a fad. In the case of the proposals made at the Danwood Group, this phenomenon may account for the proposals being received less enthusiastically than

would have occurred if they had not been described as knowledge management proposals. In practice, however, the knowledge management terminology had not been over stressed and the proposals were generally seen as being the result of the process improvement research project, so the attitudes to knowledge management did not really account for the low priority status that the proposals obtained. Nevertheless, this finding did ensure that the research team were more careful with their terminology in future collaboration with the company.

- The fact that the research team had been unable to put figures on the return on the investment for the proposals had clearly reduced the enthusiasm for the changes required. Although attempts were made to obtain fully costed details of the return achieved, these counted for little at the time of assigning the funding for the change as the costings were not available at that time. The lessons from this are simple, a means has to be found to show some form of payback for an investment while it is still in the planning stage, regardless of how difficult it is to achieve this.

- All the above problems, however, faded in significance when compared with the main reason found for the research proposals' failure. The main reason found was simply that the company did not "own" the problem. They had been unaware that they had a problem before the knowledge audit and analysis was carried out and, although they could see the logic of the resulting proposals, they also knew that it hadn't stopped the company functioning. Although the Customer Services department encountered some inconvenience in using the two current systems, they were still able to undertake their jobs and had far more urgent and significant problems to attend to than this inconvenience. No-one from the company was inspired enough to champion the changes required. From their point of view, they had many problems associated with their jobs but could not see that they were solving any of these with the system merger proposals put forward by the research team, so why should they take them seriously?

8. The resulting new approach to knowledge management process improvement

It was interesting to note that the one part of the proposals that was, in due course, acted on, was the relatively minor upgrades to the Call Query Logging system to turn it into the Intelligent Query Logging System. This had suffered the same disadvantages of having to compete with 100 other change requests, being labelled a "knowledge management" improvement and having no figures for a return on investment. The difference was that the users in the Customer Services department recognised that the system did not fully match their needs and therefore wanted some improvements to that system before the research project was ever undertaken. In other words, they "owned" the problem, they had already "bought in" to changes being made and were prepared apply pressure to get the necessary changes financed.

This experience led to a questioning of the starting point of the research, the knowledge audit. The objective of the audit was to identify inefficiency and ineffectiveness and, potentially, to identify ways to address these problems. However, every organisation has its problems and most employees will be aware of at least one aspect of the company processes that inconveniences them or hinders them in some way. These are the problems the work force understands and recognises and it is for these that they want to see some form of solution. Why then, should a process improvement initiative start with an activity to look for other problems? It was concluded, therefore, that the starting point for such research should be a *problem audit* rather than a knowledge audit. The first step should be to talk to employees to discover what problems are giving them concern and the extent that these problems are impacting employees and the company as a whole. Those problems with the greatest impact should then be the focus for process improvement.

Starting with a recognised problem has the added advantage that the problem provides a benchmark cost against which to compare improvement costs. If the problem has an impact, then some means of measuring the cost of that impact should be available, whether it is wasted man-hours, the cost of recovery from an error, or the cost of not being able to do something. Once this cost has been determined it can be compared with the cost of whatever knowledge management solution is proposed and can, therefore, form a basis for return on investment projections. Note that the introduction of a knowledge management initiative may well give benefits other than simply solving the problem identified, but these additional advantages should not be part of the business case for the proposed improvement. As these additional benefits are not needed to solve any problem they should be simply considered a bonus for any evaluation after implementation. Before implementation, it will be far more difficult to predict the cost savings these additional benefits will bring so they are unlikely to gain the same "buy in" from either the users or the management. The business case is much more likely to be accepted on the basis of costs for known problems only.

So is a knowledge audit a waste of time? While its use as a first step may not be advocated, the knowledge audit still has its place. For example, whatever problems are revealed, it will still be necessary to evaluate the extent of the problem and it will still be necessary to find a solution. The knowledge audit may be able to help in both these respects. Having a known problem to consider will give a greater focus to the audit. Could there be, for example, an instance of best practice or use of a system in one part of the organisation that could help solve a problem in another department? Having a focus for the knowledge audit should both help increase its effectiveness and reduce the time taken.

From the above considerations, for further work at the Danwood Group, the research team adopted a seven step methodology to introduce knowledge management based process improvements:

1. Carry out a problem audit to determine what problems are known to exist and are of concern to the users.
2. Assess the impact of each identified problem, including obtaining some measure of the costs attributable to the problem.
3. Design a solution to the problem. This will often involve a knowledge management initiative, though this would not necessarily be the case. A knowledge audit may help at this stage.

4. Justify the cost of implementing the solution by comparing it with the cost of the problem only. Any other benefits that the proposed solution would bring should not be emphasised at this stage.
5. Implement the solution.
6. Evaluate the actual cost savings of the solution. At this point *all* benefits can be included if proper before and after cost comparisons can be made.
7. Use the proven cost saving success of the project to promote a wider roll out of the solution and to promote new proposals to solve further problems.

This straight forward methodology with its emphasis on problem solving has since proven to be very successful at the Danwood Group and elsewhere and has been used by the research team in all subsequent work.

9. Conclusion

This paper has described a case study where a standard pattern of audit, analysis and system design at a commercial company initially appeared to be successful, but an unwillingness of the company to prioritise the proposed changes eventually led to the failure of the initiative. Reflection on the project outcome led to further research into the reasons for the failure and a re-evaluation of the approach taken. It was concluded that the initial starting point of a knowledge audit was not appropriate and that it was better to start with a *problem audit* to identify what problems were of concern to users in an organisation. Focussing on a problem to be solved also provided a basis for cost comparisons with any solutions proposed and a seven step methodology was derived to follow this new approach.

This paper shows that a clear focus on "What problem are we trying to solve?" enables a knowledge management initiative to obtain the necessary buy-in from both management and users and enables a convincing cost justification to be made. This new approach has been very successful, but the ideas involved are not specific to any particular domain. It is therefore recommended that practitioners follow the methodology advocated

for any knowledge or information management systems implementation in
organisations elsewhere.

Acknowledgement

The authors of this paper would like to thank the Danwood Group for
sponsoring and providing the opportunities for the research reported in
this paper.

References

Balafas, P. and Jackson, T.W. (2003) "Revitalising your Systems through Cross-
System Analysis", *Proceedings of Software Quality Management 2003: Process
Improvement and Project Management Issues*, Ross & Staples (eds), Springer,
Software Quality Management (SQM), Glasgow, pp. 115 -126,
ISBN:1902505530

Burnett, S., Illingworth, L. and Webster, L. (2004) "Knowledge auditing and mapping: a pragmatic approach", *Knowledge and Process Management*, 11(1), pp.
25 - 37

Gunnlaugsdottir, J. (2003) "Seek and you will find, share and you will benefit : organising knowledge using groupware systems", *International Journal of Information Management*, 23 (5), pp. 363-380

Kemp, S. (2006), *Quality Management Demystified*, McGraw Hill Professional, ISBN:
0071449086

Liebowitz, J., Rubenstein-Montano, B., McCaw, D., Buchwalter, J., Browning, C.,
Newman, B., Rebeck, K. (2000) "The knowledge audit", *Knowledge and Process
Management*, 7(1), pp. 3-10,

Malhotra, Y. (1998), "Tools@work: deciphering the knowledge management hype",
The Journal for Quality and Participation, 21(4), 58-60.

Marwick, A.D. (2001) "Knowledge management technology", *IBM Systems Journal*,
40(4), pp. 814-830

Wilson, T.D. (2002) "The nonsense of 'knowledge management'", *Information Research*, 8(1)

Knowledge Management, an Enduring Fashion

Kenneth A. Grant
Ryerson University, Toronto, Canada

Editorial Commentary

This paper examines KM through the lens of Abrahamson's Management Fashion Theory, considering two dimensions – the publication discourse, through citation counts, and concept diffusion, through case studies in five professional services firms. The analysis demonstrates the enduring nature of KM when compared to many other management fads but also highlights a growing separation between KM as discussed in the research literature and as practiced in knowledge intensive firms. The paper includes a solid methodology description and provides a useful example of structured analysis of trade and academic literature to develop a longitudinal picture of the popularity of a research theme or topic.

Abstract: Knowledge Management has been a subject of significant management interest for some 15 years. During that time it has been subjected to a variety of criticisms including the argument that it is little more than a "fad" -- something that catches management's attention for a while and then fades away because of a lack of sustainability. It has been compared to other major management fads such as quality circles and business process re-engineering.

This paper examines the discipline of Knowledge Management (KM) through the lens of management fashion theory. It demonstrates that KM is not a fad and that it has become an enduring management activity. Management Fashion Theory (Abrahamson and Fairchild, 1999) is an extension of Rogers' Theory of Diffusion of Innovations (Rogers, 2003), that takes a skeptical view of business innovations, viewing the discourse about and the diffusion of innovations as a cultural phenomenon rather than a rational decision making process.

After a brief introduction to the field of Knowledge Management (KM), a review of the theories of Diffusion of Innovations and Management Fashion is presented, along with a description of the methodology used to apply Management Fashion Theory to the discourse on KM. Bibliometric and content analysis techniques are used to examine publications and discourse in the field from 1990 to 2009. Finally, the actual practice in five professional services firms is examined for consistency with the discourse analysis findings.

The analysis of discourse on KM demonstrates a significant period of "latency" from the late 1980s to 1994, during which foundational ideas and precursors to KM appear. Then a rapid growth period is identified, from 1995-2001 during which KM becomes an innovation of interest to most major organizations. Finally, it appears that discourse has settled at a steady state, with no decline apparent. However, detailed analysis has also indentified a potential conflict between the interests of practitioners and researchers, with a separation of the discourse into distinct groups. The field experience in five major professional services firms demonstrates widespread use of KM, although actual practice in some areas varies considerably from that proposed by researchers in the field.

In summary, this paper presents a comprehensive analysis of the evolution of discourse on and the actual diffusion of KM. It provides bibliometric evidence that there has been a sustained interest up in KM that is quite unlike that of other popular management themes over the last 30 years. While it raises some questions about the relevance of some of the research being carried out, it demonstrates that KM is an enduring management fashion.

Keywords: Management Fashion, Innovation Diffusion, Bibliometric Analysis, KM Strategy

1. Introduction

The first decade of KM has been succinctly summarised by J-C Spender (2005), who observed that:

The most obvious news is that knowledge management (KM) has become big business, growing explosively since Drucker drew attention to it in 1988 (Drucker, 1988). We now see KM conferences all over the world, a huge number of KM trade journals, and battalions of KM consultants. The majority of organizations, both private and public, have KM projects of various types and their spending is enormous...There has been a parallel growth of academic discussion about knowledge.

He then goes on to say, "As KM has risen in importance and managerial fashionability the hype and confusion has multiplied, leading some to argue that KM is a fad of little long-term significance."

Wilson (2002) describes KM as, "in large part, a management fad, promulgated mainly by certain consultancy companies, and the probability is that it will fade away like previous fads." This has led to other authors to apply a more formal framework to assess the fad/fashion phenomenon, with Scarbrough & Swan (2001) and Ponzi & Koenig (2002), both drawing on the work of Abrahamson (1999), to suggest that KM might be passing from a fad to something more enduring.

2. Background

The effective use of knowledge is often argued to be key to competitive success in the global economy of the 21st century. Not only is the effective management of knowledge argued to be a critical element of the innovations needed to be successful, Knowledge Management is, of itself, a major "innovation".

One approach frequently used to examine management decisions to adopt new innovations is the Theory of Diffusion of Innovations, initially developed by Rogers in the 1960s (Rogers, 2003) and drawing on widespread studies of promotion and adoption of agricultural innovations. For Rogers, "an innovation is an idea, practice, or object that is perceived as new by an individual or other unit of adoption" and "diffusion is the process by which an innovation is communicated through certain channels over time among the members of a social system". The participant in the innovation decision can be an individual or an organization. Over time, a successful innovation is adopted by a high proportion of its target population, with several stages of adoption. Figure 1 shows the theoretical framework of adoption.

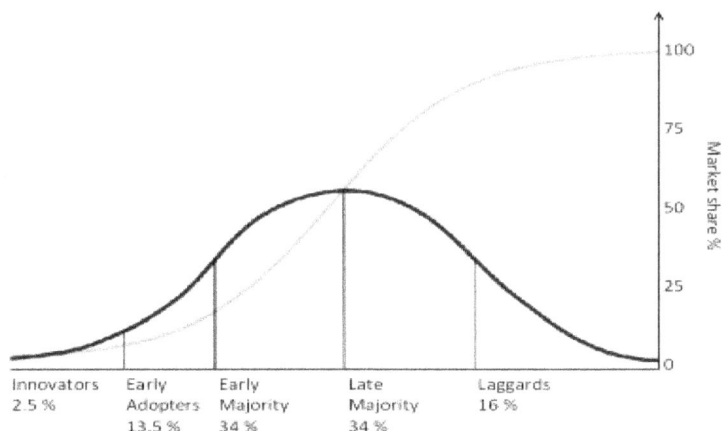

Figure 1: A Successful Innovation Adoption (from Rogers, 2003)

Abrahamson (1991), however, argues that the management innovation-diffusion literature is dominated by a perspective that assumes that rational adopters make independent and technically efficient choices and that, frequently, this is not the case. He goes on to propose that the diffusion of "innovative administrative technologies" (prescriptions for designing organizational structures and cultures) can be described as management fads or fashions.

Thus, management fashion is "largely a cultural phenomenon, shaped by norms of rationality" (i.e. sets of behaviours that are believed to be rational by a particular stakeholder group) and expectations of progress (i.e. management must be seen to be always looking for improvement) (Abrahamson, 1996). This steady user demand for new management fashions is met by a supply of new ideas promoted by management fashion setters. These fashion setters may "invent, rediscover or reinvent the management technique they attempt to launch into fashion".

The underlying expectation is that, over time, the use of a specific management fashion will eventually decline and new fashions must emerge to meet the demand for innovative ideas. Specific versions of the Fashion S-curve have been developed to show this expectation that a management fashion is typically "characterised by a long latency phase followed by a wave-like, often asymmetrical and ephemeral popularity curve" (Abrahamson and Fairchild, 1999).

Figure 2 illustrates the general argument. Following an, often extended, period of latency, where initial concepts are formulated but do not receive widespread attention, some trigger (this can be exogenous or endogenous to the field) drives a period of rapid growth in popularity, followed by a period of widespread use and then a period of decline. During this period of decline the management fashion may be subject to a re-examination and redefinition that may then act as a trigger for a new a wave of popularity.

As a result, some fashions can achieve widespread adoption and continued use for a considerable period of time. Others will decline quite quickly and these are considered to be "fads". Finally, in a given subject area during a period of decline, a redefinition can take place and multiple cycles or generations of innovation are visible where, as one proposed approach declines, fashion setters introduce a new innovation.

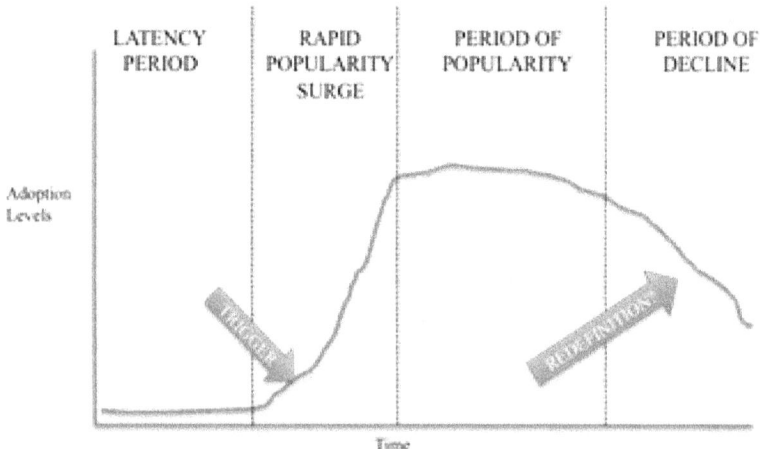

Figure 2: The Management Fashion Cycle (Abrahamson and Fairchild, 1999)

Of particular importance in the supply of management fashion is the role of the "management guru." Huczynski (1993) describes three kinds of management guru:

- The Academic Guru: An academic from a major educational institution, who has developed and popularized his or her ideas on some aspect of management. Examples include Michael Porter, Henry Mintzberg and Kenneth Blanchard.
- The Consultant guru: Senior professionals and prestigious firms who have established a reputation for creative insight and extensive experience in particular fields. Examples include Peters and Waterman, W Edwards Deming, Peter Drucker and the consulting firms of McKinsey or BCG.
- The Hero-Manager guru: A senior executive who has committed their thoughts to print, either directly or through a biographer, and whose authority comes from apparent success. Examples include Lee Iacocca, Jack Welch and Donald Trump.

Specifically, Collins (2000), in his critical examination of management fads and buzzwords, argues that the work of gurus constitutes a "ready-made science of management" that, given its influence on business decisions, must be exposed to critical review. Carson et al comment that "clearly there are some negative connotations associated with the word. Many fashion setters, such as consultants, would object to the label "fad" being associated with their intervention. (Carson et al., 1999)

Between 1996 and 2009, at least 18 studies of management fashion have been carried out, examining 28 different management topics, including Business Process Re-engineering and Quality Management. In the vast majority of cases a period of latency (perhaps 5 years or more) is followed by a rapid growth in popularity (typically from 3-5 years) with a very short peak (sometimes for as little as 1 year) and then a steady decline in interest to a much lower steady state (over a 5- 7 year period). The typical complete cycle of a management fashion seems to be in the 10-15 yea range.

3. Analysis

3.1. Methodology

Abrahamson & Fairchild (1999) distinguish between the discourse about a fashion and the actual use of the fashion and recommend that management fashions can be studied by examining two parallel life cycles – the evolution of the discourse surrounding the innovation and the degree to which the innovation is actually adopted for continued use (its diffusion):

Discourse life-cycle analysis is an approach used to examine the volume and nature of discourse about a particular fashion over time. This is typically done by bibliographic and content analysis, separating the various modes of discourse -- mass media, Internet, trade/business press, academic press (journals and dissertations).

Diffusion life-cycle analysis is an approach used to determine the degree to which an innovation is actually adopted by organizations (fashion followers) and the level of use over time. Depending on the nature of the innovation, this can be done through surveys, case studies or analysis of secondary data, such as growth/decline in the businesses of service or product suppliers and specific market sales data. Of the 18 management fashion studies reviewed for this research, all examine discourse, however only five examine the diffusion, usually by referencing secondary data. This is a significant weakness in the application of management fashion theory, since, from a practitioner viewpoint, it is the diffusion of the innovation that is important, not the discourse.

In this paper, discourse life cycle analysis is used to examine the literature on Knowledge Management. A bibliographic analysis was done using the online ProQuest Research Library Complete, which provides abstracts, indexing and full text for more than 1,800 titles from academic journals, popular magazines, business publications and newspapers and allows a separation of sources.

Preliminary findings from a diffusion analysis are also provided using evidence of five case studies in professional services firms.

3.2.   An Initial Analysis of KM Discourse since 1990

The late 1980s and early 1990s saw some pioneering efforts that led to the concept of KM emerging as a distinct recognizable discipline by the mid-to late 1990s. Figure 3 shows the results of a search for the term "knowledge management" on the ProQuest online database in April 2010, producing almost 25,000 citations. (To set this in context, similar searches for "business process reengineering" and "quality circles" produced 9,336 and 2,361 citations respectively.) Visual inspection of the graph presented suggests that a period of latency continued to about 1995, followed by a rapid growth from 1995 to 2001 and then a decade of consistent interest at about 2,000 citations per year.

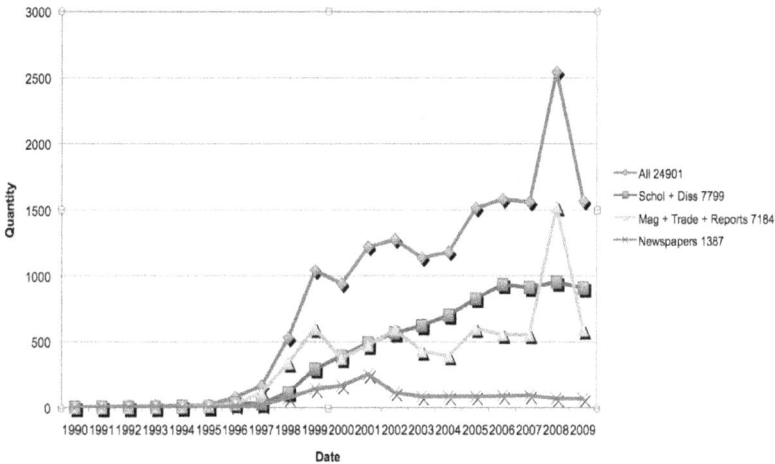

Figure 3: KM Discourse Analysis 1990-2009, Search Term "Knowledge Management"

The graph plots suggest that popular interest, as demonstrated by newspaper articles, peaked in 2001 and has since declined. Discourse within industry sources initially exceeded that from academics; however, industry interest has plateaued since about 2001, while academic interest rose steadily until 2006, after which it has also plateaued. This is consistent with Abrahamson and Fairchild's (1999) description of the management fashion cycle, but with no evidence of any decline. When comparing this with the cycles developed for other management fads and fashions (such as quality circles and business process re-engineering) this indicates a significantly longer period of popularity within the discourse analysis than has been evident for most of the other proposed innovations that have been described as management fads or fashions in other studies.

However, the field of knowledge management can be viewed from a number of different perspectives, each with its own terminology. The next sections of the analysis examine a number of themes within the KM field to determine whether the patterns identified in the overall analysis are consistent or whether there are significant differences in different subject areas.

The themes were developed from a content analysis of major KM publications, including the Journal of Knowledge Management and the Journal of Intellectual Capital. As shown in Figure 4, the themes are:

1. The management and exploitation of "intellectual capital."
2. Social views of knowledge: organizational learning and communities of practice.
3. Knowledge work and knowledge models and processes.
4. The widespread use of IT to capture, codify and share knowledge.
5. The need to manage knowledge activities at both the strategic and operational levels.

Figure 4: Common Themes in the KM Literature

3.2.1. Theme 1: The management and exploitation of intellectual capital

Perhaps the earliest coherent theme that emerged in the KM field, with some antecedents in the word of economics and innovation (which can be seen, for example, in (Teece, 1986)), is the idea of managing intellectual capital or "knowledge assets." Karl-Erik Sveiby's early work in Sweden, (for example, (Sveiby and Risling, 1986) is seen by many as the beginning of the knowledge management movement and a example of a hero-manager guru, as is Lief Edvinsson, who is widely recognized as the first CKO, appointed by Skandia in 1991. However, wider popularization of the concept likely started with Thomas Stewart's writings in Fortune magazine (Stewart, 1991, Stewart, 1994).

Figure 5 shows the bibliographic discourse analysis from 1990 to 2009, using the search term 'intellectual capital' or 'intellectual assets'

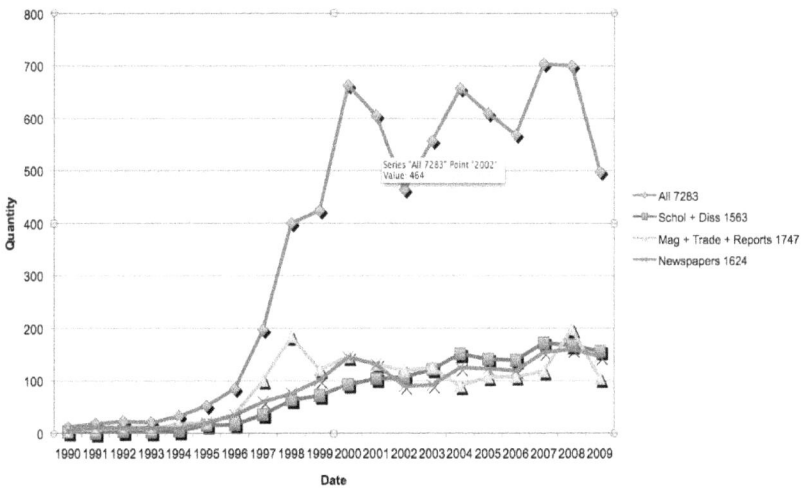

Figure 5: KM Discourse Analysis 1990-2009, Search Term 'Intellectual Capital' or 'Intellectual Asset'

Inspection of the graph shows the same rapid rise demonstrated earlier for the term "knowledge management" with an extended tool from about 2000 at about 600 citations per year. However, examination of the individual categories indicates that, over the last decade, while there has been a steady increase in discourse within the academic community, industry discourse after a fast peak in 1998, declined to a steady state thereafter.

3.2.2. Theme 2: Social Views of Knowledge: Organizational Learning and Communities of Practice

Another early theme was the consideration of learning and knowledge sharing as a social activity. This theme was popularized by Senge, an academic guru, in his book The Fifth Discipline (Senge, 1990) and evolved from the world of general systems theory.

Much of this work in organizational learning addresses a key challenge of attempting to define knowledge in a business or organizational context. Thus, while the organizational learning field takes as a given that knowledge is learned by both individuals and organizations, it provides quite varied views on what exactly that knowledge is. This discussion frequently focuses around two linked concepts - organizational memory and communities.

In Figures 6 and 7, the results of two bibliographic searches are presented. The first shows the results of a search for Organisational Learning ((using both the British and US spelling) and the second looks at Communities of Practice. The plot for organizational learning shows a steady growth in interest from 1990 to about 2003, after which it remains at a steady state of around 700 references per year. In contrast, the plot is for communities of practice discourse shows a period of latency till about 1997, followed by fast growth till 2004, when it flattens at about 240 references per year (as explained earlier, the spike in 2008 should be ignored). Of particular notice in both plots is the very high level of discourse in academic sources when compared to industry or press interest.

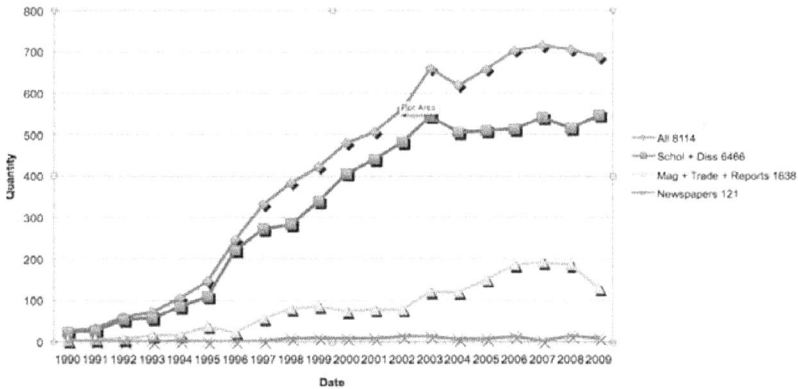

Figure 6: A KM Discourse Analysis 1990-2009, Search Terms 'Organisational Learning' or 'Organizational Learning'

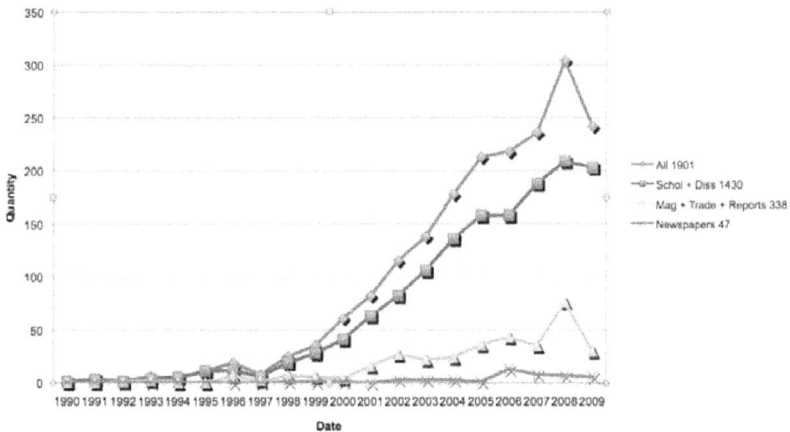

Figure 7: A KM Discourse Analysis 1990-2009, Search Term 'Communities of Practice'

3.2.3. Theme 3: Knowledge Work and Knowledge Models and Processes

Three linked sub-themes have emerged around the concept of knowledge work. One is related to the special situation of the knowledge worker and of knowledge intensive organizations. Another relates to knowledge management models, both conceptual and structural, and a third has evolved around knowledge processes. Each of these is discussed in more detail below.

Knowledge Work(ers): The early 1990s saw the beginnings of the examination of the knowledge worker as a specific topic of interest. Peter Drucker, a consultant guru, is often credited with making the distinction of knowledge-intensive work. As early as 1957, he proposed a new type of worker – the "knowledge worker"

Figure 8 shows a bibliographic analysis, using the search terms of "Knowledge Management' and 'work" or "worker". Overall, a period of latency till 1996 is followed by a very rapid growth till 1999, followed by a steady state discourse at a fairly low citation level of about 60 per year. Both the academic and industry discourse shows a sustained period of growth before flattening out in the mid to late 2000s.

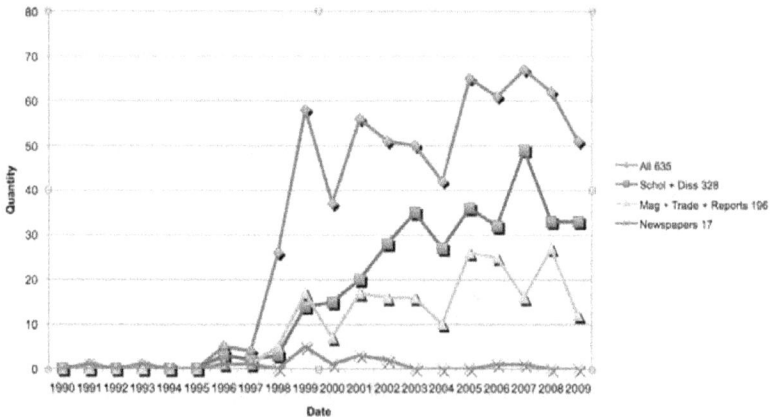

Figure 8: A KM Bibliographic Analysis 1990-2009, Search Terms 'Knowledge Management' and 'Knowledge Work' or 'Knowledge Workers'

Knowledge Models: Perhaps the most significant single KM paper published in the 1990s was Ikijiro Nonaka's The Knowledge-Creating Company (Nonaka, 1991). Nonaka "corporatized" the tacit/explicit dimension of "personal" knowledge, as originally proposed by Polanyi (1958) and proposed a spiral model for in knowledge creation and transfer which was later formalized by Nonaka (Nonaka, 1994, Nonaka and Takeuchi, 1995) as the SECI Model (Socialization, Externalization, Internalization, Combination). This model, along with its fundamental assumption that tacit technology can be transferred and can also be converted to explicit knowledge set in a corporate context, is likely the most widely adopted knowledge management concept in KM.

Over the last 15 years or so large number of other knowledge models have been proposed by academics. McAdam and McCreedy (1999) and Kakabadse et al (2003) describe several alternate categories of KM model, including "philosophy-based" models (of which Polanayi's tacit/explicit model is an example), "knowledge category" models such as Nonaka's SECI model and Boisot's I-Space (Information Space), with its six phases of knowledge evolution across the three dimensions of diffusion, abstraction and codification (Boisot, 1999); cognitive" models, often based on intellectual capital or knowledge process themes such as the Skandia IC model (Roos and Roos, 1997) or the Knowledge Life Cycle model of McElroy (1999); and "socially constructed" models of KM, such as that of Demarest (1979), who introduces social interchange processes for the dissemination of knowledge.

Figure 9 shows a bibliographic analysis, using the search terms of "Knowledge Management' and 'model". Overall, a period of latency till 1997 is followed by a rapid growth till 2006, after which interest seems to plateau at about 300 citations per year, with almost all of the growth and discourse taking place in academic journals. Industry discourse shows relatively little interest in KM models.

Knowledge Processes: The early 1990s saw a widespread interest in business process reengineering, peaking around the publication of Reengineering the Corporation (Hammer and Champy, 1993), along with an increased recognition of the importance of business processes as a primary means of adding value. A number of authors, notably Davenport et al (1996) and Davenport & Prusak in Working Knowledge (Davenport and Prusak, 1998) discussed the issues relevant to applying process models to knowledge work, differentiating between processes that apply knowledge and processes intended to create knowledge.

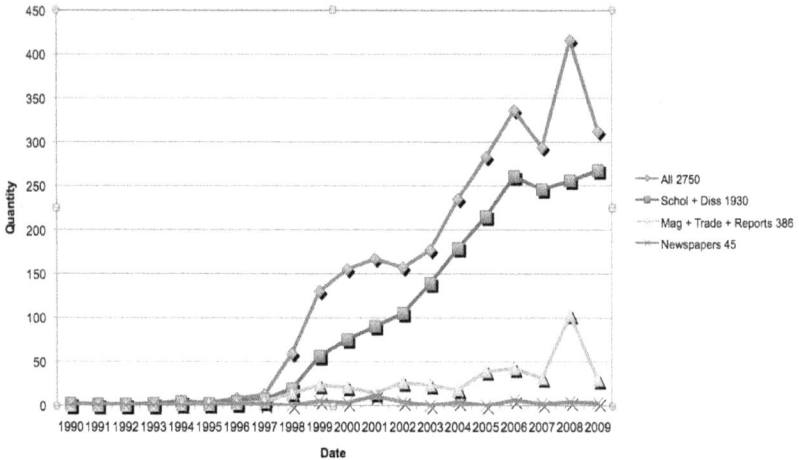

Figure 9: A KM Discourse Analysis 1990-2009, Search Terms 'Knowledge Management' and 'Knowledge Models'

While the work of Davenport & Prusak (one of the most cited sources in the literature) covers a wide range of knowledge management topics, it seems to be most frequently used for its presentation of the roles and uses of information systems as tools to capture, codify and transfer knowledge.

Figure 10 shows a bibliographic analysis, using the search terms of '"Knowledge Management' and 'Process'". Overall, a period of latency till 1997 is followed by a very rapid growth till 2001, followed by a steady state at about 600 citations per year. Academic discourse shows a sustained period of growth before flattening out in 2006, while industry discourse flattens out at a lower level by 2002. To some degree, this interest in knowledge processes can be seen as a continuation of the focus on business processes initiated in the BPR fashion of the 1990s, that going beyond the cost reduction process work that characterized much of that activity.

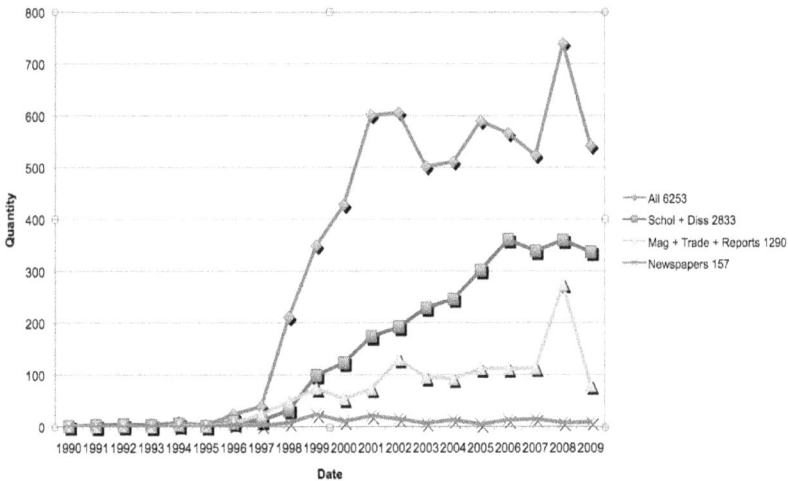

Figure 10: A KM Discourse Analysis 1990-2009, Search Terms 'Knowledge Management' and 'Knowledge Processes'

3.2.4. Theme 4: The Widespread use of IT to Capture, Codify and Share Knowledge

The discussion that concludes the previous section, suggests a long-term association between knowledge activities and information systems. In addition, by the mid-1990s, the evolution of the personal computer and personal computer applications such as word processing, spreadsheets and personal databases had reached a reasonably mature state. Telecommunications and private network applications were pervasive in many organizations, using communications applications such as email and voice mail and newer "groupware" tools such as LotusNotes were being offered to the market.

Figure 11 shows the bibliographic analysis, using the search terms of '"Knowledge Management' and 'Information Technology or 'System'". A period of latency till 1997 is followed by a very rapid growth in two years followed by a steady state at about 800 citations per year. Similar levels of interest exist in academic and business sources, although the academic discourse shows a longer period of growth before flattening out. This significant focus on IT within KM can be seen as a bringing together of several factors already discussed. The dramatically increasing capabilities of IT during the growth period proved attractive to organizations that saw knowledge as tangible objects to be stored and retrieved and created a dominant perspective of the conversion of tacit to explicit knowledge, often based on a naïve interpretation of Nonaka's SECI model.

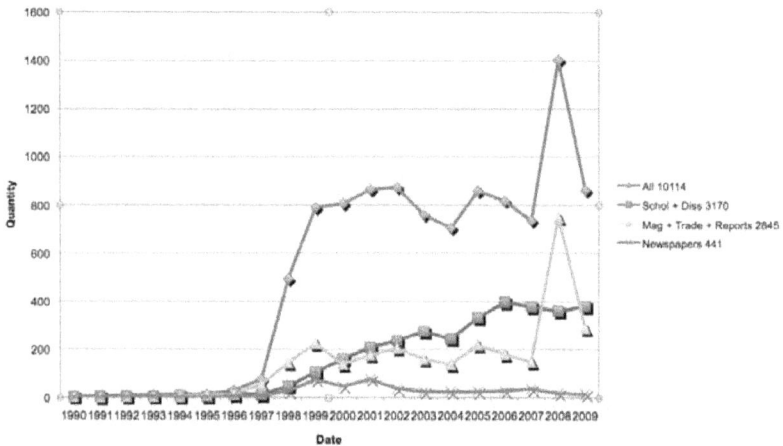

Figure 11: A KM Bibliographic Analysis 1990-2009, Search Terms "'Knowledge Management' and 'information Technology' or 'System'"

3.2.5. Theme 5: The Need to Manage Knowledge Activities at both the Strategic and Operational Levels

Starting in the early 1990s, many authors and practitioners were arguing that there was a need for explicit focus on the management of knowledge - - or at least the management of knowledge-related functions and processes within many types of organization. This goes beyond the approaches suggested in the Intellectual Capital view -- which obviously also includes some management elements.

One of the first to look at Knowledge Management as a business practice (and the individual often credited with the first use of the term "knowledge management") was Karl Wiig, founder of the Knowledge Research Institute, who set out, in a trilogy of books (Karl Wiig, 1993, Karl Wiig,

1994, Karl M. Wiig, 1995), frameworks for knowledge creation and dissemination and for its direction and management.

Figure 11 shows a bibliographic analysis using the terms "knowledge management" and "strategy". A period of latency is visible until about 1996, followed by a rapid growth over two years to a level of about 250 citations per year. The plots show a steady level of industry discourse from about 1998 but continued growth in academic discourse till about 2005. There is some evidence of a change in focus, with some anecdotal evidence suggesting that the CKO role is changing, or in some cases disappearing and that many organizations are still not clear is the most appropriate strategic approach for knowledge management.

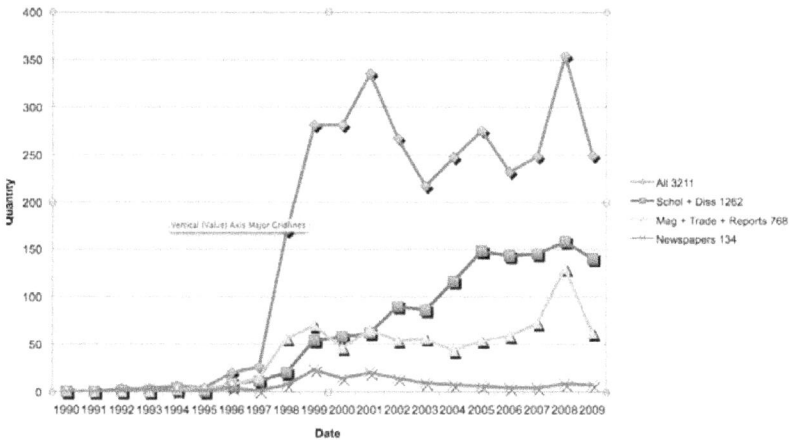

Figure 11: A KM Discourse Analysis 1990-2009, Search Terms 'Knowledge Management' and 'Strategy'

4. Next Generation of KM

After the growth phase as the discourse plateaued, several of the original KM fashion-leader authors developed arguments that there were significant inadequacies in KM as proposed and implemented in the first decade and claimed that a reinvention or "Next" Generation might be needed for success. Specifically McElroy calls for Second Generation Knowledge Management (M. W. McElroy, 2002, M. W. McElroy, 2003). Snowden (2002a) suggests that we are moving towards a Third Generation Knowledge Management and Wiig calls for what described as Next Generation Knowledge Management

5. Discussion

In the previous section, a bibliographic discourse analysis of the key concepts within knowledge management was presented in a series of graphs. A summary of the citations analysed by type is shown in Table 1. From inspection of the citations examined, the graphs and the table, the following conclusions can be drawn in applying management fashion theory to the discipline of knowledge management:

- For each of the themes, there is strong evidence of the influence of management fashion setters, including hero-manager gurus and consultant gurus. The KM field has been strongly influenced by the work of a small number of gurus, initially hero-manager gurus and consultant gurus, with some academic gurus adding their influences in the mid to late 1990s.
- With the possible exception of "organizational learning" every one of the topics analysed demonstrated a latency period followed by a rapid growth in popularity, consistent with the concept of a management fad or fashion.
- None of the topics analysed demonstrates any decline, with most showing consistent interest or increases in the discourse, thus providing no evidence of a fashion decline.
- In each topic, the early growth in discourse took place in industry and the popular press, with academic discourse initially lagging and then increasing to pass the discourse rates of the other communities.
- For the three most frequently occurring topics (Knowledge Management, KM and IT and Intellectual Capital), overall levels of discourse in academe and industry were quite similar.
    - For the other six topics, much more discourse took place within academe than in industry.
- With the single exception of Intellectual Capital, popular press in-Tanterest in the topics was fleeting, typically lasting no more than

two or three years, peaking in 1999/2000 and then declining to very low levels.

- The results for 2008 and 2009 need to be considered carefully. As has been explained earlier, the significant spike in interest within industry sources visible in 2008 for every topic, except for organisational learning is due to new edition of a specific set of industry journals end it did not indicate any increase in discourse. For 2009, although a slight decline is visible in some plots, bibliographic reviews might be expected to under-report the most recent year since many publications restrict access to the most current volumes.

This discourse analysis demonstrates a significant and consistent shift with increasing levels of interest by academics not being matched by writers in industry sources. In addition, although the field of KM was distinctive for the significant early involvement of practitioners as trendsetters, an extensive recent examination of the discourse life cycle of the body of literature in Knowledge Management/Intellectual Capital from 1994 to 2008 (Serenko et al., 2010) describes a very significant shift in authorship. In the early years of KM, non-academics constituted one-third of all authors. However, "by 2008, practitioners' contributions dropped to only ten percent of all KM/IC authors. Pragmatic field studies and experiments, which require an active cooperation of businesses and the involvement of practitioners, constitute only 0.33 percent of all inquiry methods. There has also been a decline in case studies.

In addition, Serenko et al also report that as "the number of research-oriented practitioners has been declining, so has the number of non-academic readers."

The authors suggest that this move away from practice to theory creates a communication gap between researchers and practitioners that makes it difficult for KM/IC scholarly research to be "transformed into practical managerial approaches and organizational practices""

Table 1: Discourse Analysis

	ALL #	ACADEMIC #	ACADEMIC %	INDUSTRY #	INDUSTRY %	NEWSPAPERS #	NEWSPAPERS %	DISCOURSE SUMMARY
Knowledge Management	25901	7799	30%	7184	28%	1387	5%	Latency period, rapid growth, steady level for last 10 years, similar interest in academic and industry discourse, limited newspaper interest
KM & Information Technology/Systems	10114	3170	31%	2845	28%	441	4%	Latency period till 1996, then rapid growth over 3 years, followed by steady state for academic and industry discourse at quite similar levels
Intellectual Capital/Assets	5593	1596	29%	1886	34%	2072	37%	Latency period, initially rapid then steady growth over 15 years, steady and similar levels of academic, industry and newspaper discourse
Organisational Learning	8653	6755	78%	1742	20%	156	2%	Limited latency period, rapid growth over 10 years, then steady level of growth, dominant discourse is academic, much lower levels of industry and newspaper discourse
KM Processes	6253	2833	45%	1290	21%	157	3%	Latency period till 1996, then rapid growth over 5 years, followed by steady growth of academic and flat industry discourse
KM & Strategy	3211	1262	39%	768	24%	134	4%	Latency period till 1996, then rapid growth over 3 years, followed by fairly steady growth for academic and flatter industry discourse
KM Models	2750	1930	70%	386	14%	45	2%	Latency period till 1997, then steady growth over 11 year period, with almost all discourse in academe
Communities of Practice	1901	1430	75%	338	18%	47	2%	Latency period, steady growth over 10 years, dominant discourse is academic, much lower levels of industry and newspaper discourse
Knowledge Work(ers)	635	328	52%	196	31%	17	3%	Latency period till 1996, then rapid growth over 3 years, followed by steady growth for academic and slightly flatter industry discourse, but at similar levels of interest

This increasing divide between practitioner and researchers reflects the broader debate, often referred to as Mode 1 vs Mode 2 research (Huff and Huff, 2001, Starkey and Madan, 2001, Gibbons et al., 1994). As Starkey & Madan suggest, "Business is increasingly concerned with relevance, while business and management researchers in universities cling to a different view of knowledge." Traditional Mode 1 research is often within a single discipline (consider the findings presented above for organizational learning and communities of practice) whereas Mode 2 research tends to be more heterogeneous with a more direct interaction between research and practice, thus it might be argued to have a good fit to the multidisciplinary field of KM.

5.1.   An Initial Analysis of KM Diffusion in Professional Services Firms

Professional services firms (PSFs) were chosen as a suitable environment to test for the diffusion of knowledge management concepts. These are knowledge intensive firms (KIFs), who succeed in the marketplace because of the knowledge base of the firms and their professional staff. Five firms were studied: a strategy consulting firm, two audit/ professional services firms, an IT consulting firm and a law firm. With the exception of the law firm, which was a large Canadian-based firm, the other four firms were large-scale international operations. A total of 54 interviews were carried out across the five firms, including staff at all levels within the firm, from partner to junior professional. In addition to the terms each firm's KM-related IT systems were examined.

Based on the literature review and the bibliometric analysis presented in the previous section, the actual diffusion of KM within the five firms studied was carried out using a seven Theme framework:

- The need for a Strategic Focus on KM
- The Importance of Knowledge Processes
- Recognition of the Personal and Social Nature of Knowledge
- The Use of IT
- The Management of Intellectual Property/Assets
- The Use of KM Models
- The Complexity of Knowledge

The review of the interview transcripts and evidence examined, taken along with a structured analysis of codable comments, demonstrates the importance of knowledge to all the PSFs studied and the existence of strategies, organisational units, policies and business processes to facilitate the creation, sharing and use of knowledge across each firm. Thus, in general terms, the findings in both individual and cross-case analyses demonstrate a broad level of diffusion and adoption of KM within the firms studied. Therefore, these findings do demonstrate that the practice of KM appears to be a sustainable business innovation. However, the detailed examination carried out also demonstrated that the levels and nature of this diffusion vary considerably within the seven themes examined:

Four Themes stand out as having a broad level of adoption in practice:
- Recognition of the Personal and Social Nature of Knowledge
- The Use of IT
- The Importance of Knowledge Processes
- The need for a Strategic Focus

One Theme had broad recognition as an important concept, but the practical diffusion seems to lack many of the characteristics that KM proponents argue are necessary:
- The Management of IP

Finally, there was very limited support for the diffusion of two Themes:
- The Use of KM Models
- The Complexity of Knowledge

Three Themes stand out in the overall level of interest expressed by participants -- the personal and social nature of knowledge, the use of KM processes and the use of IT. This level of interest in interview discussion was supported by detailed descriptions of the diffusion of the Theme and commentary on specific successes and limitations. In many of the comments, all three Themes were linked.

For the participants from all of the firms, these Themes were part of their daily work activities. They carried out many of their professional duties following processes, both formal and informal, relating to knowledge assets–whether those of their own firm or their clients. In some cases the processes were highly formal and often embedded in the quality assurance processes (for example, in audit procedures or legal filings). Frequently, they described a close affinity between knowledge processes and IT systems. IT systems were seen as part of most major processes, whether as repositories or as communication tools.

Throughout the interviews, participants repeatedly returned to the importance of the individual. In the strategy firm, this was seen as an essential part of their market differentiation. The specific skills and expertise of the experienced professional combined with access to available intellectual assets (processes, repositories and other professionals). Even in the IT firm, which was highly procedural, there was an increasing recognition of the importance of personal contributions and staff structures, and cross-organisation teams and processes had been implemented to make sure that this personal element was included. Expert directories, as well as informal network contacts, were seen as key to success by most participants. Participants frequently returned to the need to get to the right expert to serve their clients. All of the firms had strategies and processes in place to facilitate the formation of formal and informal communities of practice, very much along the lines caused by Brown and Duguid (1991).

To a large degree, the high level of diffusion of these three Themes is a reflection of a strong interest in KM at the strategic level. At a strategic level, the case analyses demonstrate the diffusion of a number of specific strategic recommendations across all of the firms. All have appointed chief knowledge officers (Earl and Scott, 1999); all include KM in their strategic planning (Grant, 1996). These strategic plans reflect the approaches advocated for a resource based view of strategic planning (Grant, 1991). Earl (2001) proposed seven Schools of Knowledge Management in three categories –Technocratic, Economic and Behavioural. The KM strategies adopted by the five firms studied seem to draw on all of these three categories (specifically, the Systems School, the Commercial School and the Organizational school). There is an interesting parallel here with an earlier work on strategic schools. Mintzberg, in describing 10 schools of strategic thought, concludes with the argument that at various times in a firm's strategic planning processes all 10 might be used (Mintzberg et al., 1998).

The case analysis does however, to some degree, refute the work of Hansen et al (1999), who argued for consulting firms to choose either a personalization or codification strategy. In their work, they closely associated the codification strategy with the extensive use of IT systems, suggesting that firms who follow a "strategy of reuse" should adopt the codification model with extensive and formal IT systems, while those who are expected to "create a highly customized solution to a unique product," should follow a personalization strategy with a lesser focus on IT. In examining the KM strategies of the five firms, while more elements of a personalization strategy are visible within the strategy and IT firms, many of the elements of the codification strategy, this is clearly not an either/or situation. All of the firms are highly dependent on effective use of IT systems for effective knowledge sharing. All of the firms, to some degree, recognize the need for culture and tools to share knowledge and access the personal knowledge needed to serve the client. Hansen et al suggest the need for an 80-20 split either way, suggesting that "Executives who try to excel at both strategies risk failing at both." and "Management consulting firms have run into serious trouble when they failed to stick with one approach."

Examination of the Intellectual Property Theme produced some quite mixed results. Declarations of the importance of IP were widespread, both within the firms' official documents and in the interview discussions. However, the concept of intellectual property was largely discussed and at an abstract level. Terminology varied, with intellectual property (IP), intellectual capital (IC) and intellectual assets being mentioned frequently, as well as firm-specific terms related to the topic. None of the firms appear to measure their intellectual property, whether in terms of knowledge inventories, knowledge creation or knowledge use. In most cases, while they may have had employee agreements that addressed the topic of confidentiality, this did not seem to be a concern in practice, with the exception of the IT firm. Typically participants were more concerned about client confidentiality and about misuse of the own intellectual assets. Nor did they consider areas such as methodology development and staff training as knowledge management activities. This largely contradicts the views of proponents of an intellectual capital perspective on KM, such as that presented by Stewart (1997) and Edvinsson & Malone (1997).

The two Themes that might be considered to be the most theoretical -- Better Use of KM models and the Complexity of Knowledge – proved to be of very limited interest to the participants. Indeed, as has been discussed earlier, the majority of the codable comments were somewhat indirect references to the theme, interpretations by the researcher as opposed to direct commentary by the participants. In addition, the majority of the theme-specific comments were made by the KM-expert professionals. In general, professionals were familiar with the concept of tacit explicit knowledge and of the need to access knowledge at various levels of abstraction, as well as the usefulness of metadata can help set the context for the use of retrieved knowledge objects.

Underlying all of the discussion on various Themes was a somewhat paradoxical refrain that, while participants were unanimous in recognizing the importance of and practice of various aspects of knowledge management within their firms, there was a significant degree of reluctance to treat much of what they were doing as "knowledge management". Despite the fact that these are knowledge intensive, indeed knowledge dependent, businesses, the professionals did not demonstrate a great deal of knowledge regarding the discipline of KM. This does not mean the expressed a lack of interest in the use of knowledge in their work. This was a topic of familiarity. It was notable that the KM professionals interviewed as part of the study frequently described attempts to downplay the concept of formal knowledge management.

6. Conclusion

This paper has examined the discourse and the diffusion life cycles of knowledge management and its key related concepts, in the context of management fads, enduring fashions and reinvention. This discourse analysis has indicated that, while the discourse review demonstrates the existence of a latency period followed by a period of rapid growth and continued interest, as suggested by Abramson, there is, as yet, no evidence of a fashion decline.

Also, consistent with Management Fashion Theory, a small number of key fashion setters, individuals who had a significant influence over the initial growth of the KM field have recommending the adoption of a Next Generation of KM -- in management fashion terms, a Re-invention.

The diffusion analysis indicates that knowledge management is a widely recognised practice and that specific elements of the KM discipline are broadly diffused within all of the firms studied. KM was seen as a subject of strategic importance in all the firms and extensive investments had been made, with reasonable success, in KM activities. More detailed examination, however, identified some significant differences in levels of interest and practice within the various Themes identified within the KM literature as being important elements of the discipline.

It is also interesting to note that, although several of the firms studied had, in the past, provided professional services in Knowledge Management, none of them currently do so. Clients did not come to them for Knowledge Management projects, nor was Knowledge Management seen as a specific discipline that should be brought directly to bear within their consulting projects. Thus, it can be argued that, to the degree that KM was a management consulting fad, advocated by consultants for market advantage and to sell services, this is no longer a significant factor and the brief window for specific services in the KM area has disappeared, at least from the perspective of major service providers.

Thus the KM discipline appears to have moved into an "enduring fashion" position and has not followed the "fad" pattern evidenced by most of the other management innovations previously studied. However, perhaps the greatest concern from this review is the increasing divide between practitioner and researcher in this field.

7. Limitations and Next Steps

From a methodological perspective, the discourse analysis carried out is, of course, dependent on the quality of classification systems offered by the online academic publishers.

The diffusion analysis focused on five professional services firms. Further work might consider the generalizability of these findings to other types of knowledge intensive organization and beyond.

References

Abrahamson, E. (1991) Managerial Fads and Fashions: The Diffusion and rejection of innovations Academy of Management Review, 16.

Abrahamson, E. (1996) Management Fashion. Academy of Management Review, 21.

Abrahamson, E. & Fairchild, G. (1999) Management fashion: Lifecycles, triggers, and collective learning processes. Administrative Science Quarterly, 44.

Boisot, M. H. (1999) Knowledge Assets, Oxford University Press.

Carson, P. P., Lanier, P. A., Carson, K. D. & Birkenmeier, B. J. (1999) A historical perspective on fad adoption and abandonment. Journal of Management History, 5.

Collins, D. (2000) Management Fads and Buzzwords: Critical-practical perspectives, London, Routledge.

Davenport, T. H., Jarvenpaa, S. L. & Beers, M. C. (1996) Improving Knowledge Work Processes. Sloan Management Review, Summer 1996, 53-65.

Davenport, T. H. & Prusak, L. (1998) Working Knowledge: How organizations manage what they know, Cambridge, MA, Harvard Business School Press.

Demarest, M. (1979) Understanding knowledge management. Long Range Planning, 30.

Gibbons, M., C., L., Schwartzman, S., Nowotny, H., Trow, M. & Scott, P. (1994) The New Production of Knowledge: The Dynamics of Science and Research in Contemporary Societies, London, Sage.

Hammer, M. & Champy (1993) Reengineering the Corporation: A Manifesto for Business Revolution.

Huczynski, A. (1993) Management Gurus, London, Routledge.

Huff, A. S. & Huff, J. O. (2001) Re-Focusing the Business School Agenda. British Journal of Management, 12.

Kakabadse, N. K., Kakabadse, A. & Kouzmin, A. (2003) Reviewing the knowledge management literature: Towards a taxonomy. Journal of Knowledge Management, 7, 75, 17 pgs.

McAdam, R. & Mccreedy, S. (1999) A critical review of knowledge management models. The Learning Organization, 6.

McElroy, M. W. (1999) The Knowledge Life Cycle: An Executable Model For The Enterprise. ICM Conference on Knowledge Management,. Miami, FL.

McElroy, M. W. (2002) Second Generation Knowledge Management. Vermont, Macro Innovation Associates Inc.

McElroy, M. W. (2003) The New Knowledge Management, Burlington, MA, Butterworth-Heinemann.

Nonaka, I. (1991) The Knowledge Creating Company. Harvard Business Review 69.

Nonaka, I. (1994) A Dynamic Theory of Organizational Knowledge Creation. Organizational Science 5.

Nonaka, I. & Takeuchi, H. (1995) The Knowledge Creating Company: How Japanese Companies Create the Dynamics of Innovation, Oxford Oxford University Press.

Polanyi, M. (1958) Personal Knowledge: Towards a Post-Critical Philosophy, Chicago, University of Chicago Press.

Ponzi, L. J. & Koenig, M. (2002) Knowledge managment: another management fad? Information Research, 8.

Rogers, E. M. (2003) Diffusion of Innovations, Fifth Edition, London, The Free Press.

Roos, G. & Roos, J. (1997) Measuring your Company's Intellectual Performance. Long Range Planning, 30.

Scarbrough, H. & Swan, J. (2001) Explaining the Diffusion of Knowledge Management: The Role of Fashion. British Journal of Management, 12.

Senge, P. M. (1990) The Fifth Discipline: The Art and Practice of the Learning Organization, New York, Doubleday.

Serenko, A., Bontis, N., Booker, L., Sadeddin, K. & Hardie, T. (2010) A scientometric analysis of knowledge management and intellectual capital academic literature (1994-2008). Journal of Knowledge Management, 14.

Spender, J. C. (2005) An overview: what's new and important about knowledge management? Building new bridges between managers and academics. IN LITTLE, S. & RAY, T. (Eds.) Managing Knowledge: An Essential Reader. London, Sage.

Starkey, K. & Madan, P. (2001) Bridging the Relevance Gap: Aligning Stakeholders in the Future of Management Research. British Journal of Management, 12.

Stewart, T. A. (1991) Brainpower. Fortune, 123, 44-50.

Stewart, T. A. (1994) Your Company's Most Valuable Asset: Intellectual Capital. Fortune

Sveiby, K.-E. (2001) A Knowledge-based Theory of the Firm To guide Strategy Formulation. Journal of Intellectual Capital, 2.

Sveiby, K.-E. & Risling, A. (1986) öretagetKunskapsf ("The Knowhow Company") Sweden.

Teece, D. J. (1986) Profiting from technological innovation: Implications for integration, collaboration, licensing and public policy
. Research Policy, 15, 285-305.

Wiig, K. (1993) Knowledge Management Foundations: Thinking about Thinking – How Organizations Create, Represent and Use Knowledge Texas, Schema Press.

Wiig, K. (1994) The Central Management Focus for Intelligent-Acting Organizations Schema Press.

Wiig, K. M. (1995) Knowledge Management Methods: Practical Approaches to Managing Knowledge Schema Press.

Wilson, T. D. (2002) The nonsense of 'knowledge management'. Information research, 8

.

A Case Study of Knowledge Elicitation on Intellectual Capital Performance in the Fund Service Industry

Jie Gu, Rongbin W.B. Lee and Cherie C.Y. Lui
The Hong Kong Polytechnic University, HKSAR, China

Editotial Commentary

Gu, Lee and Lui examine Intellectual Capital development in the fund services industry in this study of the business development unit within an international bank in Hong Kong. Starting with a solid review of the IC literature and models, they present a 3-stage study methodology (knowledge elicitation and capture, knowledge audit, and IC performance study). A detailed description of their approach to grounded theory and keyword code generation and use is presented. A mixed methods technique is used, combining focus groups, workshops and interviews with follow-up questionnaires.

The paper demonstrates a useful approach to quantifying IC development success.

Abstract: The fund services industry is one of the most knowledge-intensive sectors in the financial industry. Professionals in this industry have to work independently as each one has to look after portfolios of clients and markets on their own. Besides, relatively there is little tacit knowledge sharing. How to evaluate the performance of this industry is of practical business interest. A case study was conducted in the business development team of the fund services division in an international bank. The team provides tailored financial services to the fund managers, institutional investors and other commercial banks.

The objectives of the case study are: to elicit and capture tacit and implicit business knowledge of the team members through narratives, study on the IC performance by conducting a knowledge audit, and investigate the value creation efficiency and growth potential. The methodology is based on a combination of different knowledge elicitation techniques from questionnaire survey, focused group discussion and interviews. The key IC elements to be measured in the survey are extracted from narrative database. Respondents are asked to rate both the importance and performance of various IC elements in the construction of the IC value tree. The findings help to identify strength, IC values and risk factors of the business operation from a more balanced perspective. The findings can be used for organizational development and business performance enhancement.

1. Introduction

Knowledge is an invaluable asset of a company and knowledge management is the key leading to the success and continuous growth. Company performance is closely related to how well it manages its knowledge as a source of critical intangible assets. Surprisingly most companies think they know clear what intellectual capital (IC) they own but actually they do not. If they want to make good use of their intellectual capital, they have to visualize and measure it first. Identifying IC is a difficult task. Each IC component contributes to the firm's current and future revenue streams. Designing and implementing initiatives to manage grow, and leverage IC to serve strategic visions is the next task coping with the complex knowledge economy. The Case Study was conducted in Business Development Team (BD Team) of institutional fund services (IFS) in an international bank. Most of the income of IFS comes from the pitch of new business with both new and existing relationships, so relationship managers in BD Team are always directly involved. Staff are required to understand their clients, clients' current business needs through forming partnership. In order to provide a full package of service to the clients, BD Team is required to work hand in hand with other teams for providing one-stop-shop service to clients. The problems of the BD Team include: lack of knowledge codification, knowledge loss due to turnover of staff and deficiency in knowledge sharing channels. Hence, the BD Team was selected with its significance to the company from both monetary and knowledge points of view. In addition, the knowledge of BD with the unique job nature needs to be captured so that the skills and processes involved in handling their work can be stored as corporate asset. The variation in methods of managing various clients under different situation is due to their own past experience and skills which are valuable to the company.the aim of this case study is to elicit and capture tacit business knowledge of the team members through narratives and knowledge audit, study on the IC performance by a qualitative survey, and investigate the value creation efficiency and growth potential.

2. Literature Review

2.1. Intellectual Capital

Intellectual Capital is regarded as an essential competitiveness factor of a company (Wiig, 1997) that does not often appear on balance sheet (Edvisson, 1994). IC is regarded as key drivers of company's value creation (Gupta and Roos, 2001). Developments in terms of intellectual capital reporting are closely linked to individuals such as Sveiby (1997) and Edvinsson and Malone (1997) who wished to obtain a better understanding of value creation within the company. Nonaka (2001) regard the creation and utilization of intangibles as the core activities of a company in order to secure its sustainability. This is particularly valid with regard to the current financial crisis to an international financial service sector.

IC can be classified into various distinct types of intangible asset in the past decades. These classifications aim to give a better explaining of what IC consists of. It appears that the classification of IC into Human Capital, Structural Capital and Relational Capital is increasingly used as a standard perspective (Edvinsson and Kivikas, 2007). According to Devenport, human capital comprises skills, experience, and knowledge which managers could not ignore in formulating a firm's competitive strategy (Devenport, 1997) Structural capital includes organizational routines, procedures, feedback systems, information technology infrastructure, and the organization's environment, etc (Stewart, 1997; Edvinsson & Malone, 1997; Sullivan, 2000). Relational Capital relates to "knowledge of marketing channels and knowledge that embedded in relationships external to the firm" (Bontis, 1998), which is all about the contribution of the clientele towards the organizational growth- the amount of revenue generated through large customers, their commitment levels measured through repeat business (Kamath, 2006). Managing firms' relationship with employees, customers, suppliers, distributors, partners, agencies, government, charities and even media, – is key to establish more business opportunities and enhance company images. Further collaboration with different parties will also help firms to generate more wealth and create new products. Beodker, Guthrie and Cuganesan (2005) published the sub-components of each kind of intellectual capital which we do not see on the balance sheet. (Figure 1)

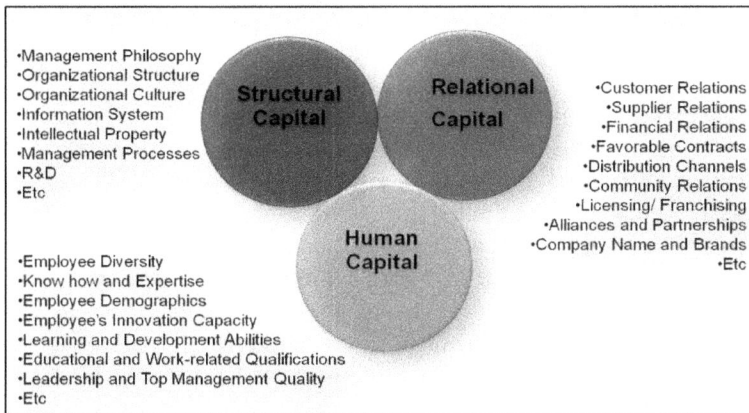

Figure 1 IC Sub-components (Boedker, Guthrie and Cuganesan, 2005)

Sveiby (2001) has reviewed 34 measuring methods of IC. All these methods aim to find out what IC that a company is already in possession and in general share the same purpose of taking a snapshot of the current business environment and identifying the growth constraints under the current IC portfolio (Sveiby, 2001). IC Rating ^{TM}, one of the methods in Sveiby's review, is very commonly used to evaluate intellectual capital performance. It is selected to represent the scorecard method. In addition to the classification used in the IC model, the IC Rating ^{TM} looks at the organization's intangible assets from three different perspectives, namely effectiveness, risk and renewal. A lot of the criticism directed at traditional accounting and financial management and measurement has been that it looks at history to try and predict the future.

The IC Rating ^{TM}, however, consider three forward looking perspectives, and in addition to looking at the current effectiveness of the organization, the model looks at the efforts and abilities to renew and develop itself and also at the risks that the current effectiveness declines. The methodology used for the IC Rating ^{TM} includes the evaluation of more than 200 intangible factors contributing to a company's performance which are further classified into the IC taxonomy. The main source of information is the company's most knowledgeable internal and external stakeholders. Personal in-depth interviews are therefore conducted with internal employees and management and external customers, partners, government bodies etc.

The questions are answered using an 8-point scale and the respondents are also encouraged to provide a short explanation of their grade. Depending on the complexity of the rating, a full rating takes approximately 4-6 weeks to complete. The rating result is then presented on three levels which are The Executive Level, The Operational Level and The Respondent Level. The Executive Level is an overall comprehensive summary showing the three perspectives effectiveness (i.e. a snapshot of how well the intellectual capital is performing today), the risk that the effectiveness decreases, and the renewal (i.e. how well the current initiatives are improving the effectiveness). The Operational Level provides additional detail by using a polar chart. Polar charts can be made using all of the factors considered in the rating. In order to create the polar chart the 1-8 scale of the grading done by respondents is converted to a 0-100 scale.(The larger the number the better the score.) The radar chart provides good input for more detailed discussions and can also form the basis for identifying important inputs to a business management system. The Respondent Level is a written document where respondents clarifying comments are anonymously categorized according to questions and categories. This is where all non-quantifiable knowledge appears (Jacobsen, Nordby and Hofman-Bang, 2005). In summary, IC Rating ^{TM} as a qualitative measurement tool provides an organization with better understanding of intangible assets rather than quantitatively calculate the financial value. It gives the organization an opportunity to increase transparency internally with a shared language and terminology. IC Rating ^{TM} shows areas where improvements are necessary and it provides an excellent analysis and starting point for internal performance measurement system that can be used to track performance and improvements over time.

2.2. Knowledge Audit

A knowledge audit is a fact-finding, analytical, interpretative, and reporting activity (Dow, 1997). Knowledge audit, according to Hylton (2002b, 2002c), is a systematic and scientific examination, review, assessment and evaluation of a company's knowledge health in terms of its existing explicit and implicit knowledge resources, its information and knowledge policies. It is a thorough examination to reveal what an organization knows, who knows what, how knowledge is being created and how it should do to improve the management of existing knowledge of an organization. A knowledge audit also helps to access the efficiency and effectiveness of corporate, departmental and process-driven knowledge lifecycles. (Hylton, 2002b). Cheung et al. (2005) suggests that a knowledge audit is vital assessment of knowledge assets to indicate where the company should focus its KM efforts. In summary, knowledge audit is a tool to check the health status of knowledge assets and then based on the result to lay a foundation for making a KM strategy for an organization. The most commonly used audit tools are based on survey questionnaires, focus groups and interviews. Most common knowledge audit analysis techniques are knowledge mapping, knowledge inventory, and gap analysis, etc.

2.3. Knowledge Capture and its associated methods

To capture invaluable knowledge assets of a firm the knowledge elicitation process is the starting point. Knowledge elicitation is the extraction of information through in-depth interviews and observations. Subject matter experts are often the ones who provide the piece of information. It involves extracting knowledge in the conscious and sub-conscious mind, helping the expert in recalling and redefining their rules of thumb, work practices with the help of knowledge engineer (Morecroft et. al, 1994). *Questionnaire survey* is one of the most traditional methods for the elicitation of knowledge. However, it has become less popular for knowledge elicitation nowadays due to the inability to look into respondent's responses. With the standardized questions asked in a survey, only areas of interests is asked, recorded, codified and analyzed in most of the time. *Ethnography*, focused on qualitative information, is another way to capture knowledge. Undoubtedly, it enables us to know deeply what people have come across, but it may take a long time to collect sufficient information or researchers may find difficulty to obtain information that they need through merely observation. *Interviews* on qualitative research seek to cover both a factual and meaning level through understanding what the interviewees say (Kvale, 1996). Unlike questionnaire, interviewer can easily put the answer back on track with the rephrase of the question if the interviewees misinterpret the questions. Interviews are good for revealing particular experience of interviewees and capturing complicated cases. Narrative technique is implemented as a form of unstructured interview so as to capture hidden assumptions and knowledge in relationship managers' minds. In the past, narratives are restricted as stories about specific past events (Labov, 1972). Nowadays, narratives are considered as a mode of recounting organization, a way of interpreting organizational life, or the stuff of which organizations are made (Czarniawska & Gagliardi, 2003). Both stories and anecdotes can be categorized as narratives. Stories refer to retellings of events that lead to an outcome which are of value to certain audiences (MSDN, 2005). For strategy, stories can be applied as a valuable tool to understand a company's current situation, anticipate possible futures and to prepare the organization for action (Snowden, 1999(a)). Anecdotes are narratives of detached incident and unpublished details of history (Snowden, 1999 (b)). They are also named as short tales narrating interesting or amusing biographical incidents. They are always based on real life, incidents involving actual persons in real places (Callahan, 2007). They are typically oral and ephemeral and used to obtain a better understanding on the culture of an organization through collecting anecdotes from the respective staff. Narrative technique is a traditional approach for sharing and affirmation of ideas, issues and values. It is effective in revealing the complex, interconnected and unpredictable messiness that exists in organizations (Callahan & Ciuro, 2008). International organizations, such as World Bank (Denning, 2007), British Council (Cheuk, 2006) and 3M (Knudsen & Jones, 2001) have implemented stories. Gordon Shaw of 3M complemented stories make them see themselves and their operations in complex and multi-dimensional forms so that they can bring up with winning ideas in strategic change through discovering opportunities (Shaw et al, 1998). Storytelling is a method to share knowledge through narratives and stories. Table 1 (Brown et.al, 2004) shows the characteristics of stories and storytelling.

Table 1 Significance of stories and storytelling (Brown et al, 2004)

Stories	- have salience to the lives of people in organizations - help us make sense of organizations
Storytelling	- quick, powerful, memorable and free - communicates naturally, collaboratively, persuasively, context, entertainingly, feelingly & interactively - builds authenticity - re-connects the knower with the known

Focus groups, like anecdote circles, is one of gatherings aiming to generate and collect anecdotes or stories about some issue or topic. It is facilitated to elicit stories, experiences and anecdotes rather than judgment and opinion (Callahan et al, 2006). The collected stories are usually placed in a narrative database or repository for sense-making. Stories can serve a lot of purposes, like trust building, value transmission and co-ordination.

Grounded theory is a method for shaping qualitative interview, like narratives and guide analysis of stories (Charmaz, 2003). It generally provides a set of rigorous research procedure leading to the emergence of conceptual categories (Rhine, 2009). These methods consist of systematic guidelines for gathering, synthesizing, analyzing and conceptualizing qualitative data to construct theory (Charmaz, 2001). In other words, theory is derived from a large amount of data and information with the application of grounded theory. Firstly, a specific social process is selected for analysis. Data are then collected in reference with emerging interpretations. The literature review was conducted mainly after data were collected, and the central themes were allowed to emerge from the data rather than being forced to fit a preconceived theoretical framework (Glaser and Strauss, 1967).

Open coding	•identify, name, categorize and decribe phenomena found in the text •read each line to find out 'What is this about? What is being referenced here?'
Axial Coding	•relate codes (categories and properites) to each other •emphasize casual relationship •fit things into a basic frame of generic relationships
Selective coding	•choose one category to be the core category •relate all related codes to the category by elimination of unrelated codes
Memo	•write to oneself as one proceeds through the analysis of a corpus of data

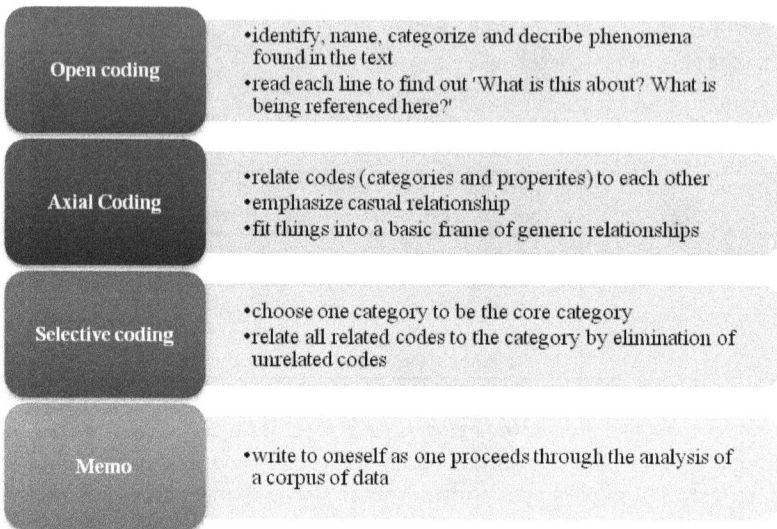

Figure 2: Methodology of grounded theory (Borgatti,1996)

Through the above techniques (Figure 2), codes, concepts, categories and theory are generated accordingly. Codes are the words and phrases that highlight an issue of importance or interest to the research. They are usually noted and described in a short phrase. For narrative analysis, they can be terms directly from the stories or slightly modified to represent theme of certain paragraph or even the whole passage. By relating the codes with high order commonality, concept is formed through grouping of the codes. Concepts are then grouped to find yet higher order commonalities called categories. The concepts and categories eventually lead to emergence of a theory (Allan, 2003)

3. Methodology and Implementation

The case study has been divided into three stages which are Stage I: Knowledge Elicitation and Capture; Stage II: Knowledge Audit; and Stage III: Intellectual Capital Performance Studies. The three stages can be regarded as separate approaches but reinforce to each other. Meanwhile, individual findings of each stage can be compared for consistency. (Figure 3)

Stage I: Knowledge elicitation and Narrative Database Construction Phase 1: Identification of project theme and scope Phase 2: Narrative collection Phase 3: Data validation Phase 4: Narrative analysis Phase 5: Construction of narrative database and concept map	Stage II: Knowledge Audit Phase 1: Process Selection and Form Filling Phase 2: In-depth interview Phase 3: Knowledge inventory building Phase 4: Data Analysis Phase 5: Data Validation
Stage III: Study on Intellectual Capital Performance Phase 1: Define IC and IC Model Phase 2: Determine IC elements to be studied Phase 3: Design the qualitative IC evaluation questionnaire survey Phase 4: Distribution of the questionnaire Phase 5: Conduct quantitative analysis	

Figure 3 Methodology and Implementation

In *Stage I*: Narrative technique is applied to elicit knowledge and skills of client relationship management and sales through narrative interviews and focus groups. In total, three focus groups and ten narrative interviews were organized. The major purpose of both focus group and interview was to collect as many narratives as possible for further analysis. Stories are recorded and transcribed into scripts for analysis. Keywords are extracted and categorized through the application of grounded theory for the construction of narrative database. There are eighty one codes extracted from the stories after the application of selective coding. Twenty three concepts and five core categories are generated from the thirty stories. Concept map is formed in accordance with the result grounded theory to visualize the causal relationship of the codes. Concept map was chosen instead because cognitive map is single directional and involves sign and strength of casualty that are not necessary in revealing the skills and techniques of a relationship manager should do for achievement of team's objectives. Also, the presentation of concept map is more understandable by including actions in the link for expressing the relationship among nodes. In *Stage II*: It is a vital assessment of knowledge assets determining what knowledge is needed, available, missing, who needs what knowledge and how this knowledge is applied. Several qualitative methodologies, i.e. surveys, workshops, and in-depth interviews, are taken into practice in the target team. The relationship managers are asked to identify a business process which they consider as their most critical process. Process that has experienced people and various knowledge located in them must be documented and shared to other people can be considered as critical. The knowledge audit in the BD team focuses on two processes: clients' enquires and new business take-on. The forms aiming at identifying the document flows, implicit knowledge flows, knowledge owners and users, communication channels and ratings of importance for the knowledge items in each task of the selected critical business processes are customized designed, completed and validated for knowledge inventory construction and further analysis. Through workshops and interviews, the collected data is compiled into knowledge inventories showing skills, experiences, expertise, know-how, location of documents and ratings of importance for each document. The purpose of compiling knowledge inventories is to prioritize knowledge assets through locating, describing and classifying. In *Stage III*: The methodology implemented in this stage basically composes five phases including: define IC and IC model, determine IC elements to be focused on, design IC evaluation questionnaire, distribution of the questionnaire survey and conduct analysis. The whole IC performance study uses qualitative method to evaluation the IC performance and quantitative method in the questionnaire analysis.

The IC model has been formed which includes three categories: Human Capital (HC), Structural Capital (SC) and Relational Capital (RC) following the most common IC classification. Bearing in mind the project scope, time, and resource, the case direction will focus on a qualitative study of the target team's IC performance through a questionnaire survey. Although there are many IC elements that can indicate the IC performance, however, different industry or company may have their unique emphases. It has been identified that one of the most critically important phase in this stage is to determine what IC elements are to be studied that perfect-fit the explanation of IC performance. Through individual interviews or focus groups, IC elements can be disclosed from participants' opinions. Additionally, bottom-up approach is adopted by extracting IC elements from the narrative database and knowledge inventory that were constructed in previous stages. Meanwhile, top-down approach is also implemented by inviting senior managers to decide and validate the IC elements to be investigated and focused on. The outcome is a structured IC value tree including HC, SC, RC and their corresponding IC elements. (Figure 4)

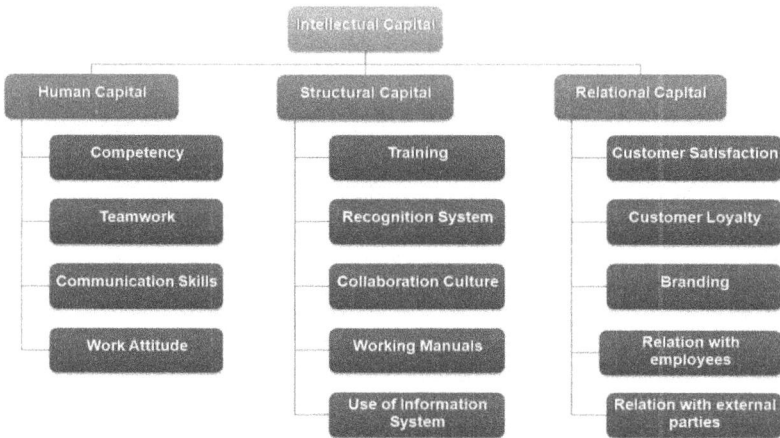

Figure 4 IC Value Tree

The IC performance evaluation questionnaire is designed with five sections including Briefing Letter to all respondents, Introduction, Part I: Demographical Information, Part II: Importance of each IC elements, and Part III: Current Status of each IC element. Part I: requires respondents to score the importance of each IC element on a 10-point scale based on their perceptions; and finally Part III requires respondents to score each question relating to corresponding IC elements on the extent to which this is available or in use within the team at present. The rating is a 10-point scale as well. To ease the IC questionnaire completion process and minimized the time it takes, all respondents are required to rate the IC elements' importance with 10-point scale (from 1: Not importance at all to 10 the most important) instead to assign exact percentage value and bear in mind that all IC elements sum up equal to 100%. The finalized questionnaire was distributed to the whole team. The survey is strictly confidential and only can be accessed by the researcher.

4. Analysis and Findings

There are total twenty-seven sets IC questionnaires completed and returned. The overage of the team reached 100%. However, one of the questionnaires was void due to invalid answers. From the Demographical data
(Table 2), it has been found that most staff in the team are 25-45 years old
within which people are equally distributed with 10 years interval. There is
no one younger than 25 years old. Therefore, it indicates that mature people are more demanded. The number of female staff is almost equal with
male ones. Also, most staff are with 3-5 years of experience in the team.

Table 2 The demographical data of all IC questionnaire respondents

Age	<25	25-35	35-45	45+
Number of Re-spondents	0	12	12	2
Gender	Male	Female	/	/
Number of Re-spondents	12	14		
Years of Experi-ence	1-2 years	3-5 years	6-8 years	8 years+
Number of Re-spondents	5	8	7	6

About rating result corresponding to the questionnaire Part II: Importance
(What should be) and Part III: Current Status (What it is), the average
scores of each rating is calculated with the following formula.

$$Avg(importance) = \frac{\sum importance}{number\ of\ respondents}$$

Figure 5a: Average scores calculation formula

$$Avg(current) = \frac{\sum current}{number\ of\ respondents}$$

Figure 5b: Average scores calculation formula

In order to reveal the difference between Importance and Current Status, radar charts are used (Figure 6). These radar charts also have shown the IC elements rating into three categories: HC, SC and RC.

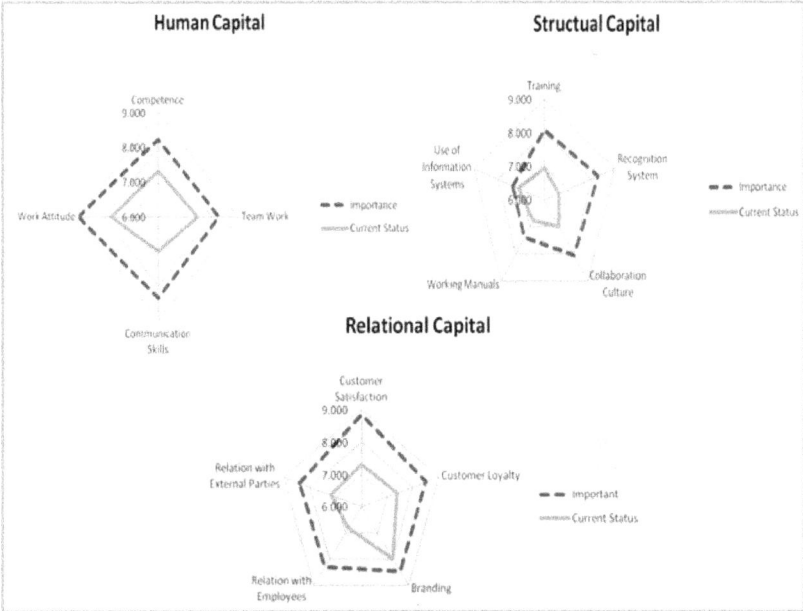

Figure 6: Importance VS. Current Status Radar Chart

As mentioned previously, in order to ease the IC questionnaire completion process, it is designed with 10-point scale to each IC element. The format conversion therefore is needed at backstage after the rating has been done by all respondents. By applying the following formula (Figure 7), the percentage value can be found.

$$\text{Importance percentage of factor } f = \frac{\text{Importance of factor } f}{\text{Sum of all importance}} \times 100\%$$

$$= \frac{im_f}{\sum im}$$

Figure 7: The formula that converts 1-10 scale to percentages

Here is an illustration of how score can be converted into percentage. Firstly, to find out the importance percentage of HC to IC, the original HC score (say 8.231) is divided by the sum rating score of HC, SC and RC (8.231+7.769+8.500 = 24.5), then times 100% which result will be: HC% = 33.6% Similarly, the percentage value of each IC element to corresponding HC, SC or RC can be then calculated. For example, to find out the importance percentage of competency to HC, the rating score (8.231) is divided by the sum of all HC elements (8.231+8.269+8.346+9.000=33.846), then times 100% which result will be: Competency % = However, the desired percentage is to IC rather than to HC. Therefore, this value (24.3%) has to be further timed with HC% to IC (33.6%) which will be 24.3% x 33.6% = 8.2%. Figure 8 has made a good illustration which summarizes and visualizes how each IC element takes up the weighted importance percentage.

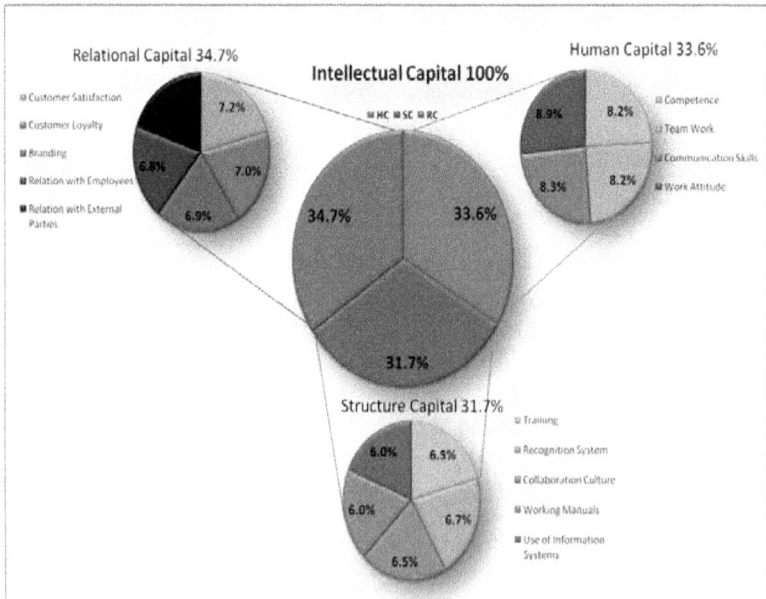

Figure 8: The Weighted Importance of each IC factor in percentage

There are three approaches in analyzing the result of the IC survey which includes Weighted Strength, Weighted Weakness and Gap Analysis. (Figure 9) shows the calculation formulas.

Strength	The Highest Score of $$(Importance \times Current\ Status)$$
Weakness	The Lowest Score of $$\left(\frac{Current\ Status}{Importance} \right)$$
Gaps	The Highest Score of $$(Importance - Current\ Status)$$

Figure 9: The guiding formula for result categorization

Table 3 summarizes the result after calculating the strength, weakness and gap score of each IC element. The next step is to identify the highest or lowest score respectively.

Table 3: Result of strength/weakness/gap score calculation

	Importance	Current Status	Strength	Weakness	Gap
Human Capital					
Competence	8.231	7.327	60.31	0.89	0.904
Team Work	8.269	7.471	61.78	0.90	0.798
Communication Skills	8.346	7.000	58.42	0.84	1.346
Work Attitude	9.000	7.750	69.75	0.86	1.250
Structural Capital					
Training	8.077	6.942	56.07	0.86	1.135
Recognition System	8.280	6.606	54.70	0.80	1.674
Collaboration Culture	8.048	7.000	56.34	0.87	1.048
Working Manuals	7.385	6.760	49.92	0.92	0.625

	Impor tance	Current Status	Strength	Weak ness	Gap
Use of Information Systems	7.346	7.106	52.20	0.97	0.240
Relational Capital					
Customer Satisfaction	8.846	7.317	64.73	0.83	1.529
Customer Loyalty	8.520	7.386	62.93	0.87	1.134
Branding	8.462	8.000	67.70	0.95	0.462
Relation with Employees	8.308	6.816	56.63	0.82	1.492
Relation with External Parties	8.385	7.200	60.37	0.86	1.185

In order to make the comparison easier, strength, weakness, and gap analysis charts have been plotted. (Figure 10, Figure 11, Figure 12)

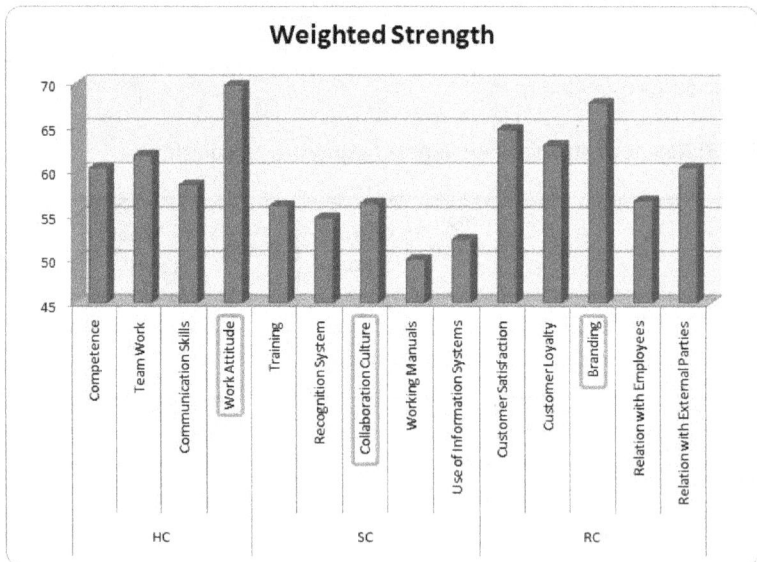

Figure 10: Weighted Strength in Performance

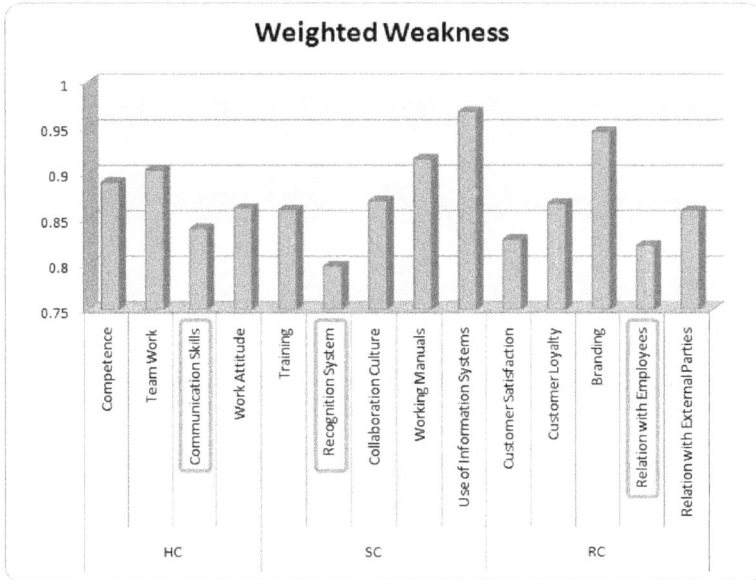

Figure 11: Weighted Weakness in Performance

The ones highlighted in square box in Figure 10 are the weighted strength in performance. They are Work Attitude of the staff under HC, Collaboration Culture under SC, and Branding under RC. The ones lighted in square box in Figure 11 are the weighted weakness in performance. They are Communicational Skills under HC, Recognition System under SC and Relation with employees under RC.

The radar chart in Figure 12 is plotted after calculating the overall Importance versus Current Status difference of each IC element. It is clear to identify the biggest gaps are at communication Skills under HC, Recognition System under SC and Customer Satisfaction under RC. The analyzed results of strength, weakness, and gaps can be categorized into two groups which are Performance Excellence and Room for Improvement. The Performance Excellence is where the strength of the team. It includes Work Attitude, Collaboration Culture, and Branding. Room for Improvement is the combination of weakness and biggest gaps. It includes Communication

Skills, Recognition System, Customer Satisfaction and Relations with employees.

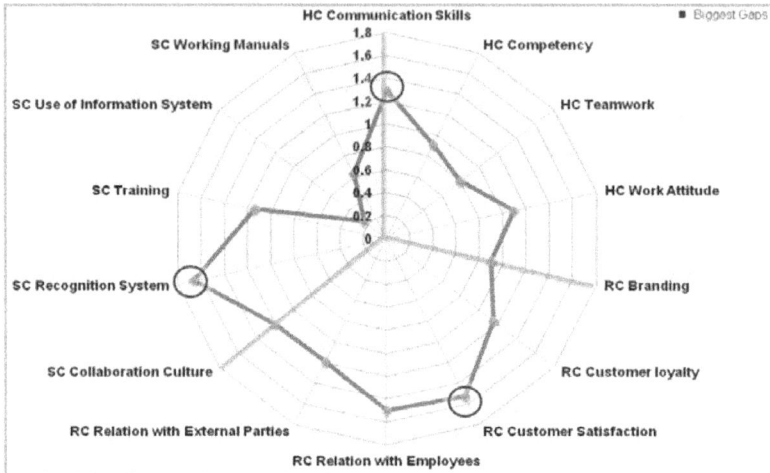

Figure 12: Highlighted Gaps between Importance with Current Status

5. Recommendation and Future Work Opportunities

For Performance Excellence, it is suggested that it is better for the team to keep the good work attitude, especially at the bad time when the financial crisis continues and the staff turnover rate is high; to secure brand name and public image and reinforce to the clients' satisfaction and loyalty; to foster a good knowledge sharing and retention with its good collaboration culture; and to continue monitor the IC dynamic and flow, have periodic IC assessment in order to benchmark the best practices. For Room-For-Improvement, it is suggested that it is better for the team to diagnose the training provided and see if it is effective and sufficient, especially on communication skills; to encourage vertical communication and provide more frequent and useful feedback; to review the recognition system, measure the effectiveness and collect feedback from the downstream; to capture and retain employee's tacit knowledge, e.g. Apply Knowledge Harvesting Tools; to pay more attention to employees' career development and host more get-together activities, such as sports day, hiking, and carnival, etc. Apart from the above, it is highly recommend to the BD team to keep the practice of IC management and expand it to other teams because it provides a better understanding of non-financial assets, and increase transparency internally.

It is suggested continue to monitor and manage the IC dynamics. Maybe the BD team can conduct the study again after a period of time for bench-marking. Moreover, it is also suggested that the IC performance study can be expanded to other teams and departments in the target international bank.

References

Allan, G. (2003) A critique of using grounded theory as a research method Available at: www.ejbrm.com (accessed 28 March 2009)

Boedker, C., Guthrie, J., & and Cuganesan, S.(2005b). The strategic significance of human capital information in annual reporting. Journal of Human Resources Costing and Accounting.

Bontis, N. (1998) Intellectual capital: an exploratory study that develops measures and models. *Management Decision* 36(2), 63-76.

Borgatti S. (1996) Introduction to Grounded Theory Available at: http://www.analytictech.com/mb870/introtoGT.htm (accessed 26 March 2009)

Brown J.S, Denning S. & Groh K (2004) Storytelling in Organizations: Why Storytel-ling is Transforming *21st Century Organizations And Management Butterworth-heinemann*

Callahan, S., Rixon, A. and Shenk, H. (2006). The Ultimate Guide to Anecdote Circles – A practical guide to facilitating storytelling and story listening. Available at: http://www.anecdote.com.au (accessed 18 March 2009)

Callahan   S.   (2007)   Definition   of   anecdotes   Available   at: http://www.anecdote.com.au/archives/anecdotes (accessed 27 March 2009)

Callahan, S. and Ciuro (2008), Walking in Two Worlds Available at: http://www.anecdote.com.au (accessed 18 March 2009)

Charmaz K. (2003) Qualitative Interview and Grounded Theory Analysis inside In-terviewing: New Lenses, *New Concerns Sage Publications*

Cheuk B. (2006) Case study- The British Council Inside Knowledge Volume 10 Issue Available at: http://www.ikmagazine.com (accessed 24 March 2009)

Cheung C.F., Ko K.C., Chu K.F., Lee W.B. (2005). Systematic Knowledge Auditing With Applications. Journal *of Knowledge Management Practice*, August 2005.

Czarniawska, Barbara, and Pasquale Gagliardi, eds. 2003. Narratives We Organize By. *John Benjamins Publishing.*

Denning S (2007) The Secret Language of Leadership: How Leaders Inspire Action Through Narratives Jossey-Bass

Davenport, T.H. (1997). 'Known Evils: Common Pitfalls of Knowledge Management', *CIO*, June

Dow Chemical (1997). *Annual Report 1996.*

Edvinsson, L. and Malone, M. S. (1997). Intellectual Capital: Realizing Your Company's True Value by Finding It Hidden in Brainpower. *New York: HarperBusiness*

Glaser B.G., Strauss A.(1967) Discovery of Grounded Theory Strategies for Qualitative Research *Sociology Press*

Gupta and Roos (2001), Mergers and acquisitions through an intellectual capital perspective, *Journal of intellectual capital electronic resource, vol.2*

Hylton A. (2002)b. Measuring & Valuing Knowledge: Role of the Knowledge Audit. http://www.annhylton.com/siteCon-tents/writings/wrtings-home.htm (accessed 25 March, 2009)

Hylton A. (2002)c. A KM initiatives is Unlikely to Succeed without a Knowledge Audit. http://www.annhylton.com/siteCon-tents/writings/wrtings-home.htm (accessed 25 March, 2009)

Jacobsen, K.; Hofman-Bang, P.; Nordby Jr, R. (2005) The IC Rating™ model by Intellectual Capital Sweden, *Journal of Intellectual Capital,* Vol. 6, No.4, pp. 570-587.

Knudsen, S. and Jones, R. (2001). Organizational storytelling: managing the exchange of identities.

Kvale, S. (1996) Inter Views: An introduction to qualitative research interviewing, Sage Publications

Labov, W. (1972) Sociolinguistic patterns. Philadelphia, PA: University of Pennsylvania Press

Morecroft, J and Heijden, K. (1994). Modeling the Oil Producers: Capturing Oil Industry knowledge in a Behavioral Simulation Model. *Productivity Press.*

MSDN Academic Alliance Developer Center (2005). Available at: http://www.msdnaacr.net/curriculum/glossary.aspx (accessed11 March 2009)

Nonaka, I., Toyama, R. and Konno, N. (2001). SECI, Ba and Leadership: a Unified Model of Dynamic Knowledge Creation. In: Nonaka, I. and Teece, D. eds, *Managing Industrial Knowledge. Creation, Transfer, and Utilization*, Sage, London, pp. 13-43.

Sveiby, K.-E. (1997) The Intangible Asset Monitor, http://www.sveiby.com (Accessed 30 March 2009)

Wiig, K. M. (1997) Knowledge Management: An Introduction and Perspective, *The Journal of Knowledge Management*, Vol. 1, No. 1, pp. 6-14.

KM Effectiveness Gap Analysis: The Case of an Indian IT Firm

Manasa Kakulavarapu and Ved Prakash
Wipro Technologies, Bangalore, India

Editorial Commentary

This is an examination of the KM performance of a large Indian IT services firm. Kakulavarapu & Prakash present a methodology for KM performance assessment, based on a gap-analysis approach with three parameters -- culture, process and technology. An audit questionnaire was developed in brainstorming sessions and administered to over 400 employees in some 88 project units. The survey findings were further investigated through follow-up interviews.

The study presents some solid insights on the successes and challenges of KM strategies and specific initiatives in a knowledge-intensive firm, as well as the difficulties of engaging senior managers in KM strategies. Specific recommendations are made to improve the likelihood of KM successes.

Abstract: Can we calculate a return on knowledge? Can we monitor a firm's knowledge management performance? Such questions have always been central to debates on measurement and evaluating effectiveness on enterprise-wide knowledge management programs. A sound metrics system helps monitor the effectiveness of any corporate-level program and acts as a guide for deciding future directions. Despite the wide recognition that a sound knowledge management process is crucial in organizational performance and growth, comprehensive and robust approaches for measuring and monitoring knowledge creation/utilization trends in firms are not yet available. Therefore, firms have to rely on other mechanisms to monitor the overall health and assess gaps in their knowledge management processes. This paper shares the findings and implications of a gap analysis exercise conducted by an Indian IT firm to evaluate the health of its enterprise-level KM program. The gap analysis was conducted over a span of two months and analyzed knowledge management in 88 project teams across the organization. Knowledge management program was evaluated against three key parameters – culture, process and technology reported by the teams. The results highlighted significant trends in knowledge sharing and acquisition patterns among these projects and also provided guidelines for identifying high and low priority areas for directing enterprise-wide KM efforts.

Keywords: Knowledge management, gap analysis, effectiveness, IT industry

1. Background

Knowledge Management is considered as an integrated systematic approach for identifying, managing, and sharing all the information assets of the organization, including databases, documents, policies and procedures as well as previously unarticulated expertise and experience held by individuals, groups and departments. Gartner (2001) defines "enterprise KM" as a centrally guided KM program that supports multiple business objectives, especially most of the KM needs of one or more strategic business processes across more than one major business unit. Effective knowledge management pays off by resulting in fewer mistakes, fewer redundancies, quicker problem-solving, better decision-making, reduced research development costs, increased worker independence, enhanced customer relations, and improved service (Becerra-Fernandez, 1999). KM also enables organizations to identify, select, organize, disseminate, reuse and transfer important information and expertise which are necessary for problem-solving, dynamic learning, strategic planning, and decision-making (Gupta et al., 2000; Shankar and Gupta, 2005; Singh et al., 2003b). However, few firms have been able to establish a causal relationship between KM activities and firm performance (Davenport, 1999).

In a survey of 431 US and European organizations by the Ernst & Young Center for Business Innovation, the most difficult obstacle faced in KM practices was reported to be "measuring the value of knowledge assets and/or impact of knowledge management" (Ruggles, 1998). Kalling (2003) tried to find the link between knowledge and performance by identifying knowledge development, knowledge utilization and knowledge capitalization, and by observing different impacts on performance. However, the analysis was qualitative in nature, and the study design with three cases limited the ability to generalize the findings. Ahn and Chang (2004) introduced the performance-oriented concept in KM and used the data envelopment analysis (DEA) approach to find areas for performance improvement. However, when measuring the knowledge contribution, their analysis was based on a relative productivity concept rather than an absolute value of business performance. In the management oriented literature, a number of academics and practitioners have expressed interest in the relationship between knowledge management and project management (Kamara et al., 2000; Gilbert & Holder, 2000) but these original contributions provide only limited, anecdotal guidance for practitioners wanting to improve their capability to manage knowledge in project environments.

Despite the wide recognition that a sound knowledge management strategy is crucial in organizational performance and growth, comprehensive and robust approaches for measuring and monitoring knowledge creation/utilization trends in firms have not yet been established. Moreover, there are no models that measure the relationship between KM practices and firm performance (Marqués & Simón, 2006). For most organizations investing and implementing in enterprise-wide knowledge management, this calls for alternate approaches to monitor the overall health or effectiveness and assess gaps in their knowledge management processes. In such a quest to evaluate the effectiveness of its existing KM efforts, a gap analysis exercise was conducted by the KM team at Wipro Technologies to evaluate the health and effectiveness of its enterprise-level KM program that reaches out to more than 65,000 employees working across the globe.

Wipro Technologies (NYSE:WIT, www.wipro.com) is a global provider of consulting, IT Services, outsourced R&D, infrastructure outsourcing and business process services , delivering technology-driven business solutions to meet the strategic objectives of its clients. With over 25 years in the information technology business, Wipro is one of the pioneers in the remote delivery of services, and has constantly innovated to provide a comprehensive range of integrated services. It has over 20 'Centers of Excellence', which create solutions and build domain expertise around specific needs of individual industries. Wipro delivers unmatched business value to customers through a combination of process excellence, quality frameworks and service delivery innovation. Being the World's first PCMM, CMM and CMMi Level 5 certified software Services Company; Wipro is the first company outside USA to receive the IEEE Software Process Award.

Given that the competitiveness in managing IT projects is growing coupled with increasing uncertainty, decreasing time to market for project results along with high quality requirements, effective and efficient management of project histories and past learning are vital for the success of future projects. Moreover, most of the projects are decentralized resulting in knowledge de-fragmentation thereby generating islands of knowledge often isolated from each other. Failure to capture and transfer these project learnings often leads to "reinvention of the wheel" and impaired project performance. In the context of software development and system support activities, the broad range of project experiences could refer to working experiences with a new software tool or a new release of a tool, knowledge insights about business procedures and dependencies, detailed knowledge about existing customer's business and processes and much more. The breadth and depth of knowledge management in such firms revolves around one or more rules like being reusable in a variety of contexts; exemplifying a unique, innovative concept, approach or solution applied to a client situation; creating or enhancing a methodology, technique or architecture; providing unique and effective visual representations/graphics of concepts, processes, etc.; presenting a comprehensive, updated summary of information/context. These could be further termed or categorized as best practices, know-how and heuristic rules; patterns, reusable software codes, business processes and models; architectures, technology and business frameworks; response for information/proposals (RFI/Ps), workplans, reports, meeting agendas, presentations, designs, instructional materials, or even process maps; tools used to implement a process such as checklists, surveys or questionnaires; models, templates, etc.

Centralized capture and dissemination of such project knowledge/lessons learnt as well as the ability to connect people across the organization have been the key focus areas for the KM initiative at Wipro. In order to support these goals, all efforts of the KM implementation team are focused on establishing a *collaborative culture* through several change management initiatives as well as rewards and recognition schemes; *integrating KM* activities with various project management *processes* closely; and enabling a customized *KM System* to serve as the backbone for most forms of knowledge capture and dissemination across the organization. Having evolved, matured and scaled up over a period of nearly six years, it was vital to measure its effectiveness and overall impact on the project delivery experience.

2. Methodology

The KM effectiveness gap analysis exercise was launched as a pilot project to evaluate the strengths and weaknesses of existing KM practices at Wipro in June 2006. All quantitative and qualitative data/insights were gathered over a period of three months, mainly around the 3Ps namely People, Process and Portal forming the three pillars of the KM framework. *"People"* refers to employee attitudes, overall culture and mindset towards KM. *"Process"* refers to integration of KM with the organizational processes. *"Portal"* represents the KM system and applications to support knowledge capture and usage across the organization. As an outcome of several brainstorming sessions, the team evolved an in-house audit questionnaire encompassing questions pertaining to the 3Ps of Wipro's KM practice. The responses on the KM practices audit questionnaire (see Appendix I) were captured using a 4-point rating scale ranging from "strongly disagree" to "strongly agree". The 5-point rating scale with the "neutral/cannot say" option was deliberately avoided to prevent response bias. The responses considered for this study were from project delivery teams consisting of responses captured from a minimum of five team members each which defined a "project unit". Each project unit included one new role incumbent (at project engineer level), one senior project engineer, one team/module/project lead, project manager and the associated technical manager. A total of eighty eight hand-picked project units (441 employees) participated in the audit exercise. These project units belonged to different vertical and technology practice groups across the organization. The data were gathered online coupled with personalized face-to-face interviews as well as telephonic conversations. The findings of the study have been presented and discussed further in the following pages.

3.   Significant findings

The survey findings for each of the 3Ps were categorized and interpreted as a function of (a) the vertical or technology practice groups in which the project units belonged and (b) the respondent's role in the project. Some of the key trends are presented and discussed below.

Familiarity with KM concepts (76%) as well as satisfaction with rewards/recognition (78%) for KM was found to be significantly lower across the enterprise than other aspects of culture like intrinsic motivation and encouragement from seniors to participate in project and organizational KM activities (Figures 1 and 2).

Lack of familiarity with KM concepts emerged higher despite higher participation reported in knowledge sharing activities reported within team (68%). The trends also suggest that personal (intrinsic) motivation to participate in KM could be linked to high support from seniors within the team (84%) even though satisfaction with formal rewards/recognition systems was perceived as low (Figures 3 and 4).

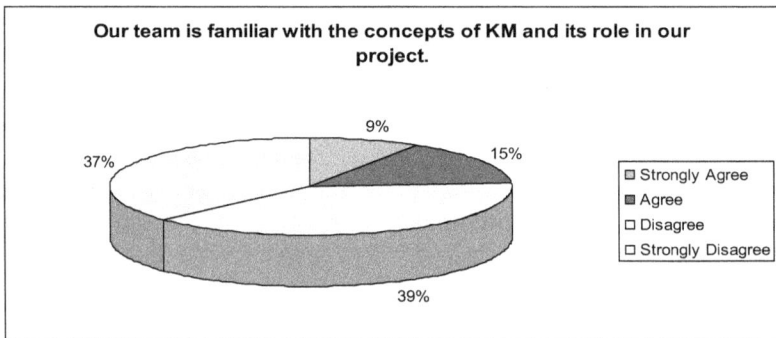

Figure 1: Familiarity with KM concepts

Knowledge sharing behaviors are appreciated in the team
through formal rewards/ recognition events.

5%

17%

42%

□ Strongly Agree
■ Agree
□ Disagree
□ Strongly Disagree

36%

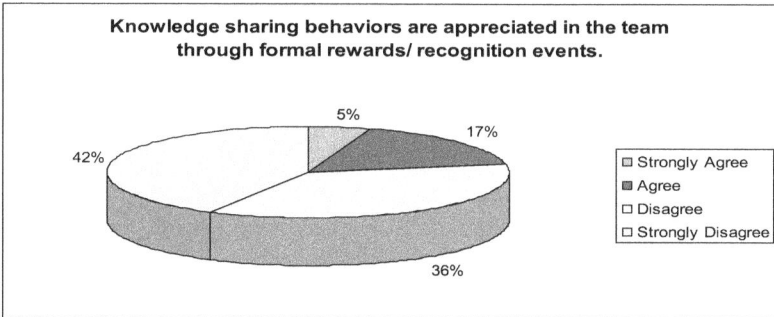

Figure 2: Rewards and recognition programs for knowledge sharing

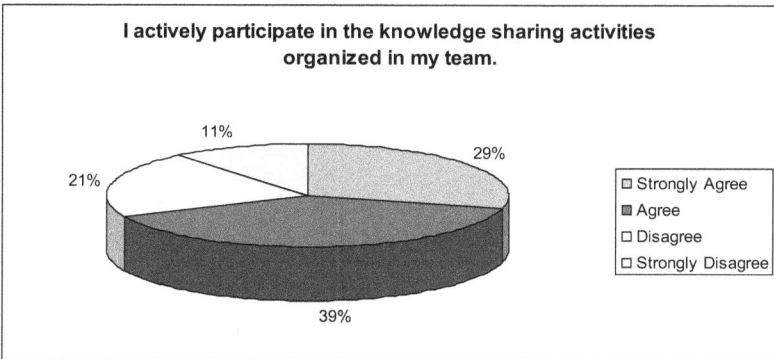

I actively participate in the knowledge sharing activities
organized in my team.

11%

29%

21%

□ Strongly Agree
■ Agree
□ Disagree
□ Strongly Disagree

39%

Figure 3: Participation in knowledge sharing activities

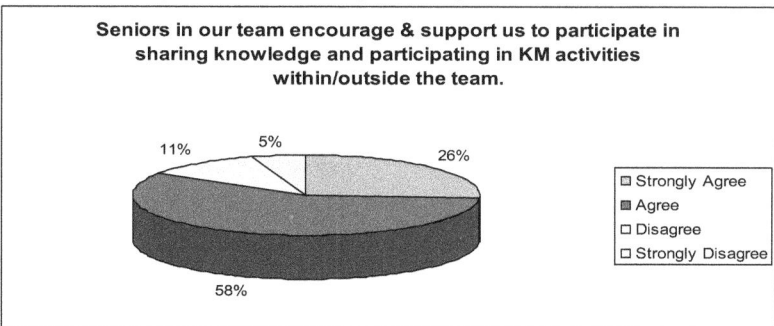

Seniors in our team encourage & support us to participate in
sharing knowledge and participating in KM activities
within/outside the team.

11%   5%

26%

□ Strongly Agree
■ Agree
□ Disagree
□ Strongly Disagree

58%

**Figure 4: Support/encouragement from seniors in knowledge manage-
ment activities**

Further, role-wise trends in KM culture suggested that experts' responsiveness within teams was reported higher by Project Engineers & Project Leads (92%) as opposed to PMs and TMs suggesting that effective expert help groups were a ground reality in a majority of project scenarios at Wipro (Figure 5).

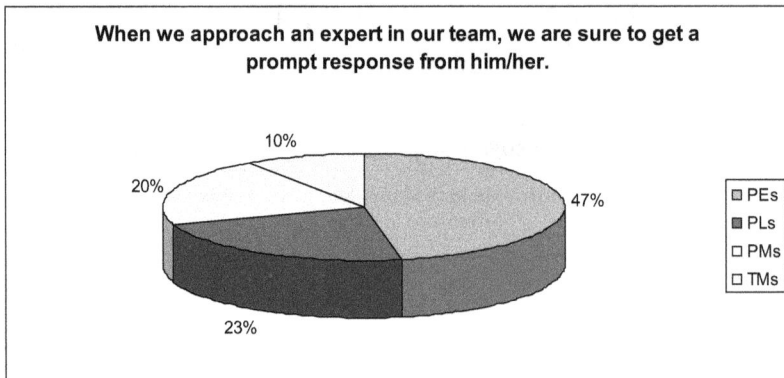

Figure 5: Experts' responsiveness in handling queries

Willingness to share knowledge was reported much higher (93%) by Project Engineers (<2 yrs. Work exp.) while PLs showed lowest personal motivation to participate in KM coupled with reports of lowest satisfaction with enterprise KM rewards & recognition schemes. This suggests a possible trend that enthusiasm and positive mindset for involvement in KM is maximum when new role incumbents enter the organization which gradually erodes as the person moves up the hierarchy (Figure 6).

The findings on KM process integration suggested that formally appointed knowledge officers (KOs) were either lacking or ineffective in most of participating project units (89%). Since knowledge officers own the responsibility of championing KM in their projects through focused KM plans, most project units reported low awareness of project-specific KM plans (96%). (Figures 7 and 8).

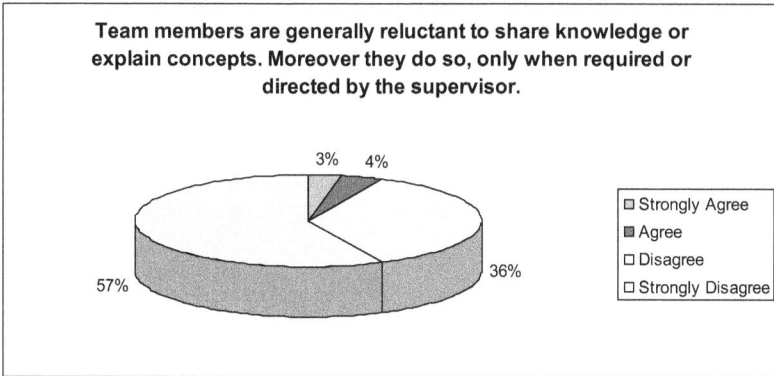

Figure 6: Willingness to share knowledge by project engineers

Figure 7: Formally appointed knowledge officers

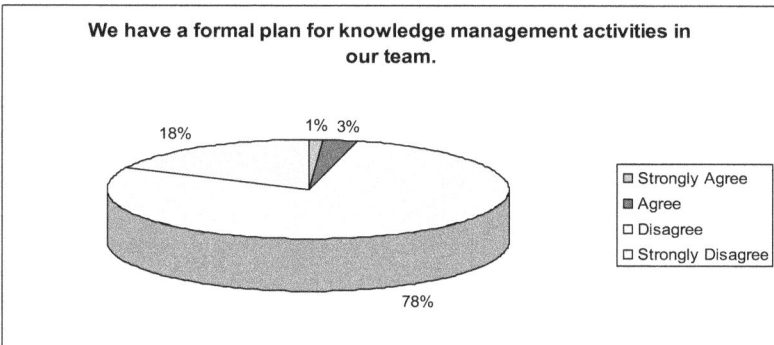

Figure 8: Project-specific KM plans

Despite lack of KOs and formal KM plans, most project units (78%) reported KM-related G&Os associated with annual performance appraisals. Process improvements, customer domain knowledge building and customers' buy-in/awareness of integrated project knowledge management were also reported as significantly higher (77%) by the project units. Role-wise trends indicated that enforcement of KM G&Os could account for higher individual participation in enterprise-wide KM activities even in the absence of satisfactory rewards/recognition programs (Figures 9 and 10).

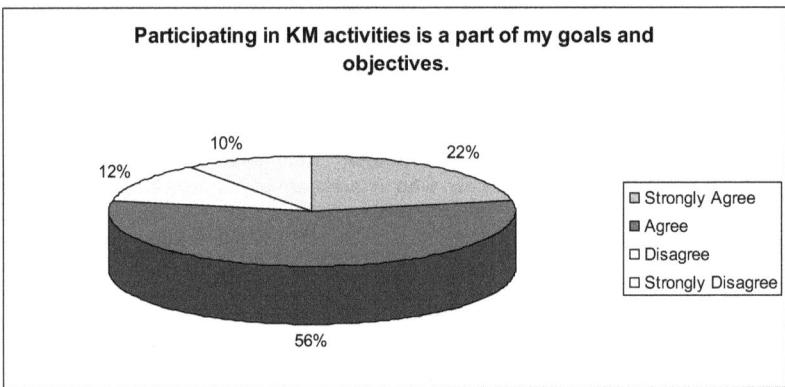

Participating in KM activities is a part of my goals and objectives.

10%
12%
22%
56%

□ Strongly Agree
■ Agree
□ Disagree
□ Strongly Disagree

Figure 9: KM-related G&Os for project members

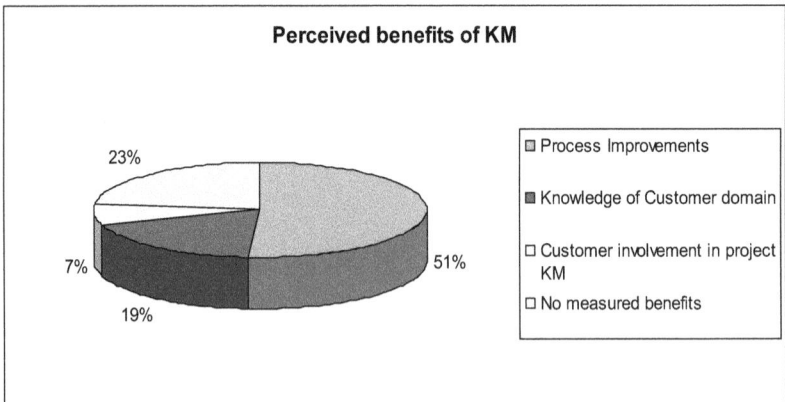

Perceived benefits of KM

23%
7%
19%
51%

□ Process Improvements
■ Knowledge of Customer domain
□ Customer involvement in project KM
□ No measured benefits

Figure 10: Process improvements, customer domain knowledge building and customer involvement in project knowledge management

Overall trends on KM portal indicated that although centralized KM repositories were established for most projects (79%), the usage of such systems
was reported to be much lower than expected (34%). (Figures 11 and 12).

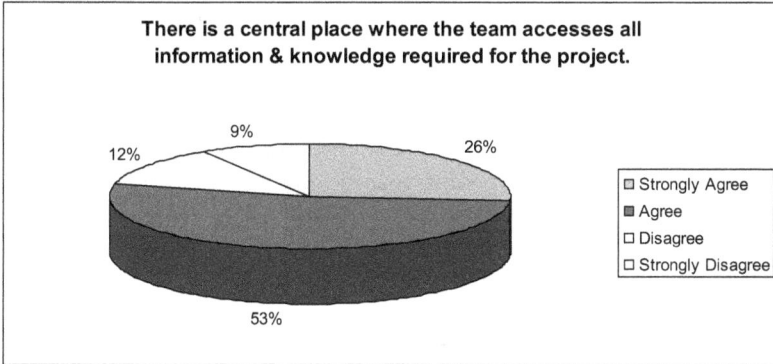

There is a central place where the team accesses all information & knowledge required for the project.

9%
12%
26%
53%

☐ Strongly Agree
■ Agree
☐ Disagree
☐ Strongly Disagree

Figure 11: Establishment of project KM repositories

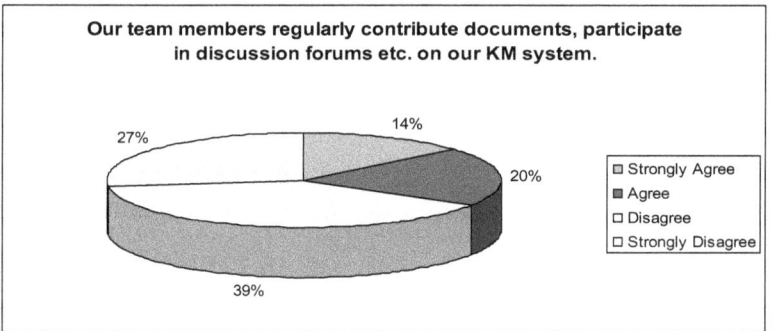

Our team members regularly contribute documents, participate in discussion forums etc. on our KM system.

14%
27%
20%
39%

☐ Strongly Agree
■ Agree
☐ Disagree
☐ Strongly Disagree

igure 12: Usage of project KM repositories

Due to decentralized projects across the organizations mostly operating as
Offshore Development Centers (ODCs) behind firewalls, familiarity with
and access of the enterprise-wide portal (KNet) was reported to be significantly low (37%). However, the overall satisfaction with KNet's knowledge
artifact quality and availability of the portal were reported to be contrast-
ingly high (74%) which emerged as a significant strength of the KM initiative. Amongst role-wise trends, TMs reported lower levels of satisfaction

with the knowledge artifacts compared to the rest though majority of the contribution and usage happens by PLs and below (Figures 13 and 14).

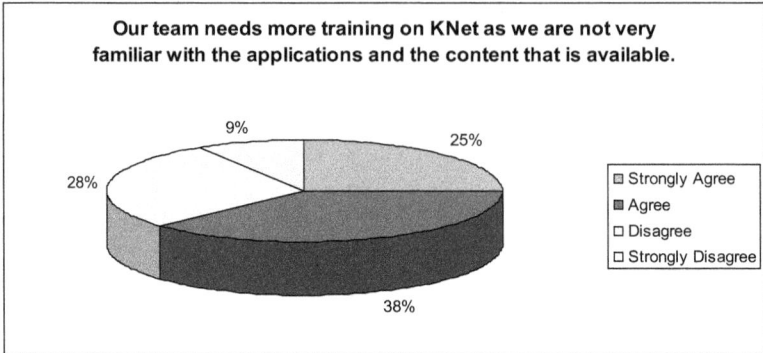

Figure 13: Awareness and access of KNet portal Graph

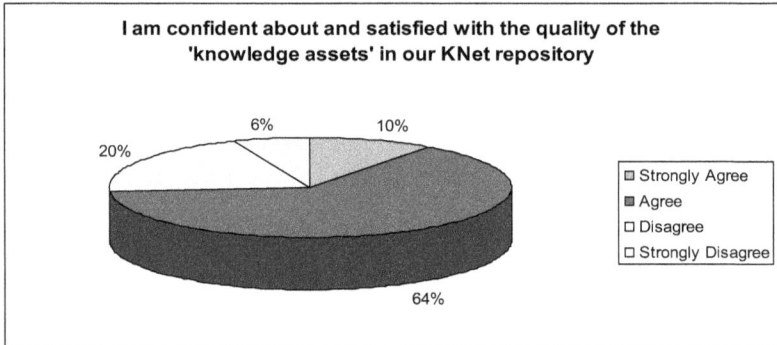

Figure 14: Artifact quality and availability of KNet portal

3.1.   Qualitative insights

Face-to-face interviews and telephonic interviews also yielded insights into several gaps and areas of improvement for the KM initiative. These are summarized below.

- Face-to-face knowledge sharing sessions/opportunities can be fa-cilitated for authors/contributors of knowledge artifacts to pre-sent and reflect upon the documented learnings.

- Increased hand-holding and customized training sessions could be organized in order to address issues of awareness and employee buy-in.
- Internal marketing and awareness campaigns at various levels and stages as necessary to increase awareness and invite higher participation from employees.
- Robust process integration is required to ensure that the knowledge is captured form members who are onsite i.e. at client locations for long durations before they move to different account or domain or company.
- Organization's induction programme must focus heavily on the concepts and spirit behind knowledge management.
- Project schedules should account for time spent in knowledge management activities in order to ensure higher participation and better quality of knowledge contributions.
- Success stories and KM best practices should be appropriately and regularly used for evangelization and spread of KM awareness.
- Customer involvement and buy-in for KM should be gained in order to account for time/effort investment in KM during the span of project delivery.

4. Conclusion

The findings from this study were presented to the senior management which was used as important input during the framing of KM strategy and the organizations' three year KM roadmap. Culture/people trends suggested that since PLs/TLs most often happen to be the technology/domain experts and also mentor/train the new role incumbents, hence, customized orientation workshops as well as rewards/recognition programs emerged as an important area of focus for KM. Formally appointed, project-level knowledge officers and a steering committee at the account or vertical level to execute and review project-related KM also emerged as a vital area to be addressed. Finally, increased internal marketing, customer involvement/buy-in and allocation of time for contribution towards KM activities in project schedules were other important action areas that emerged from this gap analysis study.

5. Implications

Apart from aiding senior management's KM strategy at Wipro, this study also offers significant insights about KM trends and patterns that could be applicable across the IT industry. One significant trend that comes across is that engaging and involving employees higher up in the hierarchy becomes increasingly difficult for any knowledge management initiative. Since knowledge and experience becomes much more enriched and tacit with growing seniority, the complexity and challenges of KM increase drastically hence calling for a different set of approaches. Secondly, people and process go hand-in-hand in the management of knowledge. Motivating people to share/use knowledge without institutionalized processes in place will not aid effective KM. Similarly, existence of well-defined processes to streamline KM activities may not work well if sufficient motivational/conducive climate is not present. Finally, technology presents its own set of challenges and obstacles to free flowing knowledge. Over-reliance on technology may result in de-personalized, passive and reactive knowledge management. Hence, it is recommended that in order for KM to yield desired results, all the 3Ps of KM should be optimally balanced depending upon the organization's dynamics.

References

Ahn, J.H. and Chang, S.G. (2004), "Assessing the contribution of knowledge to business performance: the KP3 methodology", Decision Support Systems, Vol. 36 No. 4, pp. 403-16.

Becerra-Fernandez, I. (1999), "Knowledge management today: changing the corporate culture", Proceedings of the 5th International Conference of the Decision Sciences Institute, July 4-7, Athens, Vol. 1, pp. 474-6.

Davenport, T. (1999), "Knowledge management and the broader firm: strategy, advantage, and

performance", in Liebowitz, J. (Ed.), Knowledge Management Handbook, CRC Press, Boca Raton, FL, pp. 1-11.

Gartner (Jan 2001). The Monthly Research Review, pp. 5-8.

Gilbert, M. and Holder, N. (2000), "An approach to project knowledge management", Proceeding of the BPRC Knowledge Management: Concepts and Controversies Conference, held at the University of Warwick, p. 193.

Gupta, B., Iyer, L. and Aronson, J.E. (2000), "Knowledge management: a taxonomy, practices and challenges", Industrial Management & Data Systems, Vol. 100 Nos 1/2.

Kalling, T. (2003), "Knowledge management and the occasional links with performance", Journal of Knowledge Management, Vol. 7 No. 3, pp. 67-81.

Kamara, J., Leseure, M., Carillo, P. and Anumba, C. (2000), "A framework for cross-sectoral learning", Proceeding of the BPRC Knowledge Management: Concepts and Controversies Conference, held at the University of Warwick, p. 177.

Marqués, D. P. and Simón, F. J. G. (2006), "The effect of knowledge management practices on firm performance", Journal of Knowledge Management, Vol. 10 No. 3, pp. 143 - 156.

Ruggles, R.L. (1998), "The state of notion: knowledge management in practice", California Management Review, Vol. 40 No. 3, pp. 80-9.

Shankar, R. and Gupta, A. (2005), "Framework for knowledge management implementation", Knowledge and Process Management, Vol. 12 No. 4, pp. 259-77.

Singh, M.D., Shankar, R., Narain, R. and Agarwal, A. (2003b), "An interpretive structural modeling of knowledge management in engineering industries", Journal of Advances in Management Research, Vol. 1 No. 1, pp. 28-40.

Appendix I: KM practices audit questionnaire

Details:

Vertical/Horizontal:	
SBU/BU/Practice:	
A/c Name:	
Project Name:	
Project Type:	
Role in project:	
Work Experience:	

Instructions

Given below are statements that describe different aspects of knowledge management in your team. Please rate each statement to the extent to which you agree/disagree to each. Please make sure to provide your ratings for **all** of the statements below.

Rating Scale Options are as follows:

1 = Strongly disagree with the statement
2 = Disagree with the statement
3 = Agree with the statement
4 = Strongly agree with the statement

S. No.	Statement	Rating	Comments/Observations
1	KM is only a management fad and does not benefit the project in any way.		
2	Our team is familiar with the concepts of KM and its role in our project.		
3	I actively participate in the knowledge sharing activities organized in my team.		
4	Seniors in our team encourage & support us to participate in sharing knowledge and participating in KM activities within/outside the team.		
5	Knowledge sharing behaviors are appreciated in the team through formal rewards/ recognition events.		
6	When we approach an expert in our team, we are sure to get a prompt response from him/her.		
7	Team members are generally reluctant to share knowledge or explain concepts. Moreover they do so, only when required or directed by the supervisor.		
8	A KM lead/officer has been appointed / nominated for our team as part of our KM process who actively drives KM activities in our project.		
9	We have a formal plan for knowledge management activities in our team.		
10	Participating in KM activities is a part of my goals and objectives.		
11	Our team meets frequently to share & discuss significant learnings and insights related to the project.		

S. No.	Statement	Rating	Comments/Observations
12	Formal knowledge management is important as this has resulted in improved processes in our team.		
13	We have adequate focus for building knowledge about our customer's domain (understanding about the needs of our customer's customer)		
14	Our customer is aware of our KM processes about domain knowledge-building efforts and has acknowledged the benefits of the same.		
15	There is a central place where the team accesses all information & knowledge required for the project.		
16	Our team members regularly contribute documents, participate in discussion forums etc. on our KM system.		
17	Our team needs more training on KNet as we are not very familiar with the applications and the content that is available.		
18	Our team regularly contributes and uses KNet for sharing & accessing organization-wide knowledge.		
19	I am confident about and satisfied with the quality of the 'knowledge assets' in our KNet repository		
20	Operational performance/accessibility of the KNet system has not bothered me till now.		

What are the three things you would like to see from the KM initiative this year?
1.
2.
3.

Reconfiguration of knowledge management practices in new product development- The case of the Indian pharmaceutical industry

Dinar Kale, Stephen Little and Matt Hinton
The Open University Business School, Milton Keynes, UK.

Editorial commentary
This project uses a case study approach at the industry level, examining the Indian pharmaceutical industry's transition from a knowledge imitator (by reverse engineering molecules) to a knowledge creator, through increased R&D. Kale, Little and Hinton investigate how the industry is changing due to the external pressures of international trade agreements regarding intellectual property. They selected five "innovative" Indian pharmaceutical companies and collected data about each company from internal and external interviews as well as from a variety of secondary data sources.

The paper presents a fascinating narrative of a knowledge-intensive industry under pressure to change and adopt more aggressive R&D/Intellectual Capital strategies to remain competitive.

Abstract: This paper explores the approaches used by Indian pharmaceutical firms for the acquisition of new knowledge and combination of it with existing accumulated knowledge to create knowledge required for innovative R&D. The preliminary analysis shows that Indian pharmaceutical firms are following the network model of R&D to acquire the capabilities of innovative R&D and crucial role of personnel transfer as a primary mechanism for transferring the tacit knowledge and the significant impact of information technology in transferring the explicit knowledge.

Keywords: Research & development, Knowledge management, Pharmaceutical industry

1. Introduction

The drivers of the globalisation are bringing in the 'competency destroying changes' (Tushman and Anderson, 1986) for firms in different industries. The established firms' needs the restructuring of the existing competencies to avoid the failure in face of such endemic changes (Henderson and Clark,1990). New regulatory environment or radical new innovations are the changes which makes existing competencies redundant (Pettigrew, et al. 2001). New environments and realities forces countries and firms to reconfigure their competencies to survive and succeed in a new business environment.

The pharmaceutical industry in many developing countries are undergoing a difficult transformation from reverse engineering led R&D to innovation based R&D due to World Trade Organisation agreements and specifically TRIPS (Trade related intellectual property rights) agreements. The TRIPS agreements are bringing in product patent regime in many countries and thereby preventing the reverse engineering of patented molecules. These agreements are influential in changing the patent laws, inflicting 'paradigm shift' in the external environment of firms in developing countries where the scope and rapidity of economic and political change adds to the complexities. The Indian pharmaceutical industry along with other developing countries will be facing change in the patent law in 2005 as per the requirement of WTO agreements. The new patent regime will not allow the reverse engineering of molecules after 2005 and this realisation is already forcing Indian firms to transform their R&D activities and management practices.

During the last three decades the large private Indian pharmaceutical firms focused their R&D efforts on reverse engineering oriented process R&D and activity was limited to applying known knowledge or to small adjustments in the contents (Wendt, 2000). Some public laboratories under the Council of Scientific and Industrial Research (CSIR) also did some work in pharmaceutical R&D specifically imitative process R&D. The technology of production was well mastered and the lag period between the launch of a new product in its first market and India thus was reduced, in some cases as low as two years (Lanjouw, 1996). In a way, the Indian pharmaceutical industry represents a successful case of indigenous self- reliant development. But the objective of indigenisation rather than innovation made R&D in Indian pharmaceutical firms' more insular, with a knowledge base firmly rooted in imitative reverse engineering process R&D. As a result the Indian pharmaceutical firms have accumulated extensive knowledge in process R&D (synthetic and organic chemistry) but severe weakness in other scientific disciplines. The ease of imitation in reverse engineering further resulted in intense competition among Indian firms for market share, hampering the development of a complex web of networks of research institutes, academia and industry (Ramani, 2001). The lack of trust resulting from the weak regulatory environment further prevented the development of research networks.

Indian pharmaceutical firms' success was based on effectively using reverse engineering or imitation as mechanisms of knowledge acquisition from the developed world. The change in patent law will force the firms in the Indian pharmaceutical industry to generate or create their own products, which will require new ways of knowledge acquisition and subsequent reconfiguration of knowledge creation processes. The distinction between the ability to produce a product by imitation and the capability to generate it, have profound implications in pharmaceutical R&D. The existing accumulated knowledge needs to be combined with new knowledge to develop the capability required for innovative product research.

This paper explores the approaches used by Indian pharmaceutical firms for the acquisition of new knowledge and combination of it with existing accumulated knowledge to create knowledge required for innovative R&D. The analysis is done by using a conceptual framework based on the global pharmaceuticals firms' approaches of knowledge reconfiguration as a response to bio technological change.

The paper is organised as follows: Section 2 reviews of the literature on the effect of TRIPS and the response from pharmaceutical industry. This section also presents the theoretical framework, which guides the research and explains the basis of the framework in large pharmaceutical firms' approaches to technological changes. Section 3 provides the characteristics of Indian pharmaceutical industry and further elaborates the area of research. Section 4 presents the methodology of the study and rationale behind using such a research design. Section 5 discusses Indian firms' approaches towards reconfiguring the knowledge creation process in pharmaceutical R&D. It covers the preliminary analysis of five firms. Conclusions are drawn in section 6.

2. The Research context

2.1.   2.1 World Trade Organisation Agreements – TRIPS

World trade agreements, especially TRIPS agreements, are instrumental in setting uniform standards in intellectual property rights (IPRs) all over the world. The strength of the patent regime plays an important role in knowledge intensive industries and especially in the pharmaceutical industry. The pharmaceutical industry is significantly different from other high tech industries in that the R&D process is stringently controlled by regulation making it very costly and risky. In the pharmaceutical industry patents provide strong appropriation and profit maximisation by conferring limited monopoly rights to inventors. As a result the strength of an IPR regime is an important issue for pharmaceutical firms but sensitive for countries. Even different developed countries tighten up their patent laws after assessing the capability of the domestic pharmaceutical industry. The degree of patent protection given to pharmaceutical products in the past was clearly related to the development of the domestic pharmaceutical industry.

But due to TRIPS agreements for the first time in international law, all countries are now required to provide protection to both process and product inventions made in all field of technology, subject to classical parameters. In the case of pharmaceuticals patents will now be granted both for products and processes for all the inventions in all fields of technology; the patent term will be twenty years from the date of application, applicable to all members of the WTO. Importantly in the case of a dispute on infringement, the responsibility of proving innocence lies with the accused rather than in proving the infringement of the accused by the patent holder. This broad regulatory framework will now guide and control the pharmaceutical industry in WTO member countries.

Number of studies has been carried out on effect of change in patent law on pharmaceutical firms in developing countries focusing on economic and technological development. Lanjouw (1996) studied the economic and social effects of a strong patent regime in the context of Indian scenario while Sequeria (1998) investigated the influence of change in patent regime on technological and innovative development of the Spanish pharmaceutical industry. D'Este (2001) analysed the extent of capability accumulation in Spanish industry after the change in patent law and resultant inter-firm heterogeneity. Madanmohan et al., (2003) has explored the adoptive strategies of Indian firms to the environmental change focusing on horizontal and vertical integration strategies at product as well as process ends. In a similar way Halemane et al., (2003) investigated the innovation management in Indian pharmaceutical industry as a response to environmental change using a theoretical framework based on theories of strategic groups from industrial economics.

In some developing countries like India and China the absence of product protection was one of the main factors along with local skills and expertise in the development of the domestic pharmaceutical industry and would be severely affected by TRIPS (Watal And Mathai, 1995). The TRIPs agreement is a big and difficult step for firms in such developing countries. In the new environment firms have to acquire the knowledge to do innovative R&D and combine that with accumulated existing knowledge.

2.2.   Theoretical framework

In an environment of increasing pressure and uncertainty, internal resources and capabilities becomes a key determinant of survival and success (Grant, 1991). The knowledge based view expanded from resource and capability theory, defines organisational capabilities as the ability of firm to generate new combinations of existing knowledge and exploit new technological opportunities (Kogut and Zander, 1992). Some events such as fundamental regulatory reform or radical technological advance create the need for reconfiguration of knowledge creation processes first for survival and then for success. Henderson and Clarck (1990) analysed reconfiguration of existing knowledge as a response to architectural innovation in the semiconductor industry. They point out that communication channels, information filters and problem solving strategies embody a firm's architectural knowledge and as a response to architectural innovation, require the reconfiguration of an established system to link together existing components in new way.

Advances in molecular biology proved to be a significant innovation for large pharmaceutical firms, representing a shift in the scientific knowledge base of an industry (Henderson et al., 1999). The large pharmaceutical firms responded to technological advances by reconfiguring the linkages in component knowledge bases. Many researchers have focused on different areas to analyse the restructuring process in large pharmaceutical firms. Zucker and Darby (1997) focused on the internal R&D transformation of large pharmaceutical firms and the role of research collaborations and star scientist with expertise in biotechnology. Suoniemi and Brannback (2000) looked at the alliances between the biotech firms and large pharmaceutical firms as a game between "mice" and "elephants". Nicholls- Nixon (1993) presented the absorptive capacity model to explain the use of internal R&D and technology sourcing linkages in the development of capabilities required in a new technological paradigm. She points outs that large pharmaceutical firms developed new capabilities by investing in biotechnology related R&D activities and accessing new external technological linkages. Galambos et al., (1998) analysed the R&D strategies used by large pharmaceutical firms to acquire and develop biotechnology capability. Gamberdella (1995) explained the mechanisms of knowledge transfer used by large pharmaceuticals with universities, research institutes to complement internal capabilities in biotechnology and the resultant transformation of new drug discovery and development in large pharmaceutical firms from a totally in-house activity to a networked activity.

The case of the molecular biology revolution and the response from firms provides the detailed mechanisms of industrial transformation at the firm and industry level, with the evolution of scientific knowledge on one side and organisational capabilities on the other side (Henderson et al., 1999). The large global pharmaceutical firms acquire biotech capability by changing their research teams, accessing in new external sources of knowledge and building the absorptive capacity by investing in the internal R&D.

These mechanisms guide the theoretical framework (Fig.1) which covers issues like the reconfiguration of mechanisms used for knowledge transfer, intra firm and inter-firm networks along with absorptive capacity. The theoretical framework is used to analyse Indian pharmaceutical firms' responses to regulatory change, which represents change in the scientific knowledge base similar to the technological change faced by large pharmaceutical firms.

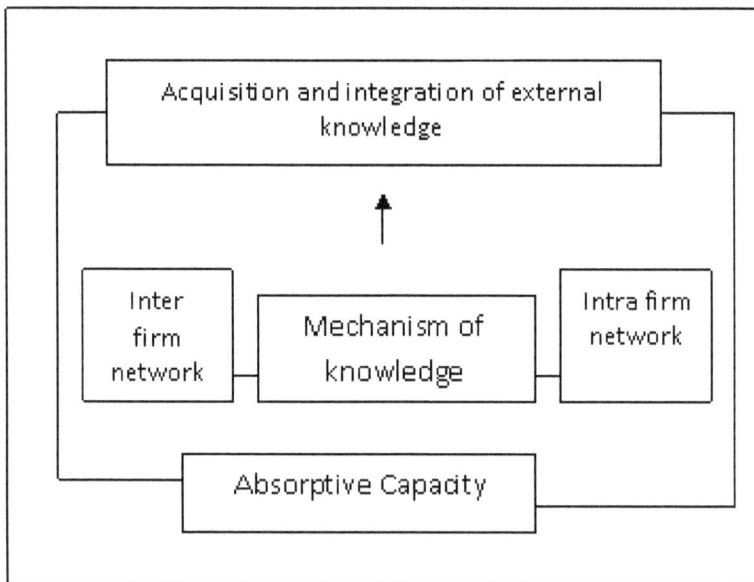

Figure 1: Theoretical Framework.

3. The Indian Pharmaceutical industry

The Indian pharmaceutical industry is a successful; high technology based industry that has witnessed consistent growth over the last three decades. It is the 12th largest in the world accounting for a market of US$ 2.5 billion

(Ramani, 2002). The Indian pharmaceutical industry has developed enough capabilities to make the country self sufficient in it's health care needs and the industry's recently acquired export ability makes it one of the crucial sectors in Indian economy. The Indian pharmaceutical industry exports generic drugs to CIS countries, Africa, and recently to highly regulated US and European markets. The Indian pharmaceutical industry structure is characterised by a low degree of concentration, a large number of firms with similar market shares, a low level of R&D intensity ratios with a high level of brand proliferation. The need and incentive for innovation was undermined by the ease of imitation and horizontal product differentiation; features that are representative of an industry behind the technological frontier (D'Este; 2001).

The growth of the Indian industry was slow till the 1970. The patent act of 1972 and government investment in the drug industry infused life into the domestic pharmaceutical industry. The act removed the product patents for pharmaceuticals, food and agro-chemicals, allowing patents only for production processes. The statutory term was shortened to seven years on pharmaceutical patents and automatic licensing put in place. It started the era of reverse engineering where firms developed new products by changing their production processes. The 1970 patent act therefore changed the pattern of competition towards volume / price led competition rather than traditional competition based on the development of new medical treatments (Wendt, 2000).

From 1970 on-wards Indian pharmaceutical firms slowly started dominating the domestic market reducing the market share and influence of Western companies. Today the market share of domestic firms is around 60-70% compared to 10% in 1970 (Ramani, 2001).

With the signing of WTO agreements in 1994, the Indian government has agreed to implement the TRIPS agreement in its entirely. TRIPS provides a 10 year transition period for developing countries with special provisions like exclusive marketing rights (EMR) for products that were granted patent protection elsewhere. Interviews with individuals associated with the industry reflect divisions within the industry over the strength patent regime that should be brought in. But in general, the expectation is that the patent law should be modelled on the TRIPS rather than US/European models. This reveals certain ambiguities (compulsory licensing) in TRIPS as well as a few drawbacks (life long patenting) in the patent laws of the developed world. However, in a product patent regime, Indian firms will have to look for new sources of growth in the future and the biggest source will be the productive R&D, which can deliver patentable innovations. But to achieve that they will need the upgrading of capabilities specifically in all area of pharmaceutical R&D management.

The extensive literature that deals with the pharmaceutical industry is focused on the technological frontier firms in the developed world. But not enough attention is paid to the capability acquisition process by firms in developing countries and to the changed patent law whose impact represents change in the scientific knowledge base for firms. This paper explores the neglected area of new knowledge creation as a response to environmental change by using firms the Indian pharmaceutical industry as case studies.

4. Methodology

The main research strategy used for the research is a case study method as the nature of the research question requires a qualitative oriented research methodology but an attempt has been made to support it with quantitative data.

The realisation that the new patent regime will restrict, not end, reverse engineering and so the non-requirement of innovative R&D in the immediate future means only a handful of pharmaceutical firms in India has started moving towards innovative activity. The products that are already on the Indian market at the time the TRIPs agreement was signed will remain free of patent protection and are one reason for a lack of diffusion of innovative R&D among all industry players. This puts a restriction on number and nature of firms chosen for the study. There are a number of firms (10 to 12) who have invested in innovative R&D and have products in advanced stages but for analysis only those firms, which has filed patent in USA and India for new drug delivery systems or new chemical entities have been chosen. The patent data was taken as the indicator of a firm's ability in innovative R&D. However this data also has some limitation as publication and patents were not the priority area till 1995 due to lack of trust in the case of former and lack of value in the case of later. The R&D intensity (R&D expenditure proportion to sales) reflecting the importance of R&D in the firm along with trends in the firm's networking activities are considered as an input variable.

Firms	No. of patents		License to MNC
	New Drug delivery systems	New chemical entities (IND)	
DRL	0	9	3
Ranbaxy	3	4	1
Wockhardt	2	2	
Torrent		4	1
Lupin	1		1

Figure 2: Patent and licensing data on innovative firms

The qualitative data collection involved interviews with academics, consultants and executives from innovative firms using semi-structured questionnaire. The issues in the questionnaire mainly covered the area of the firm's reconfiguration of organisational processes based on the theoretical framework and also issues such as effect of change in patent law on industry structure and emerging challenges.

The data was analysed using case study method and to identify patterns of reconfiguration, interview transcripts were content analysed. The secondary data was collected from industry journals, industry association publications and annual reports of Indian firms.

5. Reconfiguration process
The growth of the Indian pharmaceutical industry reflects the rise of the industry up the value chain of activities involved in pharmaceutical R&D.

The industry came a long way from importing the bulk drugs to exporting formulations to highly regulated markets in the developed world. After 1995 firms started moving up the value chain (Fig.3) in innovative R&D by concentrating on analogue research, chiral research and new drug delivery systems. The knowledge accumulated in process R&D is not directly relevant in innovative R&D but acts as a base. The experience in process R&D acted as a stepping stone for firms to do innovative R&D and without that knowledge it would have been very difficult to do innovative research.

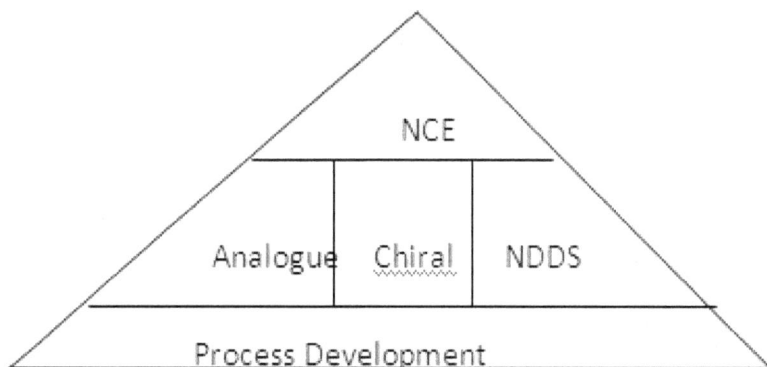

Figure 3: Pharmaceutical R&D value chain.

The TRIPS challenge demands innovative R&D and in a way it means that firms will have to create an environment that will motivate 'out of box' thinking from the scientist and competence in regulatory management. This paper will cover the preliminary analysis of five firms (Figure.2.) who are at the forefront of the Indian pharmaceutical industry and who have proven their innovative capability with patents in new drug delivery systems and new drug discovery.

The interviews with the executives suggest that firms have realised, innovation being the platform, R&D has become the key bolt in firm strategies. These firms' choose the strategy of collaborative research involving milestone payment and limited marketing rights to cover cost involved in the research. As one respondent describes the early efforts of these firms, "These companies seen writing on the wall and worked towards developing the expertise in new area of drug discovery and development research. They realise that it is imperative for their survival and growth in the global markets and have embarked investments in this for the future. Please note considering the low resources available to them in comparison to those of MNCs, they have adopted the strategy of the collaborative research through licensing route, by gaining up-front milestone and royalty payments for the molecules licensed by them to MNCs for development".

These firms started by setting up separate 'state of the art' R&D centres totally dedicated to new drug delivery and new drug discoveries. Firms used different R&D structures, starting new divisions to manage IPR as well as establishing new disciplinary divisions. They increase investment in R&D from 1995 but this gained momentum in 2000, which resulted in building the absorptive capacity required in understanding of the advances happening at the technological front. As the ability of firms to make use of outside knowledge depends upon their installed knowledge base (Cohen and Levinthal, 1990), without the investment in creation of knowledge in particular areas, it would be difficult for a firm to build capabilities to acquire, absorb and apply external knowledge.

Firms	No. of R&D labs	R&D intensity R&Dspend % of sales		
		2000	2001	2002
DRL	5	3.3	4.4	6.3
Ranbaxy	3	4.2	3.8	5.5
Wockhardt	2	7.2	6.2	7
Torrent	1	5.0	4.6	5.4
Lupin	2	2.7	4.9	5.6

Figure 4: R&D intensity of innovative Indian firms

The R&D intensity of Indian firms is much less compared to the R&D intensity of large pharmaceutical firms. But according to some respondents, the cost of the development of a drug in India could be a tenth of the international cost and Indian pharmaceutical firms' follows the resource allocation models of large pharmaceutical firms' for their R&D investment. As one R&D director suggests,

Reconfiguration of knowledge management practices in new product development- The case of the Indian pharmaceutical industry

"We benchmark ourselves on how much multinationals are investing, generic companies are investing. We know whatever the cost is in USA, 1/10th is in India. So MNC firms spending 15%, generic companies are spending 7%, then firms in India will spend 3-4%".

The significant aspect is the increase in R&D expenditure actually spent on innovative R&D from 20% in 1995 to 60% in 2002. All these firms are run by leaders who are scientists and according to the respondents that played a crucial role in the directing firm's efforts in innovative R&D. As one respondent puts it, "These leaders realised early that developing a molecule through basic research will be very costly and so looking at available resources they decided to invest in analogue research or new drug delivery systems which is a patentable, legitimate innovation".

According to one executive these firms focused on people or R&D scientists and firms started investing in them (Figure.5.).

Firms	No. of scientist working in innovative R&D	Total no. of R&D personnel
DRL	260	550
Ranbaxy	400	700
Wockhardt	90	220
Torrent	160	290
Lupin	60	250

Figure 5: Number of scientist working in innovative R&D

They started hiring scientists who have worked in the laboratories of multinational companies and have experience in innovative research. They made these scientists head of their laboratories and gave them freedom to work on chosen therapeutic areas. The approach of Indian firms was similar to the large pharmaceutical firms who hired star scientist to acquire biotechnology capabilities along with other efforts (Darby and Zucker ,1997).

Another important part of the strategy to acquire knowledge in innovative R&D was networking. Large pharmaceutical firms used networking with biotechnology-based firms, research institutes and university laboratories to acquire knowledge in biotechnology (Galambos, et al., 1998; Nicholls-Nixon, 1993). Similarly, these Indian firms started building networks with local as well as overseas research institutes; universities and research based companies.

They changed the nature of their R&D by opening the insular in-house R&D to the collaborative network model. Networking became the key mantra and some firms even established their laboratories in developed countries to make use of the knowledge spillover.

Joint ventures' with overseas research-based companies were another way used for acquiring knowledge in cutting edge technologies.

It was not enough to just hire the scientist or build new R&D centres, the creation of an environment for combination of knowledge for innovative research was another important requirement. To achieve that these firms built cross-disciplinary teams of scientists from different disciplines like pharmacology, medicinal chemistry, intellectual property rights etc. They started the process of knowledge upgrading of local scientists who were expert in process research. Respondents list measures like encouraging scientists to take training in new scientific tools or allowing them to pursue their academic ambitions while working in organisations. These firms have manufacturing and marketing centres all over the world including US and Europe and as a result of that, they could make the best research facilities accessible to their scientists. These firms are doing lot of projects with Indian as well as overseas universities, which allows scientists from these firms to pursue academic interests and this is also encouraged by firms. For example, a post-graduate working in these firms can continue his PhD when in the firm.

These Indian firms changed the R&D internally to create environment in which innovative research will prosper. Publication in journals and conferences is now valued more and encouraged, although all the respondents shared the viewpoint that this will really prosper after 2005 and lack of trust is still preventing full-fledged publication from firms.

Knowledge upgrading in terms of management of regulatory compliance is a necessary requirement for a strong patent regime. Regulatory competence is closely associated with information management and here firms' investments in information technology played an important role. These firms invested substantially in information technology tools like enterprise resource planning. Every firm has an Intranet, which carries tools like connect forum or open house for interaction between top management and employees. These Intranets facilitate the seamless flow of information across the organisation and locations through software like CDMS (clinical data management systems) and MIS helping the collection of the information required for regulatory compliance.

One R&D director explained that some firms acquire the regulatory expertise by filing patents in regions like South-East Asia, which requires the same amount of data as regulators from the developed world but are less stringent. This proved to be an effective mechanism for gathering the knowledge required for the successful filing of patents in US and Europe. The experience was further strengthened by successful filing of the patent application for generics (ANDA) in the US.

The result of the analysis shows the transformation in the R&D activities and subsequent changes in the management practices. The firms are filling up the knowledge gaps by hiring the experienced scientists, developing new units and building the external networks. Along with that they are also establishing new ways doings things to achieve the effective coordination and integration of specialised knowledge bases.

In the Indian pharmaceutical industry only a small number of firms' have invested in innovative R&D raising concerns about the survival of other firms in the long term. This research analysed their approaches but the innovative R&D and process of knowledge reconfiguration are recent phenomena in Indian pharmaceutical R&D, which is still at an emergent stage.

A good deal of additional analysis is necessary to understand the real depth of the processes involved in knowledge reconfiguration.

6. Conclusion

The TRIPS agreement represents an enormous challenge for pharmaceutical firms in developing countries. The analysis of R&D in Indian pharmaceutical firms shows that, as a response to changes in patent law, Indian firms are changing the insular in-house nature of their R&D and are embracing the network model of R&D by collaborating with research institutes, universities and other firms. The networking is helping these firms to augment and leverage organisational capabilities in innovative R&D.

The reconfiguration of the knowledge creation process in the R&D was achieved by increasing the R&D investment and hiring the new scientist embodying the knowledge about innovative R&D. Information technology supports the management of explicit knowledge but these scientists carried the crucial tacit knowledge with them and played a significant role in creating an environment required for 'out of box 'thinking by changing the mindset of the organisation.

The change in the scientific base of R&D activities as a result of change in patent law resembles the biotechnology challenge before the large pharmaceutical firms. This paper shows that the reconfiguration of the knowledge creation process of Indian firms' follows and converges with the large pharmaceutical approaches to transform their technological identity due to molecular biology advances.

References

Cohen, W., M. and D. A. Levinthal (1990) "Absorptive capacity: A new perspective on learning and innovation", Administrative Science Quarterly. Vol. 35, pp128-152.

D'Este, P. (2001) "The distinctive patterns of capabilities accumulation and inter-firm heterogeneity: the case of Spanish pharmaceutical industry", Nelson and Winter conference, DRUID2001.

Grant, R. M. (1991) "The resource- based theory of competitive advantage: implications for strategy formulation", California management review. Vol. 33, No. 3, pp114-135.

Reconfiguration of knowledge management practices in new product development- The case of the Indian pharmaceutical industry

Galambos, Sturchio, L. and Jeffrey, L. (1998) "Pharmaceutical firms and the transition to biotechnology: A study in strategic innovation", Business History Review,Vol. 72 ,No. 2,pp 250-278.

Gambardella, A. (1995), Science and innovation: The US pharmaceutical industry during the 1980s, Cambridge University press.

Halemane, M. D. and Dongen, B. (2003) "Strategic innovation management of change in the

pharmaceutical industry", International journal of technology management,Vol.25, No.3/4, pp314-333.

Henderson, R. and K. B. Clark (1990) "Architectural innovation: The reconfiguration of existing product technologies and the failure of established firms", Administrative Science Quarterly, Vol. 35, pp9-30.

Henderson, R. and I. M. Cockburn (1994) "Measuring competence? Exploring firm effects in pharmaceutical research", Strategic management Journal, Vol.15, pp63-84.

Henderson, R., Orsenigo, L. and Pisano, G. P. (1999) The pharmaceutical industry and the revolution of in molecular biology: Interactions among scientific, institutional, and organisational change. In Mowery, D. C. and Nelson, R. R. (eds) Sources of industrial Leadership: Studies of seven industries Cambridge University Press, Cambridge

Kogut, B. and U. Zander (1992) "Knowledge of the firm, combinative capabilities, and the replication of technology", Organizational Science, Vol. 3, No. 3, pp383-397.

Lanjouw, J. O. (1996) The introduction of pharmaceutical product patents in India: Heartless exploitation of the poor and suffering? NBER working paper.

Madanmohan, T. R. and Krishnan, K. T (2003) "Adaptive strategies in the Indian Pharmaceutical industry", International Journal of technology management, Vol. 25, No. 3/4, pp227-246.

Nicholls-Nixon, C. L. (1993) Absorptive capacity and technology sourcing: implications for responsiveness of established firms, Ph.D. thesis, Purdue University.

Pettigrew, A., Woodman, R. and Cameron, K, (2001) "Studying organisational change and development: Challenges for future research", Academy of Management Journal, 44, 4, 697-704.

Ramani, S. (2002) "Who is interested in Biotech? R&D strategies, knowledge base and market sales of Indian biopharmaceutical firms", Research Policy. Vol. 31, No.3, pp381-398.

Sequeira, K. P. (1998), The patent system and technological development in late industrializing countries: The case of the Spanish pharmaceutical industry, D.Phil. thesis, University of Sussex.

Suioniemi, S. and Brannback, M. (2000) "Can elephant and mice play?-Organizational and market implications of the restructuring process in the drug industry", Technical Reports No.2.

Tushman, M. and Anderson, P. (1986) "Technological discontinuities and organizational environments", Administrative Science Quarterly, 31, 439-465.

Watal, J. and Mathai, A. (1995) "Global Trade liberalization: Implications for industrial restructuring", United Nations Industrial Development Organization (UNIDO) report.

Wendt, R. A. (2000) "The Pharmaceutical Industry in India", Working Paper No. 24, International Development Studies, Roskilde University

International Strategic Alliance and Organisational Learning: Factors for Promoting Learning: A Malaysian Case

Zuraina Dato Mansor
University Putra Malaysia, Selangor, Malaysia

Editorial Commentary

In this paper, Mansor examines the contribution of strategic alliances to the organisational learning of a Malaysian manufacturing company, Polyethylene Malaysia. A framework based on six categories of "key facilitating learning elements" is developed and used to investigate the relationship between the company and a UK-based partner, BP Chemicals. Primary data collection was done through interviews, supported by observation and document review.

The joint venture was successful. The study findings demonstrate the impacts on the success of joint ventures by explicitly designing organisation strategy, structure and systems to support organisational learning and identify key activities that promote such learning.

Abstracts: Intense competition and the augmentation of business opportunities are amongst two major factors for the globalization of worldwide markets and economies. These trends are currently exploiting the industries manufacturing and non-manufacturing, calls them to take advantage of globalization process and to adopt a more sophisticated approach to strategic marketing and planning including performing collaboration. Companies have to constantly increase their knowledge base if they are to remain competitive. One way of increasing knowledge is by forming alliances. The purpose of this study is to identify the factors that promote learning through the formation of strategic alliances between a Malaysian manufacturing organisation with a UK partner and have included learning into their alliance objectives. It is a qualitative and in-depth studies of the company where the data collection process involved one time forum with personnel who were directly involved under the project, interviews with selected respondents, questionnaires, plant observation as well as secondary resources such as company reports and brochures.

Keywords: international strategic alliance, organisational learning, key elements for promoting learning

1. Introduction

In this new era of globalisation, it is undeniable that many more firms have come to rely on alliances as a strategic necessity for sustaining competitive advantage and creating customer value (Iyer, 2002). Aside from explicit strategic and operational motives, learning has become one of the primary motives in the recent partnership agreement. Extant literature regarding how alliances could promote and facilitate learning are found for example from Hamel, 1991: Inkpen 1996, 1998, 2000: and many more. Inkpen (1998) for instance has stated that alliances are vehicles of opportunity that provide a formal structure for creating a laboratory for learning.

This study was conducted with the objective to identify the factors that promote learning through the formation of strategic alliances between a Malaysian manufacturing organisation with a UK partner and have included learning into their alliance objectives. The paper has presented the case and findings as a qualitative and in-depth studies of the company.

2. Research methodology

This study covers research on International Strategic Alliances (ISAs) and the organisational learning (OL) process, which involves strategic co-operation between a local parent partner, foreign partner and 'child' alliance company. For the purpose of this study, the child company/business is defined as a company/business that is established upon the formation of alliance, and is based in the local partner country. The focus of the study identified the foreign parent partners as the sources of learning, and the child as the receiver of this foreign partner knowledge. For this paper, a case from a manufacturing company is presented. The company is known as Polyethylene Malaysia Sdn. Bhd.. It was incorporated on 11 July 1991 as a 'child' business established under the Strategic Alliance MOU signed by PETRONAS and BP Chemicals, with the equity ratio of 60%:40%. This alliance marked the beginnings of the upstream petrochemicals industry development, as well as economic and industrial development in Malaysia and was incorporated to be the major customer of the Ethylene Malaysia Sdn. Bhd., which has also formed an alliance with BP and Idemitsu Petrochemicals Co. Ltd. This ethylene project and plant is located in the same area as the polyethylene plant (sharing plant facilities under Integrated Petrochemical Complexes (IPCs)), and thus, Polyethylene Malaysia Sdn. Bhd. receives supplies of feedstock directly from the ethylene plant, without involving lengthy transportation. The data collection process on this company was drawn based on interviews with selected personnel, and access to company annual reports and brochures, and plant observations. The interviews, which are the main source of data, were conducted with the General Manager (a BP expatriate), the senior manager of operations, training manager, technical superintendent, and ex-laboratory engineer (all were key personnel of the child company). Interviews were also conducted with two junior engineers and all question were set differently (the questions designed to each of the interviewees are all different to reflect their position and responsibilities).

3. Strategic alliance and organisational learning

In the modern business world, the main goal for organisations is to perform well, to find the right strategies, and to make the right decisions that help them to be more competitive through co-operation and competition (Zineldin, 1998). Serrat (2009) emphasizes that everywhere, organisation has discovered that they cannot "go" it alone and must now turn to others to survive. Strategic alliances (SAs) are becoming a popular and prominent strategy in the global economy to satisfy the rapid market changes. It is reported that the formation of SAs or co-operative activity has increased dramatically in recent years (Dyer and Singh, 1998) due to the effect of globalisation (Imai and Itami, 1984; Narula and Hagedoorn, 1999; Buckley et al., 2002). SAs can be defined in various ways and provide a variety of firms' motives for its formation. For example, Inkpen (2000), who suggests alliances provide a platform for learning, has described an alliance as two or more organisations that are brought together because of their different skills, knowledge, and complementary strategies. These partnerships of two or more corporations or businesses are also set to achieve strategically significant objectives that are mutually beneficial. SAs can be used as a mechanism for growth strategies and entering new markets (Harrigan, 1986; Contractor and Lorange, 1988; Kogut, 1988; Glaister and Buckley, 1996); obtaining new technology (Lei and Slocum, 1992; Faulkner, 1995), reducing financial risk and sharing costs of R&D (Pucik, 1988); learning and developing new knowledge (e.g. Hamel, 1991; Grant 1996; Khanna et al., 1998; Beamish and Berdrow, 2003, Senthil and White, 2005) and as a source for achieving competitive advantage (e.g. Grant, 1991; Ireland et al., 2002).

In identifying the facilitating factors for promoting learning through strategic alliance, this study has made used of the framework suggested by Morrison and Mezentseff (1997) in their studies on alliance within a cooperative learning environment with objective to achieve long-term success. The Morrison and Mezentseff (1997) learning framework is chosen as a based for continuing research in this study. This framework is particularly interested as it has suggested a few key learning elements that facilitate learning process in alliance case. Though the authors of the framework have suggested it for the use of parents in assessing learning, but this research would use and adopt it to suit with the child partner process of learning from its foreign partner. Morrison and Mezentseff (1997), in defining the terms in their framework suggested that element 'systemic thinking' helps alliance companies form their mutual dream for the relationship. It is very important that the dreams of the partners are mutually agreed, so that there is a collective driving force to achieve this goal. Element 'share mental mode' suggested that people within these relationships need to test share their ideas and perceptions about the learning environment. This process facilitates decision-making, action, and learning. Further, the authors suggested a learning environment that builds 'learning relationship' between partners. This relationship can be achieved through a knowledge connection and a network that influences how well the firm can learn and build new core competencies. Additionally, they agreed that 'joint learning structures' can be sustained through; first, identifying and becoming aware of new knowledge, second, transferring/interpreting new knowledge, third, using knowledge by adjusting behaviour to achieve intended outcomes, and finally, incorporating such knowledge by reflecting on what is happening and adjusting learning behaviours.

3.1. Objectives for forming international strategic alliance for our case

To complement the back-up of rich natural resources, the company Polyethylene Malaysia Sdn. Bhd formed strategic alliance with the UK partner with the objectives to seek tangible assets such as financial support, plant and equipment technology, as well as technical and managerial capabilities. It also sought intangible assets, such as firm reputation, brand equity and superior customer services reputation, especially in the polyethylene business. From the interviews, the respondents also stated that both the parent and child company agreed that the prime objective of this alliance should involve acquiring learning on manufacturing polyethylene products. The alliance also brought together a strong JV set-up, which gave access to the foreign parent partner's best practices, multi-cultural workforces that drive various ideas and contributions, international image, experienced manpower, and strong financial backing. Further, the alliance also contributed in terms of an integrated supplier partnership where it could bring benefits in terms of accessing secure and reliable feedstock, and at a more competitive price. Additionally and indirectly, since the start of its operation, Polyethylene Malaysia has also developed other related strength, in terms of:

- Proven gas-based technology.

- Good technical service capability.

- Stable workforce (few industrial disputes).

- Modern product range.

- Regional marketing expertise.

In summary, it could be said that by forming the alliance, the child business, Polyethylene Malaysia Sdn Bhd would gain technology, skill and experience in manufacturing the polyethylene related products, 'standard prototype plant', to be built by the vendor selected by the parent partner organization and finally, programmes under 'shadow posts' who are loaned to the child company plant to guide and supervise the local staff.

4. Summary and findings

4.1. Alliance history

Based on the interview, it has been revealed that both parent partners already had other established business ties prior to this alliance thus apparently this alliance did not involve too much 'paperwork' and therefore Polyethylene Malaysia Sdn Bhd was incorporated with few problems or disagreements. Within the alliance agreement, BP agreed to license the polymer technology, design the polymer plant and transfer the knowledge (which included skills to operate the plant), and manufacture the polyethylene product using up-to-date technology. BP would find a suitable contractor to build the child company plant so that it would be a 'prototype' or similar to the BP polyethylene plant.

4.2. Implementation

In terms of implementation and commitment, it was agreed in their alliance contract that whenever Polyethylene Malaysia plant commenced its operations, BP expatriate staff would be loaned on a 'shadow post' basis, to guide and observe the local staff working on the plant equipment and machines. BP would also facilitate the transfer of technology by providing intensive courses for the local staff and would put no restrictions on R&D, which allowed the child company to improve product development based on their experience and new ideas. The alliance agreement placed no restrictions on Polyethylene Malaysia for using BP Chemicals' Innovene Gas Phase technology, and for using BP's marketing strategy under the pre-marketing activities based on their product. The child company would also be invited to join international seminars with other BP subsidiaries, as long as the company paid the membership fee.

4.3.   Communication

To encourage the process of learning, all staff are encouraged to communicate regularly, either formal or informal. For example, the child company holds regular meetings with all staff, along with the specific issues to be discussed in each meeting. Table 1 summarises the types of meeting that staff attended and the themes that are to be discussed.

The foreign parent organisation staff and the alliance managers, who are based at Polyethylene Malaysia, also communicate regularly. For example, the GM himself communicated with the UK parent organisation by eMail and attended board and shareholders' meetings. As expatriate staff who was loaned and responsible for assisting the learning process at the child company, occasionally, the GM attended the company's morning and monthly meetings, where he would share ideas and help to solve any problems.

Table 1: Types of meetings at Polyethylene Malaysia Sdn. Bhd

Time	Members/staff	Issues
Every morning	Compulsory for all operational staff, others welcome	To solve/share ideas on everyday problems
Every week	All supervisors and operation manager	To solve and bring ideas on operational problems
Every month	Managers, GM, committee members	To discuss operational issues, and new ideas
Annual shareholders' meeting	Shareholders, GM	To discuss financial issues
Annual Board Meeting	Board of directors, GM	To discuss operational issues, financial issues, etc.

(Sources: adapted from interview with respondents)

Daily morning meetings between the key managers and technical and operational staff were important for these people to share ideas and information, because during the meetings, the managers took the opportunity to open up discussions with the staff to ask question or discuss problems. For example, as stated by one of the respondents:

"The managers try to identify any technical or operational problems from the staff through question and answer sessions, and give feedback to correct mistakes or errors. In case they were unable to solve the problem, then they would bring the issue to the upper level management for a solution."

Other than that, staff communicates informally when they meet either during working hours or during their leisure time. In summary, all respondents agreed that communication between partners took place when local staff communicates with the parent staff and vice versa and when the local staff communicated and interacted with local colleagues, supervisors and managers. Thus, this suggests that they were all in consensus that communication takes place at almost everywhere, with everybody either through eMail, formal or informal meetings. In another point, networking or knowledge connection, which promotes 'absorptive capacity' from foreign parent to child company staff, took place when the experts were loaned to the child company on a 'shadow post' basis during the commissioning period. These expatriate staff (managers) that were loaned on rotational basis, helped promote communication and sharing of ideas and experiences with the child staff.

4.4.   Learning process

As stated before, all child staff underwent training before they were appointed to any specific post or job. A respondent said,

"The child company will make sure that new employees are competent to work before they start working. This will happen through comprehensive training – in house and abroad. Whenever the needs to train occur, the company will provide whatever they can. But, if the expert is there, then the staff will be trained individually by the expert till he has achieved certain levels which are certified by the expert and the supervisor."

Learning is very important in order to help the child company achieve its objectives. It was suggested that learning takes place *from* the foreign partners in this alliance through:

- Formal technical training
- Shadow postings

- Permanent expatriate posts located at the child company plant

4.5. Key facilitating learning elements

In identifying key facilitating elements for promoting organizational learn-ing process, elements introduced by Senge (1990) in learning organization with focus on the elements discussed by Morrison and Mezentseff (1997) in their studies on learning in collaborative partnership were used and tested and the study findings were discussed below.

4.5.1. Learning culture and climate

According to the extant literature, knowledge can happen when employ-ees have access to organisational knowledge, can find new and better ways to perform, work together, break down barriers, share a vision, fill gaps in knowledge, increase productivity, satisfy customers, and ultimately compete (Tsang, 1998). Based on the interviews, it was believed that the child had no problem in assessing the acquired learning. In this view, it can be summarised that the culture promoting the learning environment at the child company was developed and evolved through the following situa-tions:

- Mutually agreed alliance objectives between partners in the rela-tionship.
- Commitment from the top management of the child company to build a positive staff relationship.
- Each member of staff develops knowledge by working as a unit.
- Providing, sharing and expanding useful information, be it 'ex-plicit' or 'tacit' knowledge.
- Regular communications and discussions, both formal and infor-mal.
- Providing facilitative technology to enhance the transfer of knowledge (i.e. via the Internet), communication and storing use-ful information.

Additionally, the respondents suggested that in order to promote learning culture amongst the staff, the top management had initiated the following:

- Inculcating staff with the child company objectives, philosophy and values from start of employment.
- Training starts from the first day of working, either through on-the-job training or self-development programmes.

- Identifying staff competency from the beginning, so that they are assigned with the appropriate work. This is considered important for building a positive commitment and encouraging job development.
- Encouraging staff to learn in a continuous process.
- Encouraging staff to work with colleagues, share ideas and learn from mistakes.
- Requesting feedback and assessing learning outcomes.

4.5.2. Knowledge acquisition, creation and transfer

It is agreed that knowledge, whenever is shared and properly managed, should be able to increase individual as well as organisational learning. It was established from interviews with the majority of the key interviewees, as well as further observation at the child company, that knowledge acquisition from the foreign partner was mostly facilitated through technical training (during project period), 'shadow posting', on-the-job-training, as well as the initiative of local company to provide a compulsory self-development programme, internal R&D, facilitative technology and encouraging key personnel to attend international conferences and seminars. Thus, it can be summed up that learning at Polyethylene Malaysia has been acquired and considered important, based on arguments that they have successfully acquired and progressed in learning from the foreign partner, at least in terms of skill to manufacture polyethylene products. This can be proved as they stated that their knowledge has made them able to operate the plant with or without the presence of the parent expatriate staff. Furthermore, with such knowledge they have been able to share and improvise new ideas, and then bring the ideas into international discussions (seminars) where many of other parent partner subsidiaries attended.

4.5.3. Systemic thinking

Systemic thinking helps alliance organisations share their objectives. Based on the interviews, it was established that all staff at Polyethylene Malaysia were briefed to share the company's objectives and encouraged to collective efforts for achieving learning. The management was also responsible for designing the necessary mechanisms for learning to take place and evaluating its outcomes. For example learning outcomes are assessed using internal and external benchmarking and both partners – the foreign partner expatriates and the child - were collectively interacting to produce new ideas and solve problems.

4.5.4. Shared mental models

It is suggested that in a learning organisation, members need to share their ideas and perceptions about the learning environment so that it would facilitate decision-making, action, and learning. Hence, based on the information, it can be suggested that top management at this child company are responsible for directing the commitment of their staff to share ideas and perceptions about the learning environment. This was because, it was reported that each member of staff is responsible for acknowledging and promoting the shared culture and values, to give full support to colleagues, supervisors or subordinates, minimising product failure, minimising customer complaints, minimising accidents/incidents, and optimising the working time frame of 8 hours (staff have to work 8 hours per day). In addition, these interviewees also suggested that in order to help staff at Polyethylene Malaysia to cope with the everyday change in work and ideas, the following measures were adopted:

- Share alliance-learning objectives.
- Bridge and reduce cultural gap between foreign and child partners.
- Adopt a process focus in which learning is concentrated on innovating and generating new ideas.
- Work according to a common philosophy and safety statements set by parent partners.
- Direct a commitment towards helping the child company achieve its objectives
- Encourage frequent dialogue and communications.
- Revise the child company objectives at each annual board meeting

4.5.5. Building learning relationship

The management at Polyethylene Malaysia was also responsible for promoting an understanding that people at top management level play a major role in encouraging and assisting the development of the alliance relationship; they also act as an agent of learning. For example, it was reported that the GM is willing to be involved in regular morning meetings with technical and operational staff so that he can share ideas and be transparent to them. Other than that, supervisors are responsible for identifying any problems encountered by their subordinates and for solving these. This happens through frequently requested feedback on the jobs delegated to the staff. Conversely, staff are encouraged to communicate regularly with their supervisors to promote a 'supervisor-subordinate' approach in the on-the job training programme. From these, it can be deduced that the child company promotes 'leadership commitment' in order to enhance the creation of knowledge.

4.5.6. Joint learning structures/strategies/programmes

Staff at Polyethylene Malaysia have been able to learn and acquire the skills to manufacture polymer and polyethylene products faster and easier, as both alliance partners – the foreign and child - were involved in the development of joint-learning programmes. This has provided the connection for the opportunity to create new knowledge. In summary, these joint-learning programmes happened through; first, expatriate manager rotation: second, 2-yearly world-wide seminars: and third, visit plant sites. Additionally, the interviewees also suggested that it was due to the in-house R&D projects, in-house new idea generation, and commitment towards a continuous learning process that had helped the learning to successfully achieve by the local child staff. Based on information from the forum and interviews, the tacit and explicit knowledge acquired by the child company are summarised in Table 2 below.

Table 2: Types of knowledge transfer at Polyethylene Malaysia Sdn. Bhd.

Explicit knowledge	Tacit knowledge
Product formula	Skills and experience in developing polymer-based products
Manual for handling material/equipment	Skills and experience in handling plant equipment
Plant operation manual	Learning about different culture
Computer course	Learning to communicate with different nationalities
Plant safety rules	Learning to develop new ideas or new product
Plant policy	Learning to develop successful marketing skills in supplying and delivering polyethylene products

In addition, the study also tried to relate the importance of elements related to top management qualities with such as 'shared mental models', 'systemic thinking', and 'building learning relationship' in order to help the organizational learning process took place. Thus, those selected respondents were also asked to choose from a list of leadership qualities available at their workplace that help to support their learning process. The summary of those qualities were listed as shown in Table 3.

Table 3: Leadership qualities to promote learning process as described by respondents at Polyethylene Malaysia Sdn Bhd

Qualities	Percentage agreed
Manager acts as an agent of learning	90%
Communicate regularly	95%
Developed focus and shared objectives	85%
Direct shared vision	85%
Promotes learning culture	90%
Support improvement in teams	90%
Admitting mistakes and openness to new learning	70%
Work together	90%
Willingness to take risks in ambiguous situations	70%
Build trust	75%
Willingness to make special efforts	75%
Willingness to co-operate	80%
Willingness to be transparent	75%
Promote systemic thinking on this specific alliance	85%

In summary, if referred to the original key elements suggested by Morrison and Mezentseff (1997) and compared with the findings from the interviewees, it can be concluded that element 'communication and network' and 'learning mechanism', are also important and need attention. This was because in terms of the element 'communication and network', the child company emphasised the need for both partners – the child and the foreign parent - to communicate regularly, and had been able to reduce the communication gap by having a specific channel for communication and networking or an appointed agent for networking between both partner. Finally, the child company has also shown that it has given considerable attention to the element 'learning mechanism' through the process of feedback and assessment and deciding benchmarking for product quality, which helped to increase staff commitment and achieve continuous learning as well as ability to maintain the product quality as per standard required by foreign parent partner.

5. Conclusion

The paper presents the research on International Strategic Alliances (ISAs) and the organisational learning (OL). Based on the case study used in this research, it can be suggested that learning can be one of important reasons for forming ISAs. This is because learning is a key feature of the process by which firms accumulate technology in order to compete and add value to their current product. This paper has presented how, in this case, Polyethylene Malaysia Sdn. Bhd. as the child company formed an alliance with a UK company with a learning objective. The foreign parent partner (BP Chemicals) agreed to provide technology and skills in polyethylene products to the child company, and has designed a proper planning strategy for acquiring such skills. The information was mainly collected through interviews with several key persons and support staff from the child company. Based on the information, it can be suggested that this company has designed its organisational structure, strategy and system in line with achieving the specific learning objectives. For example, the motive for acquiring polyethylene technology was set up and agreed during the negotiation of alliance by both partners. Additionally, in order to achieve this learning motive, the company has reserved permanent positions for the expatriate staff, and allocated a specific budget for acquiring necessary skills and experience.

It is very important for an organisation to design a climate that creates and enhances a learning atmosphere. The findings further established that Polyethylene Malaysia deliberately designed strategies for promoting learning culture, and built systemic thinking and shared mental models so that they become committed to the learning and the jobs delegated to them. In addition, to ensure a long-term commitment between the partners, they have set up a joint-learning structure and strategies (by organising world-wide seminars, encouraging in plant R&D and continuous learning). All of these have helped the 'child' to be able to acquire and manage knowledge from its foreign parent partner. Additionally, the case shows that in order to help the alliance partners achieve their shared alliance-learning objectives, relationships must be built within a proper learning plan, from planning to control, and this needs top management strategic decisions and commitment.

References

Beamish, W. P. and Berdrow, I. (2003). "Learning from IJVs: The unintended outcome". *Long Range Planning*, Vol. 36, pp. 285-303Buckley, P. J., Glaister, K. W. and Husan, R. (2002). "International joint ventures: Partnering skills and cross-cultural issues". *Long Range Planning*, Vol. 35, pp.113-134

Contractor, F. J. and Lorange, P. (1988). Why should firms cooperate? The strategy and economics basis for cooperative ventures. In: Contractor, F. J. and Lorange, P. (eds.), *Cooperative Strategies in International Business*. Lexington Books, Lexington, MA, pp. 3-30

Dyer, J. H. and Singh, H. (1998). "The relational view: Cooperative strategy and sources of inter-organisational competitive advantage". *Academy of Management Review*, Vol. 23, No.4, pp. 660-679

Faulkner, C. J. D. (1995). *International strategic alliances: Co-operating to compete*. McGraw-Hill, Maidenhead Glaister, K. W. and Buckley, P. J. (1996). "Strategic motives for international alliances formation". *Journal of Management Studies*, Vol. 33, No. 3, pp. 301-32

Grant, R. M. (1991). "The resource-based theory of competitive advantage: Implications for strategy formulation". *California Management Review*, Vol. 34, pp. 119-135

Grant, R. M. (1996). "Toward a knowledge-based theory of the firm". *Strategic Management Journal*, Vol. 17, (Special issue), Winter, pp. 109-122

Hamel, G. (1991). "Competition for competence and inter-partner learning within international strategic alliances". *Strategic Management Journal*, Vol. 12, pp. 83-103.

Hamel, G., Doz, Y. and Prahalad, C. K. (1989). "Collaborate with your competitors and win". *Harvard Business Review*, Vol. 67, Jan-Feb, pp. 133-139.

Harrigan, K. R. (1986). *Managing for joint venture success*, Lexington Books, Lexington, MA

Imai, K. and Itami, H. (1984). "Interpenetration of organisations and market: Japan's firm and market in comparison with the US". *International Journal of Industrial Organisation,* Vol. 2, pp. 285-310

Inkpen, A. C. (1996). "Creating knowledge through collaboration". *California Management Review*, Vol. 39, No. 1, pp. 123-140.

Inkpen, A. C. (1998). "Learning and knowledge acquisition through international
strategic alliances, competitiveness and global leadership in the 21st century".
The Academy of Management Executive, Vol. 12, No. 4.pp. 223-229

Inkpen, A. C. (2000). "Learning, knowledge management and strategic alliances: So
many studies, so many unanswered questions". In: Lorange, P. and Contractor,
(eds.) *Cooperative Strategies and Alliances*. Pergamon, London, pp. 267-289

Ireland, R.D., Hitt, M. A. and Vaidyanath, D. (2002). "Alliance management as a
source of competitive advantage" *Journal of Management*, Vol 28, No 3,
pp.413-446

Iyer, K.N.S. (2002). "Learning in strategic alliances: An evolutionary perspectives",
Academy of Marketing Science, [Online] 2002 (10) Available:
http://www.amsreview.org/articles/iyer10-2002.pdf

Khanna, T., Gulati, R. and Nohria, N. (1998). "The dynamics of learning alliances:
Competition, cooperation and relative scope". *Strategic Management Journal*,
Vol. 19, No.3, pp. 193-210

Kogut, B. (1988). "Joint ventures: Theoretical and empirical perspectives". *Strategic
Management Journal*, Vol. 9, pp. 319-32

Lei, D. Slocum Jr, J. W. and Pitts, R. (1997). "Building cooperative advantage: Managing strategic alliances to promote organisational learning". *Journal of World
Business*, Vol. 32, No. 3, pp. 203-224

Lei, D. and Slocum, J. W. J. (1992). "Global strategy, competence-building and strategic alliances". *California Management Review*, Vol. 35, No. 1, pp. 81-97.

Morrison, M. and Mezentseff, L. (1997). "Learning alliances: A new dimension of
strategic alliances". *Management Decision*, Vol. 35,No. 5, pp. 351-358.

Narula, R. and Hagedoorn, J. (1999) "Innovating through strategic alliance: Moving
towards international partnership and contractual agreements". *Technovation*,
Vol. 19, Nov, pp. 283-294.

Nonaka, I. and Takeuchi, H. (1995). *The knowledge creating company: How Japanese companies create the dynamics of innovation*. Oxford University Press,
New York Osland, E. G. and Yaprak, A. (1995). "Learning through strategic alliances processes and factors that enhance marketing effectiveness". *European
Journal of Marketing*, Vol. 29, Iss. 3, pp. 52-66

Pucik, V. (1988). "Strategic alliances, organisational learning, and competitive advantage: The HRM agenda". *Human Resource Management*, Vol. 27, No. 1, pp.
77-93Tsang, W. K. E. (1998). "Motives for strategic alliances: A resource–based
perspective". *Scandinavian Journal Management*, Vol. 14, No. 3, pp. 207.

Senthil, K. M and White, M. A (2005) "Learning and Knowledge Transfer in Strategic
Alliances: A Social Exchange View". *Organization Studies,* 26(3): 415–441, SAGE
Publications(London): Access on web-site on 8th April 2009

Serrat, O (2009) "Learning In Strategic Alliance", Asian Development Bank. http://www.adb.org/Documents/Information/Knowledge-Solutions/Learning-in-Strategic-Alliances.pdf. Access on website 12 April 2009.

Zineldin, M. A. (1998). "Towards an ecological collaborative relationship management: A "co-operative" perspective". *European Journal of Marketing*, Vol. 32, No. 11/12, pp. 1138-1164

Enabling Knowledge Creation in Judicial Environments: The Case of Catalonia's Public Administration

Mario Pérez-Montoro[1] and Jesús Martínez[2]
[1]Department of Library and Information Science, University of Barcelona, Spain
[2]Center for Legal Studies and Specialist Training, Generalitat, Government of Catalonia

Editorial commentary

Pérez-Montoro & Martínez examine communities of practice in justice administration in Catalonia. This government department is staffed by quite distinct sets of professionals (such as lawyers, psychologists and educators). This large-scale project, with 14 communities and 27 working groups, has more than 2000 participants. The project approach addresses the characteristics of each type of professional group (need for continuous innovation, degree of hierarchy, group size, and need for ICT systems to do work) as well as the specific lifecycle stages for CoP evolution.

The paper is silent on methods of data collection and analysis, focusing instead on model development and project experiences. From the study, factors for success in CoPs are identified and conclusions drawn that could be used in other environment.

Abstract: The last two years has seen the implementation of a project of Knowledge Management in the justice department of the Generalitat, Government of

Catalonia. This project seeks to enable the community of workers in this administration to find a suitable context for the creation of knowledge and also to benefit from this knowledge such that each member of the community ends up contributing more efficiently to the collective aim that is being pursued: to improve and streamline day-to-day praxis. The project has been developed on a network of communities of practice, coordinated by a central organizational figure: the e-moderator, one of a few key people in the department who aims to encourage and create a collaborative environment to facilitate creation, exchange and knowledge sharing among the teams involved. Two different complementary strategies were put into practice to help these e-moderators achieve these objectives. Firstly, the chance to use an online cooperative environment was on offer. Named "e-Catalunya", this online environment allows them to develop most of the main strategies involved in knowledge management. In this way, for example, this environment permits on the one hand the development of a series of actions to manage explicit knowledge (using systems of representation and protocol creation); and, on the other, it also allows a tacit knowledge management (using synchronic and diachronic socialisation strategies). Secondly, a policy of incentives was designed to ensure return on investment in both time and effort for these e-moderators. The incentives were principally economic, rewarding those actions that could help guarantee the correct working of the community they were responsible for. The policy was complemented with actions to promote the usage by the rest of the community, the potential users and also suppliers of knowledge, and active participation in the project. This allowed us to gather systematically all the knowledge generated in the project as well as the raw material to create a collection of good practices. The project involves, by a blended methodology, 20 communities of practice, 12 professional groups, and more than 1600 people.

Keywords: Knowledge creation, judicial environments, knowledge management, collaborative environments, knowledge technologies, information management

1. Introduction

Currently, it is not difficult to see that Knowledge Management (KM) is being positively received within organisations. Since the mid-90s, a significant number of corporations worldwide –especially multinationals– are turning slowly to the implementation of projects of this kind as a way of improving the efficacy and performance of their firms. However, it is not possible to claim that these types of projects are being implemented as a matter of course in the great majority of organisations. There is a particular type of organisation in which KM has had a general lack of application:

public organisations. The reasons for this lack of application can be found in the special characteristics (like, for example, the absence of threats arising from a potential rival or the rigid civil service employment structure) that can be seen in these organisations and which has allowed them to avoid looking for new strategies in KM to guarantee their survival. Nevertheless, despite the difficulties, a series of interesting KM projects are being implemented by various public sector organisations which are not exclusively profit-based.

Within the context of public organisations, one of the most noteworthy projects is being carried out within the *Departament de Justícia* of the *Generalitat de Catalunya* (the government of Catalonia). This project seeks to enable the community of workers in this administration to find a suitable context for the creation of knowledge and also to benefit from this knowledge such that each member of the Community ends up contributing more efficiently to the collective aim that is being pursued: to improve and streamline day-to-day praxis. This paper is aimed at outlining the project. To this end, we will be examining certain points. Firstly, in section 2, we are going to show the principal characteristics that knowledge exhibits in the judicial environment and describe how the project came about. In section 3, we are going to introduce a description of the Community of Practice which served as the driving force behind this project: the community of social workers. Thirdly, in section 4, we are going to describe the map of existing communities, focusing on the figure of the e-moderator, on the functioning of these communities and on workshops on best practices. Lastly, in section 5, we will present a more or less detailed breakdown of the functions and role played by technological support, e-Catalunya, which has in this project allowed for communities to develop through a collaborative environment and social network.

2.   Knowledge in judicial environments

Within the context of the the *Departament de Justícia*, it is normal to give examples of the main problems associated with knowledge that have occurred in other similar public administrations. Such problems are due, for the main part, to the clearly identifiable characteristics that knowledge usually displays in these contexts. On the one hand, it is normal that there should not be a clear context that governs the creation of new knowledge. On the other, most of this knowledge remains exclusively within the minds of the professionals who have created it as part of their daily praxis and, as such, is not usually found represented in any of the usual types of documentary support (chiefly, electronic files or paper). This lack of representation means that the knowledge in question is geographically dispersed and poorly structured, inhibiting efforts to manage it in some way. Furthermore, training plans do not tend to reach all the collectives included in this context in the same way. And, lastly, as a corollary of all the preceding arguments, this knowledge is manifested in an almost exclusive fashion within those who already have it, only being accessible in a fragmented and superficial manner.

For these reasons, in the last two years there has been an attempt to implement a Knowledge Management project within the *Departament*. The main objective sought by this project is twofold: to take advantage of a network of communities of practice, creating a context which allows for the creation of knowledge, and to establish the circuits and mechanisms for the collective usage of this knowledge. To bring about the implementation of this Knowledge Management system, a pilot programme was first prepared and it was decided that a specific community of practice should be activated: the community of social workers. Four months after this community came online, and after having extracted and analysed the first results, it was decided to activate the rest of the network of communities of practice (psychologists, librarians, etc). This network of communities was developed around a key organisational figure: the e-moderator.

3.   The community of social workers: One of the drivers of the project

From the inception of the project, the community of social workers has become one of the central driving forces, serving as a model and allowing the development of the Knowledge Management programme. However, owing to the special characteristics of this community, it has been necessary to develop a methodology and strategies which are a little different to those of other communities. We began by showing that the collective of social workers plays an important role in judicial environments. The smooth functioning of the judicial system depends on them, along with judges and psychologists. Nevertheless, this collective has experienced numerous knowledge-related problems in the past, making it different from the rest. On the one hand, the standard of training received (university studies, mainly) has been shown to be wanting when it came to dealing with day-to-day praxis. Also, owing to different social factors (issues such as immigration, for example), the continually changing environment has accentuated these shortfalls in knowledge even more. On the other hand, there are no shared standards which can help us to standardise the quality of individual praxis. This lack of standards creates a situation in which actions of high quality share space with others which are inadequate. Lastly, the existing knowledge resides exclusively in the minds of professionals who have created it from the basis of their own daily praxis, and who are consequently not accustomed to sharing it with the rest of the collective. Faced with this panorama, the collective has historically demanded training schemes to help overcome this structural deficit and resolve any problems of knowledge.

As a strategy to solve these problems, and with the full support of the *Department*, it was decided that a Knowledge Management programme would be set up. The aim of the project was clear from the outset: to try to extract high-quality knowledge that came from individual practice and activate the necessary mechanisms so that the rest of the collective could take advantage of it. The benefits of what was being pursued were also clear. On the one hand, it was an attempt to improve the quality of praxis across the entire collective. On the other, the aim was to standardise the praxis of social workers. Lastly, we looked to offer an effective tool for the creation of collective knowledge favouring the rapid adaptation and acceptance of newly hired social workers and lessening the negative consequences of losing the valuable knowledge of people who left the collective (because of illness or retirement). In order to achieve these aims and benefits, a start was made by drawing up a Knowledge Management pilot programme. The aim of this pilot programme was to establish the system on a small scale in order to foresee the possible benefits and consequences (positive and negative) and the modifications necessary to successfully carry out, during the second stage, a more extensive and exhaustive general project. In fact, the pilot programme was developed with a small but enthusiastic community of social workers (10 people) which included an easily controllable set of parameters. The chosen strategy was to select an issue which generally concerned the collective, and which, from the perspective of the gaining of knowledge, could offer positive results quickly enough to offer positive feedback.

The issue chosen was that of reports. The main reason for this choice lay in the fact that a large part of a social worker's responsibilities reside in preparing reports which, alongside reports prepared by other professionals (jurist and psychologists, for example), allow the relevant authorities to take decisions on the prisoners involved in prison trials. Paradoxically, however, the social workers never received any prior training to help them prepare these reports in a suitable and effective manner. Once the issue had been chosen, and after carrying out certain tests, the next working methodology was decided. Using the Focus Group technique, a number of regular and exclusively live meetings (2 per month) were arranged. These meetings were attended by the group of chosen social workers, along with a specialist Knowledge Management consultant.

The group of social workers was composed of 10 people who were enthusiastic about the project and who suitably represented the diversity of the collective. Before each meeting, aided by the consultant, a daily agenda was prepared and a series of tasks was delegated to each participant. Each participant was able to develop and prepare these tasks with other social workers who were not members of the group. Later, at the live meeting, each participant was asked to present the chosen tasks, which were discussed (defended and evaluated) and, after reaching a consensus following these discussions, a series of conclusions were reached. These conclusions and all the proposals which had been generated were documented and stored in files. The objective being pursued in these meetings was clear: to identify the structural type of each report model, identify the profile of unsuitable reports (those rejected by the recipients) and bring together all the finished reports which could be considered as good models to be followed by the rest of the collective of social workers. These reports were collated with the aim of later becoming part of an archive of good practices which could serve to support the praxis carried out by social workers.

The results obtained were significant. For four of the types of reports most commonly used by social workers, the following elements were achieved: a practical manual for the creation of reports, a Word template used in the creation of reports, a collection of best and worth practices (with regard to reports) which included examples to follow (and not follow) when preparing reports of this type, and a guide including indications for the simple and effective preparation of interviews with inmates, allowing for the collection of raw data for the preparation of reports. These products assisted in the later streamlining of reports being prepared about the same person throughout his or her time in the prison system. This could in turn give us an overview of the development of the inmate and the preparation of later reports. These templates were tested with the relevant organisations receiving the reports and were presented to the rest of the collective of social workers during the programming of a number of workshops. These workshops, as well as formally presenting the products, were also used to carry out training courses to promote the suitable use of these templates by the collective. Once the pilot programme had been covered, two more workgroups were prepared: one focusing on immigration and the other on alternative penal methods. The principal aim of the immigration group was to design a help system to be used by social workers when taking decisions on immigrant inmates. The main aim of the workgroup on alternative penal methods was to build a complete action protocol (including the design of the relevant reports) for social workers in cases where the sentences have been commuted to some type of community service. These two groups are currently working with a hybrid format: they arrange a monthly face-to-face meeting with a similar methodology to that of the pilot group and, directed by the e-moderator, they take advantage of the resources offered by the e-Catalunya platform in order to keep collaborating and working online between these meetings.

4. Other communities

Alongside the running of the social worker community, a further thirteen communities of professionals were added gradually. As shown in fig. 1, the total number of professionals involved up until now (May 2007) comes to 1012, comprising 21 active workgroups and 199 involved directly in the communities, generating knowledge (see table 1).As we will show in the following points, the working premise of the collaborative workgroups is based on four key elements: the e-moderator, the working methodology of the communities based on the work of Wenger (2000 and 2002) and Collison and Parcell (2001), the policy of distribution of created knowledge via workshops on best practices, and, finally, the development of an innovative incentives package.

4.1. The e-moderator

The e-moderator has come to be the key figure in the knowledge management process. The selection process began with the formulation of a professional profile with a series of characteristics (see fig 2). From this starting point a consulting process was opened between the formal leaders of the organisation until a number of ideal candidates were found. After a series of interviews twelve (12) e-moderators were chosen for renewable yearly periods.

The design of the training given was based on the principle of 'learning by doing.' Immediately they took on leadership and promotion functions – in person as well as in virtual settings – within their respective communities. As an aid to their work a course was designed with support, animation and leadership content in a virtual environment, imparted over the same technological platform that was being used for their communities. Following the debate generated in the forum and the input presented by an external consultant, different strategies were prepared in the direction and handling of these kinds of communities. Between February and March 2007, up to four debates were developed about the type of learning which was required. Training was aimed at making sure that e-moderators were capable of assuming two types of roles: on the one hand they needed to chair debates (both in real and virtual environments), and on the other, they needed to become motivators in their community in order to gain acceptance and to be able to distribute the knowledge generated.

4.2.   Working of the communities

The work methodology followed was based on the work developed by Wenger (1998 and 2002) and adapted by Vazquez (2002) to our context. Putting it succinctly, the following steps were taken:

▪   a. Identification of the ideal collective. This needed to be a group of people who were ideally already motivated, or who could at least become enthusiastic when the idea was explained to them for the first time. In other words, people "who were up for doing the job." The ideal situation was that in addition there would be at least one group in the collective that had already begun to meet and exchange knowledge about the work they were carrying out.

▪   b. Identification of recurring problems which faced the collective, or at least those which were more current. The members of the Community of Practice were asked about which issues they found themselves discussing most often, that is, which work issues they most commonly discussed when they were not working.

▪   c. Identify the person who would be the host of the Community of Practice (e-moderator).

▪   d. Organisation of the first attended meeting of the collective in question: The issues which were discussed were those which the e-moderator had identified (after consulting various members of the collective) as the "hottest" topics.

▪   e. Continuation of the Community of Practice's conversations online, using the e-Catalunya platform and co-ordinated by the community's e-moderator.

Currently, as we indicated at the beginning of this section, the average active participation in each Community of Practice is around 15% of each professional collective. These figures are well above the typical participation reported in similar projects.

Table 1: Communities, professionals, work areas and participants

Community	No of Pros	Work Areas	Participants
Community of ins-titutions	125	Self-training. Currículum of the GES.	15
Community of educa-tors	135	Social Education content in specific treatment programmes. Knowledge pills in Social Educa-tion.	17
Community of jurists	65	Immigration. Jurisprudence and knowledge pills.	15
Community of profess-sionnals in the open environment	45	Work with juvenile reoffenders. The model of intervention. Neonazi violence. Domestic violence. Intervention in gypsy families.	15
Community of media-tors	35	New intervention methodologies in community mediation.	4
Community of social workers	95	Report models. Intervention en alternative penal methods. Social work with migrants.	25
Community of Artistic Monitors	35	Teaching pack (collection of formative tools). Art teaching method.	8
Community of Legal Librarians	35	Marketing of libraries.	6
Community of e-Mode-rators	39	Manual of procedures and con-tent for preparing Knowledge Management projects in Public Administration.	9
Community of Legal Archivists	45	Access protocol to legal docu-mentation	32
Community of linguistic motivators.	48	Preparation of a catalogue of SLAJ services. Prepare a system for resolution of doubts over terminology.	6
Community of Psycho-logists	106	Clinical interviews in Initial Clas-sification. Protocol for Intervention in Alco-hol cases in open environment	21

Community	No of Pros	Work Areas	Participants
E-rehabilitation (court orders)	9	Principal processes in rehabilitation programmes	9
Social Educators in Juvenile Crime.	120	Good practices manual	8
Professionals from the Technical Consultancy Service in Juvenile Crime	45	Good practices manual	
Total	982		190

4.3. Workshops on best practices

The Workshops on best practices have a key role in the final stage of the process, once the new knowledge has been gathered and prepared for use. These workshops are aimed at distributing and sharing with the entire professional collective all available new knowledge. They are programmed at the end of each stage in the process of knowledge management and are usually held once a year. The organisational outline revolves around these elements:

a) Distribution of the acquired knowledge: it can be presented in printed documents, presentations etc.

b) Involvement of an expert in this material. This expert is invited especially for the occasion and is asked to comment on the input made by the community to the process.

c) Gathering of proposals for new issues to be covered in the future and small group debates on the proposals which are chosen.

d) Incentive scheme and general motivation strategies.

The relevance of an incentive scheme to ensure success in the creation and transmission of individual knowledge has been stressed on repeated occasions. In the project we are describing, various combined strategies were used. On the one hand direct financial incentives were used: the moderators were assigned a modest fund and, for each knowledge input provided, its authors received direct compensation. Apart from this compensation, other important incentives were also considered: the guarantee of publication for the best workers in their own journal and certification of the hours spent in the community of practice as training hours.

Table 2: Characteristics of e-moderators

Characteristics of e-moderators
A person who: Represents the community and has good leadership skills. Participates in the institutional project. Is respected and has influence in the community. Has good communication skills. Is familiar with working in technological environments. Is a professional committed to advancing the area of knowledge in his / her professional area.

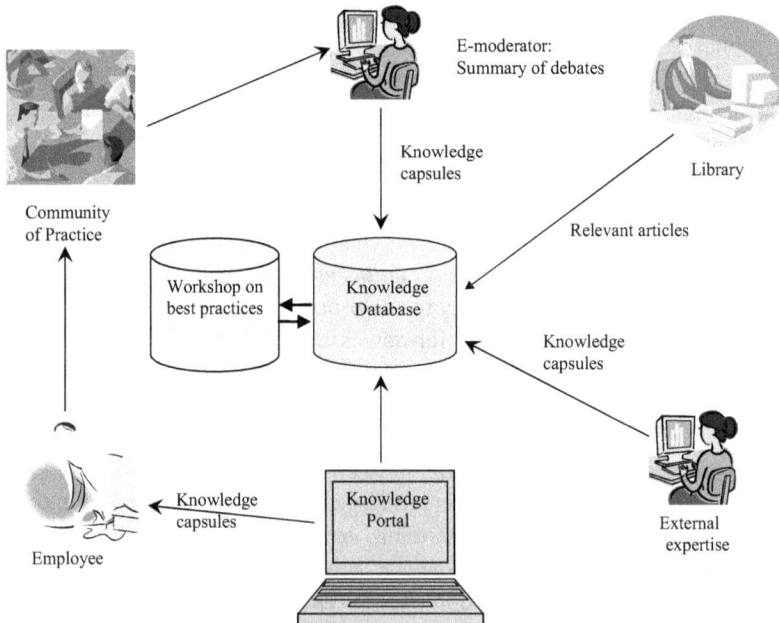

Figure 1: Knowledge management system (adapted from Vasquez Bronfman 2007)

5. E-Catalunya: A platform for collaborative work

The technological platform that allows the development of the communities is a collaborative environment and social network called e-Catalunya (http://ecatalunya.gencat.net). e-Catalunya is a platform for the creation and development of virtual communities promoted by the *Generalitat de Catalunya* so that citizens can communicate, work in teams and manage knowledge using online participation tools. So, it is clearly benefiting the *Department de Justícia* staff as it offers the ideal toolkit for online working collaboration, with Catalan government backing, and virtually no financial costs, and, in addition, ongoing use may provide ideas for improving future versions of this platform.

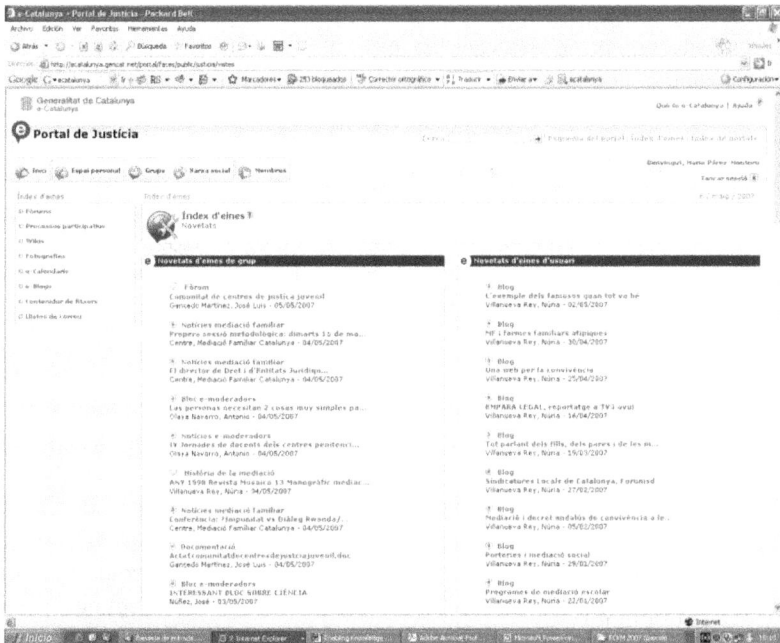

Figure 2: e-Catalunya portal

In contrast to other collaborative work solutions, e-Catalunya has been designed as a divisible and versatile system which means that workgroups can choose which tools to use according to their needs. It is a platform based on open-source software which allows users without specific technical knowledge to create and maintain communities in an uncomplicated manner. The platform – which has already had more than 100,000 visits between January and July 2007 –includes an intelligent system of social and knowledge networks, which are built on the interaction between members of the community and the activities they carry out. This allows users, among other things, to get to know one another, to broaden their network of personal and professional contacts or have access to the content which has been added or viewed by other users with similar interests (Generalitat de Catalunya 2007).

In more technical terms, this online environment offers the possibility of developing a large proportion of the principal strategies involved in Knowledge Management. In this way, for example, it permits on the one hand the development of a series of actions to manage explicit knowledge (using systems of representation and protocol creation). On the other, it also allows a tacit kind of knowledge management (using synchronic and diachronic socialisation strategies). To offer these functions, the platform includes a series of tools which can be activated or not according to the interests of the community: a photo album, a weblog (or blog), a calendar, a shared folder, a forum, a mailing list, a system of management of participative processes and a Wiki function.

- The photo album allows the publication and sharing of images.
- The weblog allows one or more authors to write and publish articles and news, as well as the comments and articles of others. The entries are presented in reverse chronological order (from more recent to less recent) and a monthly archive. It also allows the attachment of documents and the addition of recommended links to websites.
- The calendar is a virtual diary which allows group members to organise and publicise events together (e.g. live meetings, congresses, report deadlines etc). The entries can be accompanied by commentaries and it is possible to create a register of participants for each activity.

- The shared folder is a space for the management and sharing of all community files in various formats (text, multimedia, specific application files etc).
- The forum is a space for open and lively debate, where all group members can share opinions and proposals. Entries are arranged by issue.
- The mailing list collects all the mailing addresses of a group of people in one unique address. This way it is possible to send the same message in one transaction to an unlimited number of people.
- The participative processes are used to gather short, structured information from community members, using custom questionnaires. It can be used to create opinion polls or to reach a consensual decision based on a users' vote.
- The Wiki function allows the collective creation and editing of documents. The communities use the tools to create strategic documents and monitor all the changes which are made, and also to create reference materials for members.

All these tools have two update alerts without having to be connected to the platform: via RSS, which allows group members to see changes as they happen from personal e-mail accounts or from their computers; and via automatic e-mail updates. In the table 3 we can see the grade of adaptation of the tools included in the platform to the potential needs of the community.

In order to complete this description of the tool we can also comment that the platform uses a series of technological resources. Its infrastructure is based around an operating system (Linux), a web server (Apache), an application server (Tomcat), a database (MySQL) and an authentication system (OpenLDAP). As a portal infrastructure it incorporates a platform (exoPlatform) and a Single Sign-On protocol (JOSSO). As collaboration tools, it includes a Wiki (XWiki), forums (phpBB), weblogs (XWiki), mailing lists (Sympa) and a search engine (Lucene). It also includes a text editing toolbar (FCKeditor) as an additional feature.

Table 3: Potential needs of the community and e-Catalunya tools

	Forum	Blog	Wiki	Distribution list	Calendar	Participative	Shared folder	Photo album
Space for meetings, debates and discussion	✓	✓	✓	✓		✓	✓	
Communication channel between group members	✓	✓	✓	✓	✓	✓	✓	✓
Support for internal meetings (programming, material preparation, taking of minutes, etc.)	✓	✓	✓	✓		✓	✓	✓
Consensual decision-making	✓	✓	✓		✓	✓	✓	
Brainstorming	✓	✓	✓	✓				
Group activities report	✓	✓	✓		✓		✓	✓
Report on events	✓	✓	✓	✓			✓	✓
Creative collaboration on documents	✓	✓	✓	✓		✓		
Project planning and management	✓		✓	✓	✓		✓	
Support for symposia, congresses and other events	✓	✓	✓	✓	✓	✓	✓	✓
Evaluation						✓		
Storage and sharing of graphic material (photos, logos, etc.)							✓	✓

(adapted from Generalitat de Catalunya 2007)

6.   Conclusions

From experience on this project we have been able to draw a set of inter-esting conclusions and learned a series of lessons easily applicable to most of KM projects oriented towards public administration.

The first conclusion was an obvious one, namely, that the project had al-lowed us to help reduce some of the knowledge-based problems, particu-larly in relation to creativity and dissemination, which we had identified within the *Department*.

As for the second, it was clear that ensuring the success of a community of practice called for the implementation of two important measures, at least in the initial phase. While it is on the one hand vital to be able to rely on the participation of an external expert that will introduce and consolidate discussion methods for creating and capturing knowledge. It is also impor-tant during this phase to organise face-to-face meetings so that the work does not get restricted to getting done online. That initial physical meeting ensures some bonding, and provides the mechanisms for subsequently working online. New knowledge is not simply produced from the mere potential for working in the virtual world. Only in those communities where prior bonding takes place and interests are shared does the online work really bear fruit.

The third conclusion has to do with training. Based on our experience, we have detected the critical need to train community members in two as-pects: information literacy and communication techniques. Without this training, the community members are not going to be able to make the most of the platform's potential.

Conclusion number four is centred on the need for a policy of incentives. Particularly for public administration, it is necessary to introduce a public and transparent incentives policy to help the project run smoothly.

Lastly, one important fact worthy of attention: success breeds success. We have significantly noted a certain infectiousness – and competitiveness, too – among communities, with the most positive consequences. So the degree of success of each community translates into the one of the most important factors for stimulating work in the remaining communities for creating new and useful knowledge.

References

Collison, C. and Parcel, G. (2001) Learning to Fly, Capstone, Oxford.

Davenport, T. (2005) Thinking for a Living: How to Get Better Performances And Results from Knowledge Workers, Harvard Business School Press, Boston.

Generalitat de Catalunya (2007). "QueEseCatalunya", [online], Generalitat de Catalunya, http://ecatalunya.gencat.net/portal/faces/public/quecat/

Wenger, E., McDermott, R. and Snyder, W. (2002) Cultivating communities of practice, Harvard Busines School Press, Boston.

Vasquez Bronfman, S. (2007). "The launching of a knowledge management project in a public administration", Paper read at XIVth EDINEB Conference, Viena, June.

Wenger, E. and Snyder, W. (2000). "Communities of practice: the organizational frontier", Harvard Business Review, Vol. 78, No 1, pp 139-145).

Critical Success Factors for Communities of Practice in a Global Mining Company

Judi Sandrock and Peter Tobin
Gordon Institute of Business Science, University of Pretoria, South Africa

Editorial commentary

In this work, Sandrock & Tobin examine communities of practice in Anglo American Corporation, a very large mining company with global operations. With more than 300 CoPs in various stages of evolution this is a rich review of CoP successes in a variety of contexts. This is useful work since many studies of CoPs focus on CoP launch and do not examine the later stages of the CoP life cycle. This was a mixed methods study, with qualitative analysis done through literature review and focus groups, while most data were collected through an online survey of some 233 participants in CoPs.

While the critical success factors identified varied between communities, two factors stand out – the need for quality content and user-friendly technology.

Abstract: Communities of practice are often recommended as a means of sharing knowledge in organisations. For organisations which intend to elicit the maximum benefit from launching and sustaining communities of practice, it is important to understand the critical success factors required to do so. Not all communities of practice are identical or equally successful, and a large collection of potential success factors have been proposed in the literature. Authors refer to different types of communities of practice as well as stages of development for these communities. On reviewing the literature it was also found that the critical success factors for communities of practice for one organisation may not necessarily be the same for all organisations. Therefore the research was conducted in one organisation to maximise the possibility of reaching a conclusive outcome. The company selected was the Anglo American Corporation, a global resources group with over three hundred communities of practice in various stages of development. The intention of the research was to create an understanding of the critical success factors required for communities of practice in the Anglo American Corporation, in order that they could be supported to create the value they have the potential to produce. Literature research was conducted to determine the list of potential success factors for communities of practice. The literature review was followed by a quantitative study which was conducted by gathering data using a web-based survey tool. This data was analysed and the results interpreted to determine the critical success factors for the communities of practice. The results were conclusive in that clear critical success factors were found for each type of community of practice as well as the different stages in the life cycle of the communities. The web based survey method was effective, and may used by others in their investigations to determine critical success factors for communities of practice in their organisations. The conclusion of the research project included recommendations for supporting these critical success factors, as well as further topics for research in the future.

Keywords: Knowledge management, communities of practice, critical success factors

1. Introduction to the research problem

For organisations which intend to elicit the maximum benefit from launching and sustaining communities of practice, it is important to understand the critical success factors required to do so.

The factors contributing to the success of the communities of practice vary, and need to be identified. The reason for choosing the critical success factors for these communities was the speed with which a business value can be realised due to the high success rate and relatively low impact cost of implementing the communities (Snyman and Van den Berg, 2003). Not all communities of practice are identical or equally successful, and critical success factors have been researched by the American Productivity and Quality Centre (APQC, 2001) and a large collection of potential success factors has been proposed in the literature, as listed in section 2.4.

Wenger, McDermott and Snyder (2002) refer to different types of community of practice as well as stages of development for these communities which are frequently referred to in subsequent literature (Rumizen 2002, Saint-Onge and Wallace 2003).

Research on virtual communities of practice undertaken by Dube, Bourhis, and Jacob (2005) has relevance as knowledge workers are becoming reliant on virtual communication tools now that their communities have global domains. Dube *et al.* (2005) note that the critical success factors for communities of practice may have changed with the increasing prominence of virtual communication and collaboration tools.

1.1.   Context of the research

On reviewing the literature it was found that the critical success factors for communities of practice for one organisation may not necessarily be the same for other organisations (APQC 2001). Therefore this research was conducted in one organisation to maximise the possibility of reaching a conclusive outcome. The company selected was the Anglo American Corporation, a global resources group with over three hundred communities of practice in various stages of development. The research was conducted within the Anglo American Corporation to determine the critical success factors for communities of practice, depending on their type and community life cycle stage.

1.2.   The research problem

The research problem was broken down into the following questions:

- What are the critical success factors for communities of practice in the Anglo American Corporation?

- Do the critical success factors vary with the type of community of practice?

- Do the critical success factors vary with the stage in the life cycle of the community of practice?

A pictorial representation of the study is shown in the figures below:

Figure 1 shows that the importance of the potential success factors will be determined in order to identify which ones are critical success factors.

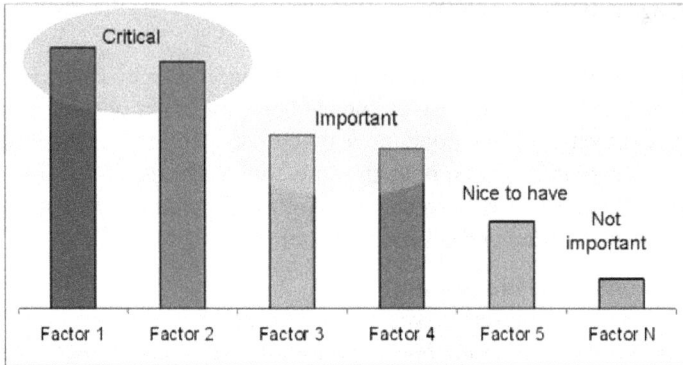

Figure 1: The identification of critical success factors.

Figure 2 represents different types of community of practice with the relevant critical success factors.

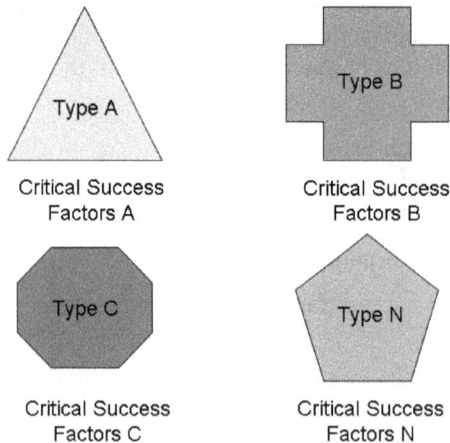

Figure 2: Critical success factors for various types of community of practice:

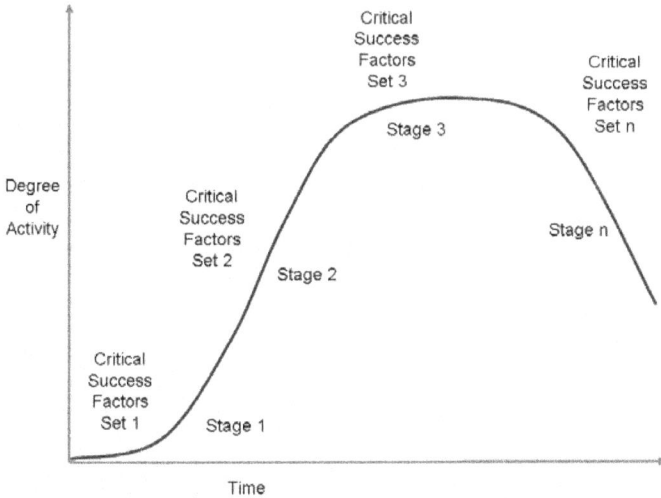

Figure 3: A representation of the stages in the life cycle and the respective critical success factors based on the work by Wenger *et al.* (2002).

Dube *et al.* (2005) conclude that the focus of their research is limited to the community of practice launching phase, and suggest that "further research should investigate critical success factors for different stages of development in the community of practice life cycle". Therefore this research project investigated the critical success factors for the different types of community of practice, at the various stages in the life cycle. The intention of the research was to create an understanding of the critical success factors required for communities of practice in the Anglo American Corporation, in order that they can be supported to create the value they have the potential to produce.

2. Communities of practice

The term 'communities of practice' is defined by Lave and Wenger (1991) as "groups of people who share a concern, a set of problems, or a passion about a topic, and who deepen their knowledge and expertise in the area by interacting on an ongoing basis". It is from the work of these authors that the term community of practice became a common term in the field of knowledge management. APQC (2001:6) states that "people have always created communities, inside and outside of organisations". What is new is the emerging prominence and formality of communities of practice as boundary-spanning units in organisations, responsible for finding and sharing best practices, stewarding knowledge, and helping members work better. This new role for communities is emerging because they nurture and harness the raw material of this millennium - knowledge.

Consistently, three dimensions of communities of practice are referred to (Rumizen 2002, Saint-Onge and Wallace 2003, Wenger *et al.*2002). Wenger *et al.*2002 have these dimensions as:

- The domain – the domain of knowledge for the community, what the members care about, their area of interest.
- The members – thought-leaders, practitioners, their relationships and the trust that exists between them.
- The practice – what the community does. Sharing of best practices, creating tools, mapping processes and other knowledge work.

Significant benefits have been derived by organisations from communities of practice.

2.1. Types of community of practice

As communities of practice are studied, it is being recognised that they are of different types. McDermott (2000) indicates four types of community:

- Communities which are linked to a strategic objective
- Communities which focus on tactical processes, process optimisation and sharing of best practice
- Project-based communities
- Communities which nurture and grow a particular body of knowledge

For the purposes of the research, the types of communities proposed by McDermott (2000) were used. Different types of communities have different life spans, and they display different characteristics depending on what stage of their life cycle we find them at.

2.2. Community life cycle

Communities of practice experience different stages in their life cycles (Wenger *et al.* 2002). It is important to identify which stage in the life cycle the community is at, to understand the characteristics being displayed. Wenger *et al.* (2002) identify four life cycle stages of communities of practice:

- Launched – the community has been identified and launched, with members, roles, domain and goals identified.
- Developing – membership is growing, the facilitator has been trained, and activity is on the increase.
- Mature – there are steady contributions, the goals are being achieved.
- Dissolved – the community has achieved its goals, the activity has ceased and all explicit knowledge has been captured and perhaps archived for future reference.

The critical success factors for communities of practice were explored in order to understand what the organisation must have in place to ensure the survival and growth of these communities.

2.3.   Critical success factors

As communities of practice can add value to organisations, the critical success factors for their success need to be identified. However, the term "critical success factors" needs to be understood first. The term "critical success factor" is a business term for an element which is necessary for an organisation or project to achieve its mission. A company may use the critical success factor method as a means for identifying the important elements of its success. Rockart (1979) was one of the first to use the term "critical success factor" and he defined it as "the limited number of areas in which results, if they are satisfactory, will ensure successful competitive performance for the organisation".

2.4.   Critical success factors for communities of practice

The most referenced work on the critical success factors for communities of practice is that of McDermott (2000). Through his studies and involvement with communities of practice McDermott has concluded that the critical success factors fall into four main categories, namely, management, community, technical, and personal challenges. The list of potential success factors gathered from the literature was clustered to produce fourteen factors for the purposes of the research and they are:

Clear goals	Core group
Facilitator	Leader
Line management support	Participation
Personal value	Promotion of the communi-ty
Quality content	Quality members
Sponsor	Strategic alignment
Trust	User-friendly technology

3. Research methods

The research methodology used was a combination of qualitative and quantitative research methods.

3.1. Qualitative research

The qualitative research was conducted in the literature review, which was very informative as to the approach to be taken. The topics covered were knowledge management, including an understanding of the term "knowledge", tacit and explicit knowledge and applying knowledge. It then went on to describe communities of practice, with definitions, the different types, stages of the life cycle, and the benefits to be realised through their implementation. While researching the critical success factors for communities of practice in the literature it became apparent that the critical success factors for these communities could vary from organisation to organisation, as well as by type and life cycle stage of community. Further qualitative research was conducted through the use of a focus group, to assist with the development of the questionnaire for the data collection process.

3.2. Quantitative research

The data collection and analysis processes were quantitative as they involved the use of a survey. A survey method of data collection is regarded as more efficient and economical than observations (Emory and Cooper, 1991). The survey was conducted using a questionnaire enabled by an online survey tool. The questions were close-ended, some giving only the choice of four options, and others using a Lickert Scale. An open text area was included to collect information which the contributors felt was important. The researcher had access to the members of the Anglo American communities of practice, and as a result convenience sampling was applied. The target population was mailed an introduction to the research and asked for their permission to be included in the survey to follow. Two hundred and thirty-three people responded positively, and the population was therefore deemed large enough to proceed.

3.3.   Questionnaire design

The questionnaire was designed with the intention of collecting the data required to answer the research propositions. Descriptions of each of the types of community, stages in the life cycle, as well as the potential success factors, were included in the questionnaire to ensure clarity and understanding.

The questionnaire design included the following:
* Type of community of practice (choose one of four)
* Community of practice stage in life cycle (choose one of four)
* Importance of success factor (four-point Lickert Scale)
* Free text areas should contributors wish to add to the research as their experience is valuable

The questionnaire was drafted and tested during a focus group session with those involved in knowledge management and communities of practice at Anglo American. It was discussed with the Research Supervisor and subsequently modified to include important insights and to make it more understandable to the research population. Thereafter, it was tested with the Anglo American executives who have knowledge management in their performance contracts for the Exploration, Coal, Gold and Platinum divisions respectively. The executive from the Anglo American Base Metals division was included at a later stage as he was on vacation at the time of the discussions.

3.4.   Data collection method

Anglo American has a standard on-line survey tool which is used for data collection within the group. The research survey was built using this on-line tool and was based on the questionnaire. The design allowed for buttons from which the respondent could select an option, and only one option. Two free text areas were included, one for the name of the community of practice, if people wanted to add that, and a large area for people to add comments. On testing the time taken to complete the survey, it was found that the period would be approximately four minutes without the text areas being used for individual comments. The survey was distributed to the sample population via an e-mail, containing a link to the survey. The survey feedback data was automatically collected in the survey tool, and the data downloaded to a spreadsheet for analysis. The data in the spreadsheet was checked for completeness and integrity.

3.5. Data characteristics by type and life cycle stage
The table below shows the numbers of responses by type and life cycle stage of community:

Table 1: Data collected by type and life cycle stage of community of practice

	Launched	Developing	Mature	Dissolved
Strategic	4	13	2	0
Tactical Process	26	67	9	2
Project	5	9	5	1
Knowledge Nurture	4	9	2	0

Table 1 show that the tactical process communities on the developing stage were the most dominant, followed by the tactical process communities in the launched phase.

4.   Results

The findings have been summarised in the table below with the critical success factors identified with "X".

Table 2: Critical success factors by type and life cycle stage of community of practice

	Quality Content	User-friendly technology	Support From Line Management	Facilitator	Clear goals	Sponsor	Leader
Entire group	X	X					

Type of Community

	Quality Content	User-friendly technology	Support From Line Management	Facilitator	Clear goals	Sponsor	Leader
Strategic	X	X	X	X	X	X	X
Tactical Process		X					
Project	X	X					
Knowledge Nurture	X	X					X

Life Cycle Stage of Community

	Quality Content	User-friendly technology	Support From Line Management	Facilitator	Clear goals	Sponsor	Leader
Launched	X	X					X
Developing	X	X					
Mature	X						
Dissolved	Inconclusive						

4.1. Discussion on results for overall data set

From Table 2 it can be seen that user-friendly technology and quality content were the two factors considered critical by the whole response population. The standard deviations for these two factors were acceptable which means that there was no significant difference of views in this regard. These two factors were rated highly irrespective of the type of community or the stage of the life cycle the community found itself at. Line management support, the presence of a facilitator, participation by community members and trust appeared next on the order of importance. The least desirable of the potential success factors were the presence of clear goals, a leader and a sponsor. It was also found that for these three the standard deviations were fairly high which means that there was a level of disagreement in the research population regarding the importance of these three factors. This can be explained later in this paper as the requirement for clear goals, a leader and a sponsor vary depending on the type and maturity of the community.

4.2.   Critical success factors for communities of practice vary with the type of community

The results of the survey had to be analysed in conjunction with the information available regarding the distribution of the types of communities within the data set.

4.2.1.   Strategic communities

The strategic type of community considered a large number of factors to be "critical success factors" relative to the whole research population. Considered "critical" were quality content, user-friendly technology, line management support, the presence of a facilitator, clear goals, a sponsor, a leader and strategic alignment.

4.2.2.   Tactical process communities

The tactical process type communities were in the majority for the responses received in the research.

The analysis of the results showed that only one factor, user-friendly technology, was regarded as "critical". Quality content, which rates as "critical" for all the other types of community, is seen by this type only as "important". A deeper understanding was gained by looking closer at the life cycle stages present in this set of communities. Sixty-four per cent of the tactical process communities were in the developing stage, and it is the data from this sub-set which rated quality content as "important" dominantly, thereby lowering its overall rating in the entire tactical process type set.

Line management support comes a close third to the above-mentioned two factors. The literature indicates that in cases of large multinational organisations, line management support is critical to allow for a mandate or permission to seek advice from others rather than having to solve problems internal to the department (APQC 2001).

The factors which rated the lowest relative to the whole list were clear goals, leader and sponsor. An observation is that this could be an indicator of the culture of the organisation and the acceptance within that culture for knowledge sharing, especially when it comes to sharing tactical processes.

4.2.3. Project communities

The two factors which were found to be critical were quality content and user-friendly technology.

The project communities rated the presence of a leader and sponsor, and promotion of the community, as the least important factors. Wenger *et al.* (2002) note that project type communities are more formal than the other types of communities of practice, as roles are well defined. Therefore, the rating of these factors could be low as the project manager and project sponsor roles are well defined prior to the launching of the community of practice. In addition, promotion of the community could be a low priority as projects have usually been justified in the approval process and therefore are felt not to need further promotion in order to succeed.

4.2.4. Knowledge nurture communities

In the research, the fewest (9 per cent) of the responses came from this type of community.
Quality content, user-friendly technology and the presence of a leader were seen as the critical factors. McDermott (2000) notes that communities set up to nurture and grow knowledge over many years require strong and dedicated leadership.

4.3. Critical success factors for communities of practice vary with the stage in the life cycle of the community

4.3.1. Communities in the launched phase

User-friendly technology, quality content and the presence of a leader were seen as critical success factors. Wenger *et al.* (2002) and Dube *et al.* (2005) note that the launch phase of the community needs to be led by a leader determined to make a success of the community of practice. It is during this phase that failure is most likely (Wenger *et al.* 2002).

In the literature (McDermott 2000, Rumizen 2002, Wenger *et al.* 2002, Saint-Onge and Wallace 2003) the role of a facilitator appears to be critical to the success of a community in the launch phase. It does appear to be the case for the community members surveyed in this research project: the presence of a facilitator appeared third last on the list of priorities.

4.3.2. Developing communities

User-friendly technology and quality content were seen as the only two factors critical to a developing community. This phase in the life cycle was the most dominant in the sample (62 per cent) and therefore it is not sur-prising that the two critical success factors identified were the same two for the whole data set .
The presence of a facilitator came a close third although the overall view was that it was important not critical.

4.3.3. Mature communities

The number of responses for this phase in the life cycle was 11 per cent which was not large enough to satisfy the law of large numbers (Saunders, Lewis and Thornhill, 2003). However, the standard deviation was accept-able which indicates that a fair amount of agreement existed within the respondents in this subset. For the mature communities, only quality con-tent was regarded a critical success factor. Little more could be deduced from the results as no other factors were voted as being sufficiently impor-tant to be regarded as critical.

4.3.4. Dissolved communities

During the survey, only three people responded that their communities had been dissolved. The results for this phase could not be included in the study as they did not have the reliability required by the theory of large numbers, and too many of the ratings of the factors were inconclusive.

5. Recommendations

The outcome of the research was to make recommendations to Anglo American for the effective support of Communities of Practice.

5.1. Quality content

The following processes and roles were found to be necessary to ensure high quality content:
- Content owners for the community areas
- Rating of content by those in the communities
- Content updating or archiving included in the role of the facilitator

As quality content was found to be a high priority, the above roles were highly recommended to support communities of practice.

5.2. User-friendly technology

In order to support user-friendliness of the technology in the Anglo American Corporation on an ongoing basis, the following components were recommended as considerations:
- Consistent and acceptable accessibility to the global network
- Help /Service desk capability to support collaborative tools and users
- Regular training on the tools as well as refresher courses on an ongoing basis
- Availability of the collaborative tools and training materials in language of the user

Within the organisation collaborative tools are available, and even though user-friendliness has improved with time, this critical success factor should always be given a high priority.

5.3.　Leader

The presence of a leader was seen as critical by the strategic and knowledge nurture communities, as well as those communities in the launched phase of the life cycle. It is recommended that the role of the leader includes:

- Communicating a clear and compelling vision for the community of practice
- Custodianship for the goals of the community
- Communicating with the sponsor and/or senior executives on the goals, achievements and requirements of the community

A further recommendation was that workshops be conducted to coach Community of Practice leaders on their roles in the Anglo American Corporation.

5.4.　Facilitator

The training materials and training workshops for this role had been developed and implemented in Anglo American Corporation at the time of writing this report. It was recommended that a network of facilitators be encouraged in order for them to share experiences and support one another.

5.5.　Line management support

Line management support can be elicited through demonstrating the value of communities of practice to all areas of the Anglo American Corporation. Knowledge sharing needs to be seen as adding to the goals of the business unit in order for line management to support the process. This factor is linked to the presence of strategic alignment, and this was seen as critical for the strategic communities. It is recommended that the capturing of success stories and value mapping be included in the support infrastructure for communities of practice, to strengthen the view that knowledge sharing is strategically aligned and that value is added to the organisation.

In conclusion, critical success factors were identified for communities of practice in the Anglo American Corporation, as well as the determination that they varies according to the type and stage in the life cycle of the community.

6. Suggestions for further research

Recommendations for further research in the area of knowledge management and communities of practice are suggested:

- The impact of the availability of collaborative tools in the user's first language on the extent of collaboration
- The organisational cultural characteristics which encourage and discourage knowledge sharing
- The development of measurement methods to determine the value of communities of practice

Acknowledgements

Special thanks go to the members of communities of practice at the Anglo American Corporation whose contributions made this research possible, and to the management of Anglo American Corporation for their support for the research.

References

American Productivity and Quality Centre (APQC). (2001). Building and Sustaining Communities of Practice: Continuing Success in Knowledge Management. APQC: Texas.

Dube, L. Bourhis, A. and Jacob, R. (2005). The impact of structuring characteristics on the launching of virtual communities of practice. Journal of Organizational Change Management 18(2): 145-66.

Emory, C.W. and Cooper, D.R. (1991). Business Research Methods, (4 edn). Homewood, Irwin

Lave, J. and Wenger, E. (1991). Situated Learning: Legitimate Peripheral Participation. Cambridge University Press: Cambridge

McDermott, R. (2000). Knowing in Community: 10 Critical Success Factors in Building Communities of Practice. IHRIM Journal, March 2000, Texas.

Rockart, J. (1979). Chief executives define their own data needs. Harvard Business Review. 1979 (2), pages 81-93. HBR:Boston.

Rumizen, M. C. (2002). Complete Idiot's Guide to Knowledge Management. Alpha: Indianapolis.

Saint-Onge, H. and Wallace, D. (2003). Leveraging Communities of Practice for Strategic Advantage. Butterworth Heinemann: Burlington, MA.

Saunders, M., Lewis, L. and Thornhill, A. (2003). Research Methods for Business Students. Prentice Hall: London.

Snyman, M.M.M. and Van den Berg, H. (2003). Managing tacit knowledge in the corporate environment: Communities of practice, South African Journal of Information Management, 5(4) (electronic journal). South Africa.

Tobin, P.K.J. (2006), The use of stories and storytelling as knowledge sharing practices: a case study in the South African mining industry, available at:http://upetd.up.ac.za/thesis/available/etd-07302006-065725/

Wenger, E. (1998). Communities of Practice. Harvard Business Review Jan-Feb, pp 139-145. HBR: Boston.

Wenger, E., McDermott, R. and Snyder, W. (2002). Cultivating Communities of Practice. Harvard Business School Press: Boston

Practice Based Research and Action Learning in a Learning Organization - The case: Patient Centred Treatment in a general hospital.

Henk Smeijsters, Hans Koolmees, Sylvia Schoenmakers
Zuyd University of Applied Sciences, Heerlen, The Netherlands

Editorial commentary

Smeijsters, Koolmees and Schoenmakers describe the evolution of a learning organization in a Dutch hospital, using practice-based research and action learning. The paper examines a project to implement Patent Centred Treatment (PCT) as part of a program commissioned by the Dutch government to develop the "Hospital of the 21st Century". After presenting a view of the learning organization, they show how practice-based research and action research can contribute to the successful implementation of a new organisation.

They provide a good description of the process followed during a 2-year period and identify examples of action learning that are being widely used across the hospital.

Abstract: The Dutch government commissioned the Maasland Hospital of the Orbis Medical and Treatment Group to develop the 'Hospital of the 21st Century'. In 2006, the board of Orbis and the board of Zuyd University of Applied Sciences signed an agreement to join forces for this development. Part of this collaboration is the project Patient Centred Treatment (PCT).

The objectives of the project are to develop a mental model for PCT with core categories and subcategories, values and behavioural guidelines, and to develop learning activities that change the actual behaviour and knowledge flows of medical professionals at their workplace.

The practice based research design is based on the naturalistic/constructivistic research methodology, with elements of grounded theory. The key characteristic of this design research is to explore and evaluate the implicit knowledge in the organization by means of iterative dialogues among professionals and between professionals and researchers. Within this process of co-creation among up to 200 participants, consensus based 'best practices' are developed. This practice based research approach organically runs into action learning activities that serve to anchor PCT at the workplace.

As a result, consensus based core categories and subcategories of PTC (patient, guest, person; cognition, emotion, self-esteem) have been developed, consensus based values and behavioural guidelines derived form the core categories and subcategories have been described, and training activities and action learning activities for PCT have been introduced at the workplace.
In terms of learning as a result of the project, the individual professionals, the teams of professionals and the organization is developing into a learning organization.

Keywords: patient centred treatment, client centred care, practice based research, action learning, learning organization

1. Introduction

This article describes how the concept of the 'learning organization' has been connected to 'practice based research' and 'action learning' by the authors. Practice based research and action learning act as tools that enable the development of the learning organization. This results in a process in which professionals reflect on their daily experiences, compare their daily experiences with each other and in the role of co-researchers develop consensus based best practices. The research methodology is based on techniques of naturalistic/constructivist inquiry and grounded theory.

The whole process of introducing practice based research and action learning actually has been a research project from 2006 till 2008 by several Research Centers of Zuyd University of Applied Sciences in Heerlen, The Netherlands. Members of the Research Center on Knowledge Management have taken the lead in developing patient centred treatment in a Dutch general hospital. This hospital will be used as a case to illustrate how the process of developing into a learning organization by means of practice based research and action learning has taken place.

The article first focuses on characteristics of the learning organization and the connection with practice based research and action learning. The case of the hospital will illustrate the outcome of this project, and how learning process and product are intertwined.

2. The workplace central in the learning organization

A learning organization is an organization that is dedicated to promoting continuous learning in the workplace, for people as individuals and as teams, and for the organization as a whole. Professionals utilize a variety of patterns of thought and action in their day-to-day activities that are 'embedded' in their professional performance over the course of time. These patterns of thought and action have become an intrinsic part of them. This also is known as 'implicit knowledge'. This implicit knowledge enables them to perform their work in a 'natural' way. An example of this is that experienced professionals know how to make eye contact and body contact with the patient in a way that the patient feels supported and understood. They know how to tell bad news verbally and nonverbally.

However, when professionals stop thinking about this implicit knowledge altogether, when they stop reflecting, we have a problem. It is important that they continuously ask themselves whether these embedded patterns of thought and actions are still appropriate. That is precisely what happens in a learning organization. This means that it is part of the work to discuss how to respond to patients.

Here, staff members work together to create a culture, in which they continuously argue about how they do their work. Together, they evaluate their work, examine their strengths and their weaknesses, devise improvements and solutions, apply these solutions and verify whether the desired result has been achieved. The organization is thus continuously learning, and continuously in movement. This is an important process for all organizations, in particular for organizations that are dedicated to professional innovation.

In a learning organization, learning primarily serves the needs of the professional's own workplace. After all, professionals have a thorough understanding of their own department and the work to be undertaken. They and their colleagues have a unique insight into those issues that provide relevant solutions to problems. In addition, they are receptive to solutions provided from outside the department or the organization. Together with their colleagues, they formulate their learning needs on the basis of their practical experiences, plan their learning activities and, correspondingly, identify changes that they wish to implement in the workplace. This involves collating, developing and implementing insights that determine the ultimate quality of their work. Staff members begin to behave like 'knowledge workers', who know and actively *want* to improve their day-to-day activities. This benefits the customer, the professional, the department in which the professional operates and the organization as a whole.

2.1.   Characteristics of the learning organization

The list of journals and articles dedicated to the concept of the learning organization is inexhaustive (e.g.: Schön, 1983/1988; Senge, 1990; Argyris, 1991; Krogh et al, 2000; Tissen et al, 2000; Lekanne Deprez & Tissen, 2002; Wierdsma & Swieringa, 2002). The list is too comprehensive to discuss in detail, and goes beyond the scope of our paper. Qualitative research by one of the authors about learning processes of educators during curriculum development (Smeijsters, 2004) showed that professionals themselves believe that the following are characteristic of a developing learning organization:

- An organization flourishes if the personal interests and the interests of the organization are in perfect harmony, if the employees sense that their work is useful and meaningful. The organization flourishes when all members of staff dedicate their hearts and

souls to embracing the mission, if they think in terms of 'our business'.

- The organizational culture is largely determined by the mentality
  with which people interact with one another and do their work. In
  a learning organization, a climate of mutual trust pervades. Professionals honour agreements, think and act consistently, show
  responsibility for their work and for each other, and tend to think
  in terms of solutions rather than problems. They have respect for
  each other's opinions, yet are not afraid to voice their own differ-
  ing insights.
- As many people as possible are engaged in change processes.
  These representatives, in consultation with their managers, are
  responsible for knowledge creation. The end product of these individual and collective learning processes is innovation.
- The learning organization knows which employees are capable of
  tapping into innovations and act as advocates to win over colleagues. They are openly and officially assigned tasks, responsibility, decision-making powers and resources. This does not automatically imply that all initiatives come from these people.
- In a learning organization, a framework is in place to direct the
  patterns of thought and action of each member of staff. This
  framework allows sufficient scope for enthusiastic employees to
  flesh out their thoughts and actions using their own creative
  processes.
- People are given the time to absorb innovation, to think about it
  and discuss it with others. In a learning organization, the management board determines the course of action, yet allows sufficient time to clarify and discuss the course. Conversely, talking
  leads to decisions being taken, bottlenecks being eradicated and
  action being taken.
- The learning organization allows room for emotions, without losing sight of the business process. If far-reaching changes evoke
  strong emotions, employees in a learning organization work together to develop 'coping mechanisms' to handle these emotions.

2.2. Creative professionality and creative leadership

A learning organization does not simply appear out of thin air. It is important that employees and managers alike have the right mentality and professional aptitude to facilitate the establishment of a learning organization. In those areas where protocols offer no viable solutions, professionals need to sense immediately what is desirable and feasible, and respond accordingly. In situations such as these, the professional sees himself as the owner of a problem who instantly identifies, develops and applies appropriate behaviour. The flexible culture of the learning organization helps the professional boost his creative powers and ensures that he is receptive to the feedback of customers and colleagues.

The learning organization also embraces the concept of creative leadership. The creative leader is a 'spirited leader' who gives his employees 'mental space', enabling a free exchange of ideas and experiences. Employees feel free to explore new avenues. The leader is innovative, dares to abandon the familiar and is able to inspire, enthuse and motivate others to embrace change and problem ownership. An open dialogue exists between management and staff members. The leader respects the fact that employees are capable of independent thought, and sees them as 'autonomous developers'. Employees are given the freedom, within reason, to experiment with new ideas. Decisions are reached on the basis of feedback and logical reasoning. Innovation is adapted to the possibilities that exist within the organization.

3. Practice based research and action learning

An organization can develop into a learning organization by using practice based research and action learning in which the professional is the core actor of the process.

3.1. Practice based research

In constructivistic research in practice the professionals of the participating institutions do not act as 'respondents' but as co-researchers (Lincoln & Guba, 1985; Kemmis & McTaggart, 2000; Schwandt, 2000). Being a co-researcher means that they are not only 'data suppliers', but also play a pro-active role during all project phases (data collection, data analysis, defining best practices, applying and evaluating). The constructivistic research can be mixed with grounded theory (Strauss & Corbin, 1998; Charmaz, 2000). Professionals thus learn how to implement and execute a development process independently. This research method is aimed at the following core characteristics:

- Enticing professionals to reflect and create clarity for themselves on the practices they adopt with whom, when, how and why.
- Enabling professionals to learn from and with each other, to compare experiential knowledge, to evaluate and to integrate into best practices.
- Enabling professionals to integrate new knowledge in their process of reflection and development.
- Developing practical knowledge. The research delivers something tangible that can be put into practice with comparatively little effort. From the point of view of learning this is called 'workplace learning'.
- Developing a 'community of practice' in which people of the same experiential background, discuss, systemize, innovate, apply and evaluate interventions.
- The research activities stimulate the organization to develop into a 'learning organization', and that the profession can turn into a 'learning profession'.
- Action learning

Action learning ranks as one of the most suitable instruments to shape workplace learning (Marquardt, 1999; Brockbank, 2003; Garvin, 2003). Action learning straddles the line between formal learning and experiential learning.

Formal learning (for example attending a traditional, generic training course) can be regarded as a highly formalized form of learning. In other words, goals are pre-defined, theory and the overall learning process have been determined. The disadvantage of formal learning is that it is typically removed from everyday professional practice. The acquired theoretical knowledge usually wanes over time.

Experiential learning can be defined as the learning processes that occur when the professional performs his work; 'learning by doing'. The disadvantage of experiential learning is that learning solely takes place within the confines of the organization. Experiences of e.g. fellow professionals in other organizations or knowledge gleaned from literature are not highlighted.

Action learning combines the best of both concepts and neutralizes the abovementioned disadvantages.

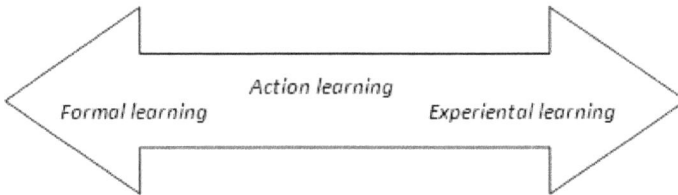

Figure 1: Learning forms

Action learning was developed in the 1940s and applied and further developed in a variety of situations. The concept has proven its worth in areas such as product development and improvement, certain forms of service provision, customer base growth, increased safety, shorter delivery times, promotional activities. It is also applied in vocational secondary education to help students develop their professional skills and devise solutions to professional problems.

Because action learning is applied in so many different situations, there are many interpretations of the term. The below description is extremely workable (Marquardt, 1999):

Action learning is a process for bringing together a group of people with varied levels of skills and experience in order to analyze an actual work problem and to develop an action plan. The ad hoc group continues to meet as actions are implemented, learning from the implementation and making mid-course corrections. Action learning is a form of learning by doing.

Action learning has a number of distinct features:
- Experience is amassed, with explicit focus on learning
- Business-relevant issues are addressed
- Participants are given a problem-solving role
- Creative solutions are sought to complex problems
- Relevant knowledge is acquired and exchanged
- Implementation is conducted in teams with co-learning group support
- Tangible results

Through action learning, the professional signals problems with others, thinks about improvement actions, test drives them and, if appropriate, implements them. He thus contributes towards shaping the policy within the department. Together, professionals systematically address the problems identified and, over time, departments begin functioning better by jointly suggesting and test-driving the solutions.

Action learning not only contributes towards solving problems in the workplace, but also facilitates organizational change: 'the organization as a learning system.'

3.1.1. The learning cycle

Within action learning, putting the learning cycle in motion is an important innovation and improvement tool. A learning cycle comprises different stages of learning to achieve a specific goal (Kolb, 1984; Wierdsma & Swieringa, 2002). Experience forms the basis for observation and reflection, and is the driving force behind learning. Thought and action play an important role during the learning process.

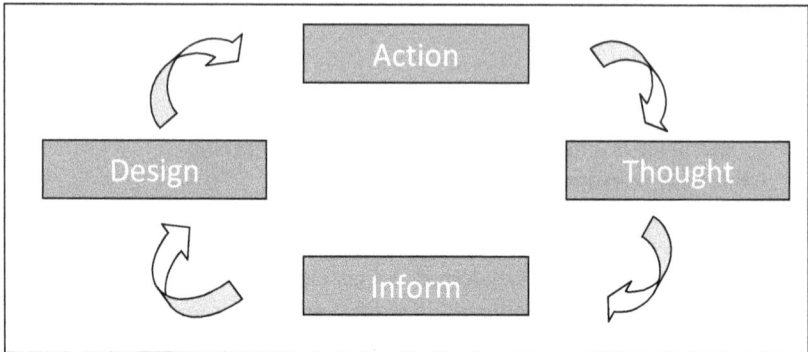

Figure 2: Learning Cycle

- *Action*
  Through action, people amass new experiences. These experiences can be similar to or different from their usual experiences, and are often geared towards a specific situation.
- *Thought*
  Reflecting whether certain actions were adequate in a given situation, making the action discussable.
- *Inform*
  Finding alternative solutions to approaching a problem or to implementing actions, helps to make arguments explicit and make choices.
- *Design*
  When the need arises, people want to choose the best solution. The situation is assessed from a multitude of angles and arguments are carefully taken into consideration before a solution is devised and accepted.

Learning is only possible if all four stages of the learning cycle have been touched upon. Acting without thinking means that mistakes are not identified. Similarly, collating information without putting it into practice will not result in behavioural change. All learning activities are characterized by constant interaction between action and thought, between thought and action.

For instance a general problem in Dutch health care is that patients get information about the treatment from several professionals in separate occasions. It is simple to check simple messages, but for the patient it is difficult to integrate these messages in the complex information about his health and his fears, the proposed care and the way to cure. Describing already existing solutions, designing new solutions, acting these solutions and reflecting on the outcome finally leads to a 'best practice' how to handle this problem. A best practice means that it is the most effective way how to handle the problem. In this example what turned out to be a best practice is to give each patient a personal guide who is able to integrate the information for the patient.

Another best practice is to improve the relation with the patient by showing human interest and some professional empathy. This can be reinforced by inviting the patient to tell about the situation at home, about the social context in which the patient lives and talking with appreciation about the care that is given by people in this context.

Action learning is possible if the organization or department jointly prepares, executes and evaluates the learning activities. The collaboration need not necessarily take place in the traditional settings of a group meeting or a team, but could equally take the form of involvement of e.g. employees and patients or an online forum. The learning process is constantly steered in the right direction by the parties concerned.

4. The case: Developing and implementing Patient Centred Treatment in a general hospital

4.1. Background

The Maasland Hospital of the Orbis Medical and Treatment Group in Sittard The Netherlands has been appointed by the Dutch government to develop the 21st century hospital. A complete new building arises that will be finished in 2008. In 2006 the board of the Orbis Group made an agreement with the board of Zuyd University of Applied Sciences to develop the so called *New Way of Working*, which includes introducing the nursing part of the Electronic Health Record System (Verwey, 2008), Patient Centred Treatment (Smeijsters et al, 2006, 2007) and Quality Indicators (Schoot,

2007). The project is embedded in the Expertise Centre Quality of Life of Zuyd University for Applied Sciences and is a joint action of several research institutes within the centre. In this article the focus is on the development and implementation of patient centred treatment by the Research Centre on Knowledge Management.

4.2. Developing a mind map, values and guidelines for patient centred treatment

First the hospital developed a mission statement on treatment in which the dialogue between people is basic. In this article the concept of Patient Centred Treatment is used, which includes cure and care. The patient is central to all activities of the physicians and nurses. The professional discusses with the patient how treatment can fulfill their wishes and needs. This mission statement has been the starting point of the practice based research by the present authors in the years 2006-2008. In the year 2006 hundred professionals of the hospital working in the primary process of treatment have been involved in the development of a consensus based mind map for patient centred treatment. The constructivistic action based research method treated the professionals as co-researchers who make their implicit knowledge explicit. By means of focus groups, coding procedures based on grounded theory and constructivistic techniques like member checking, the core categories and subcategories of patient centred treatment have been developed. These core categories turned out to be: 'patient', 'guest', 'person', which means that the patient will be treated as a guest and a human being. Within these core concepts the professionals differentiated between subcategories such as cognition, emotion and self-esteem. Patients in hospitals want to be informed about what is going on. They experience all sorts of emotions and their self-esteem is harmed by their incapability's and dependencies.

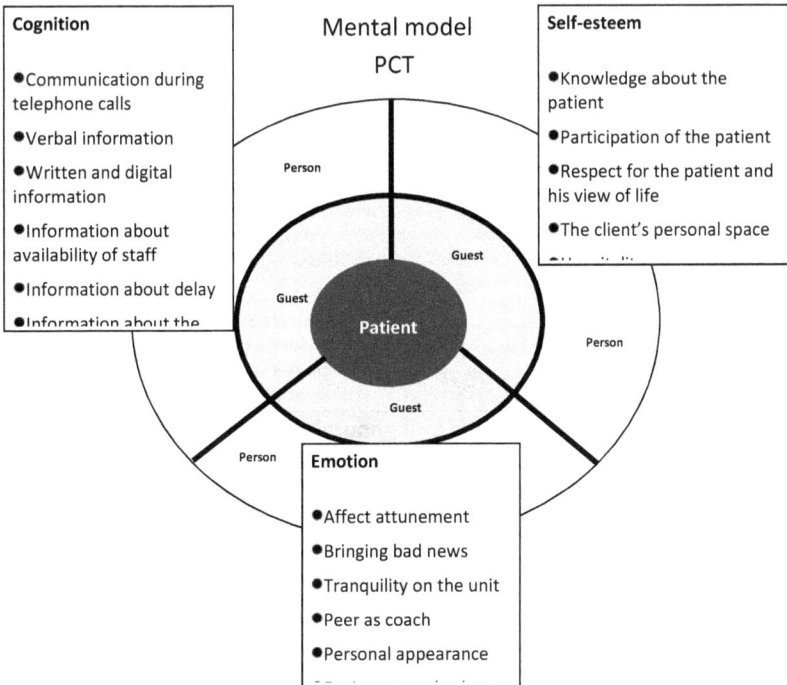

Figure 3: Core categories and subcategories of Patient Centred Treatment

In 2007, with a core group of 15 professionals and another group of 60 leading professionals the core categories and subcategories were developed into 'values' and 'behavioural guide lines' that will be leading in all departments of the hospital.

One of the central values is hospitality. As an example, this value was translated in behavioural guidelines as shown in Figure 4:

	Values	Behavioural guidelines	A few important examples of concrete behaviour
	HOSPITALITY		
1	ACCOMMODATE	I welcome and treat people as my guest	I actively approach people who need directions in the hospital. I try to help the patient and their next of kin, without belittling them. Even if I am busy, I will interrupt my work briefly to make my patient feel that I am 'really' there with him/her. I am creative and receptive to the patient's needs and ensure that his/her expectations are exceeded.

Figure 4: An example of deriving behavioural guidelines from a value

4.3. Training Patient Centred Treatment

The employees who were involved in the development of the general vision, values and behaviour guidelines with regard to patient-centric treatment expressed their interest in engaging a learning process to practice patient-centred treatment. Members of the Research Centre KenVaK, specialized in psychodrama (Welten and Oudijk) and a member of the Research Centre for Autonomy and Participation who is specialized in client centred care (Schoot), developed a training program for the professionals of the Maasland Hospital to explore the values and behavioural guide lines of patient centred treatment (Welten et al, 2008).

A video showing examples of non-patient-centred behaviour was designed to entice employees to reflect on their actions and change. The employees contributed case histories, performed role plays, exchanged their thoughts and opinions, made suggestions for improvements and put these into practice using role plays. By means of role plays, professionals, supported by skilled trainers, coached each other in giving, asking and receiving feedback.

After the training, participants had a better understanding of the patient as a human being and as a guest, his emotions, his views and wishes to keep his dignity intact. The employees were given the opportunity to reflect on themselves in relation to the patient and communicate about 'bad' and 'good' practices of patient centred treatment.

4.4.   Learning activities for action learning

By means of the work-based training program, the corner stone has been laid for an ongoing learning process that is characteristic for the learning organization. There is a close connection between the training program and the following action learning program. Several learning activities precede the training program and other learning activities are follow ups of the training program.

The whole process is characterized by learning cycles. The management board of the Maasland Hospital established a learning circle with representatives from all professional and patient groups of the hospital. Together with the authors, this learning circle reflected on the whole developmental process. During the whole process, the management board formed all sorts of focus groups and plenary sessions that were chaired by the authors in which, in a process of co-creation with the professionals, the development of the core categories and subcategories, values, guidelines and eventually the training program and action learning activities have been designed.

Several examples of action learning activities that have been developed by the authors in cooperation with the learning circle are listed below (Schoenmakers et al, 2007).

- In order to make action in everyday practice discussable, it helps to compile an inventory of good examples and problems of patient centred treatment around a specific theme, for instance 'dealing with privacy'. This could be achieved for instance by organizing activities such as a (digital) survey or 'silent wall' discussion, communicating good news and frustrations, telling stories or writing poems, a 'mirror conservation' where employees listen to what a group of patients has to report, but also discussing contemporary topics during the break, devising metaphors, etc.
- When thinking or reflecting about a theme such as 'hospitality', a particularly helpful tool is to display relevant posters, analyze a protocol, describe patient experiences, create a mindmap, etc.

Organizing intervisions or coaching processes are more formal triggers to think about one's actions.

- Enhancing one's knowledge and understanding of 'patient participation' can be achieved by reading articles, examining a book or surfing the Internet, but above all by asking questions to colleagues and patients or their coach. Considerations and arguments relating to the course of action to pursue can be addressed using a variety of (creative) work methods. A particularly useful and educational activity is to hold a demonstration or presentation about a specific theme and incorporate the patient's reactions into the professional's own opinions. Communicating about the newly acquired information helps to improve the insights of all parties concerned.
- When developing and implementing a new treatment programme, for example 'using the reception desk PC' it is useful to analyze case studies and attempt to schematically represent these in a decision tree or tree diagram, organize feedback in small teams and discuss how the new treatment can be brought to the attention of colleagues. Action learning means that, where possible, patients are actively involved in the design of a new treatment programme.

At the time of this article being submitted, these learning activities were used by all teams of professionals in all departments of the hospital. The motto is that patient centred treatment is applied by everyone: nurses, medical specialists, heads of units, board members, process managers, service employees, etc.

The goal is that professionals of the Maasland Hospital:
- adopt a patient centred approach in ordinary situations
- observe themselves and others if and how they are working patient centred
- are able to acknowledge best practices
- see themselves as a problem owner of patient centred treatment
- in dialogue with patients and colleagues, create ideas on how patient centred care can be anchored in the culture

- continuously actualize their knowledge and skills about patient centred treatment
- find and use codified knowledge to improve their behaviour

5. Conclusion

This article shows that by means of practice based research and action learning, it is possible to support an organization to become a learning organization. Each step in this developmental process is characterized by co-creation between researchers and professionals. This means that the implicit knowledge of professionals and the dialogue to develop together consensus based best practices was central. In this project of patient Centred treatment the designing process itself, the way in which knowledge is created, and the outcomes (the knowledge about patient Centred treatment) both illustrate how a learning organization works.

References

Argyris, C. (1991). Teaching smart people how to learn. Harvard Business Review, May/June, 99-109.

Brockbank, A. (2003). The action learning handbook. Powerful techniques for education, professional development and training. London: Taylor & Francis Books.

Charmaz, K. (2000). Grounded theory: Objectivist and constructivist methods. In: N.K. Denzin & Y.S. Lincoln (Eds.). Handbook of qualitative research. London: Sage Publications. pp. 509-535.

Garvin, D.A. (2003). Learning in action. A guide to putting the learning organization to work. Boston: Harvard Business School Press.

Kemmis, S. & McTaggart, R. (2000). Participatory action research. In: N.K. Denzin & Y.S. Lincoln (Eds.). Handbook of qualitative research. London: Sage Publications. pp. 567-605.

Kolb, D.A. (1984). Experiential learning. Experience as the source of learning and development, Prentice Hall, Englewood-Cliffs.

Krogh, G. van, Ichijo, K. & Nonaka, I. (2000). Enabling knowledge creation. How to unlock the mystery of implicit knowledge and release the power of innovation. Oxford: Oxford University Press.

Lekanne Deprez, F. & Tissen, R. (2002). Zero space. Moving beyond organizational limits. San Francisco: Berrett-Koehler Publishers.

Lincoln, Y. S. & Guba, E. G. (1985). Naturalistic inquiry. Newbury Park: Sage Publications.

Marquardt, M.J. (1999) Action learning in action. Palo Alto: Davies Black Publishing.

Schoenmakers, S., Koolmees, H. & Smeijsters, H. (2007). Action learning ten beho-
eve van patiëntgecentreerde bejegening [Action learning in patient centred
treatment]. Sittard/Heerlen: Orbis Medisch & Zorgconcern / Hogeschool Zuyd.

Schön, D.A. (1983). The reflective practitioner. New York: Basic Books.

Schön, D.A. (1988). Educating the reflective practitioner. San Francisco: Jossey Bass
Publishers.

Schoot, T. (2007). Kwaliteitsindicatoren voor de nieuwe manier van werken [Quality
indicators for the new way of working]. Sittard/Heerlen: Orbis Medisch &
Zorgconcern / Hogeschool Zuyd.

Schwandt, T.A. (2000). Three epistemological stances for qualitative inquiry: Inter-
pretivism, hermeneutics, and social constructionism. In: N.K. Denzin & Y.S. Lincoln (Eds.). Handbook of qualitative research. London: Sage Publications. pp.
189-213.

Senge, P. (1990). The fifth discipline: The art and practice of the learning organization. New York: Double Day.

Smeijsters, H. (2004). De praktijk van leren en creëren bij onderwijsinnovatie [The
practice of learning and creating in educational innovation]. In: Stam, C., Evers,
A., Leenheers, P., Man, A. de, Spek, R. van der (red.). Kennisproductiviteit. Het
effect van investeren in mensen, kennis en leren [Knowledge productivity. The
effect of investing in people, knowledge and learning]. Amsterdam: Pearson
Education. blz. 201-215.

Smeijsters, H., Schoenmakers, S. & Koolmees, H. (2007). Waardenprofiel en
gedragsrichtlijnen patiëntgecentreerde bejegening [Value profile and behavioural guidelines for patient centred treatment]. Sittard/Heerlen: Orbis Medisch
& Zorgconcern / Hogeschool Zuyd.

Smeijsters, H., Schoenmakers, S., Wilbers, M. & Koolmees, H. (2006). Patiëntgecentreerde bejegening binnen het Maaslandziekenhuis [Patient centred treatment
at the Maasland Hospital] . Sittard/Heerlen: Orbis Medisch & Zorgconcern /
Hogeschool Zuyd.

Strauss, A.L., & Corbin, J. (1998). Basics of qualitative research. Techniques and
procedures for developing grounded theory. London: Sage Publications.

Tissen, R., Andriessen, D. & Lekanne Deprez, F. (2000). The knowledge dividend.
Creating high performance companies through value based knowledge management. Financial Times/Prentice Hall.

Verwey, R. (2008). Procesevaluatie invoering EVD in het Maaslandziekenhuis. Een
onderzoek naar de gehanteerde methodiek bij de implementatie van het EVD
[Process implementation of the Electronic Health Record System; research into
implementation methodology]. Sittard/Heerlen: Orbis Medisch & Zorgconcern /
Hogeschool Zuyd.

Practice Based Research and Action Learning in a Learning Organization -
The case: Patient Centred Treatment in a general hospital.

Welten, J., Oudijk, R., Smeijsters, H., Schoot, T., Liem, S.L. & Soons, E. (2008). Train-ingen patiëntgecentreerde bejegening. [Courses patient centred treatment]. Sittard/Heerlen: Orbis Medisch & Zorgconcern / Hogeschool Zuyd.

Wierdsma, A.F.M. & Swieringa, J. (2002). Lerend organiseren. Als meer van het-zelfde niet helpt [Organising as a process of learning. If more of the same does not work]. Groningen: Stenfert Kroese.

Balancing Learning and Efficiency Crossing Practices and Projects in Project-based Organisations. The Case History of "Practice Groups" in a Consulting Firm

Saverino Verteramo and Monica De Carolis
University of Calabria, Rende, Italy

Editorial Commentary

Verteramo & De Carolis address the special issues of KM in project-based organizations through examination of practice groups in an Italian IT consulting firm. By combining communities of practice with project teams in a "Double Knit Organization" (a "DKO") the firm transformed more traditional practice groups into an unusual form of CoP. While the paper is largely silent on methodology, Verteramo & De Carolis tracked the implementation over a 3-year period and report that the project was successful and that the relative stability and typically smaller scale of practice groups contribute to the successful adoption of CoPs.

The paper provides an interesting insight on ways of making CoPs more effective by blending CoP techniques with permanent and project structures within the firm.

Balancing Learning and Efficiency Crossing Practices and Projects in Project-based Organisation.

Abstract: Project-based organizations have received increasing attention in recent years as an emerging organizational form to integrate diverse and specialized intellectual resources and expertise. A typical problem of these structures is the difficulty in sharing knowledge in and across projects. Besides, project teams are temporary and therefore much learning may be lost when they disband. Very often the storage of lessons learned is not effective; the databases are not widely used and the people are too engaged in their projects to share knowledge or help other people cope with similar problems. The inherent contradiction between organizing for meeting short-term, project task objectives, and the longer-term developmental nature of organizational learning processes asks for innovative organizational solutions. How can a project-based organization be simultaneously oriented to project-outputs and learning?

The processes of knowledge capture, transfer and learning in project settings rely heavily upon social patterns and processes. This situation emphasizes the value of considering a community-based approach to managing knowledge. Several authors suggest adding a new "dimension" (a "home" for learning, integration and development of specialized/technical competencies) following a "Crossing-approach" that leads to design organizational solutions in which project teams (focused on their strengths: outputs, processes or market segments) and learning groups, like CoPs, coexist.

The aim of the paper is to investigate the critical points in designing and implementing these innovative organizational solutions (e.g. group design, reward system, participation modes, support mechanisms, formalization degree) that are difficult to manage and little investigated in the literature.

We conducted an in depth case study research of an Italian IT Consulting firm: VP Tech. This analyzed firm introduced a particular kind of CoPs called "Practice Groups" (PGs) in a typical project-based organizational structure. The Practices are knowledge domains (expertises) transversal to the projects or market areas. VP senior executives chose the main strategic practices to be developed and decided to aggregate the main internal experts (PGs) around these knowledge domains. The goals of PGs are to strengthen and diffuse the knowledge developed during previous projects, to monitor the state of the art, and to support professional training and problem solving for people involved in the projects. In VP Tech, PGs represent a:

- network in which specifically useful information can be found;
- learning locus in which professional competencies can be improved;

- social network in which both knowledge exploitation and exploration take place.
- The conducted case study shows:
- the different phases and "crisis" in implementing this organizational solution;
- the specific and innovative mix between formal and informal organizational levers adopted;
- the circular and virtuous relation between projects and practices.

Keywords: Project-based organization, Communities of Practice, knowledge sharing, groups design

1. The issue of Knowledge Management in Project-based Organizations

According to Newell et al. (2006), there are several and "dichotomous" views of knowledge and Knowledge Management (KM).

Following the perspective defined "knowledge as possession", knowledge can be made explicit and shared among persons and groups. Examples of codified knowledge can be "artifacts" such as intranets, documents, databases, manuals, guidelines and reports. Critics of this view instead emphasize that knowledge is situated in social and organizational practice and relationships. Knowledge (or rather knowing) is not so much possessed as social and embedded in practice (Lave and Wenger, 1991). According to Brown and Duguid (2001), it is the shared know-how (that develops from shared experience within communities or networks of practice) that enables the sharing and circulating of explicit knowledge.

In a similar way, Swan et al. (1999) distinguish between cognitive and community approaches to KM. According the cognitive view, knowledge is referable to objectively defined concepts. On the other hand, the Community view sees knowledge as embedded and constructed in social networks and groups. Rather than study knowledge as something that people have, as an object that could be generated, codified and transferred, this approach focuses on the process of knowing regarded as something that people do (Bellini and Canonico, 2008).

At a strategic level, Hansen et al. (1999) describe KM strategy as *"codification"* and *"personalization"*. "Codification" focuses on making knowledge explicit and spreading information. In contrast *"personalization"* is based on the concept of network within people can learn though dialogue (Hansen et al., 1999). Personalization approaches require space and time to enable the "getting together" of people to develop interpersonal networks.

At the level of KM Systems, Alavi (2000) distinguishes between "repository" and "network" approaches. The former is based on building and implementing knowledge repositories and retrieval technologies. In the second approach, technology is used to connect people and to identify the location of different kinds of competencies.

The previous introduced *"dichotomies"* can be compatible rather than mutually exclusive.
This is a theoretical key point for the project-based organization that:

- generally has the tendency to follow the "Knowledge as possession" view and the "codification" approach. At the level of the project, much more often the "product knowledge" ("what" was done) rather than the "process knowledge" ("how and why" it was done) is captured. The community model or personalization strategy of KM can support the solution of these problems;
- has to face the inherent contradiction between organizing meeting short-term, project task objectives and the longer-term developmental nature of organizational learning processes (i.e. Bresnen et al., 2004).

The following are the main problems of managing knowledge and improving learning processes in project-based organization (Keegan et al., 2001):

- lack of time and reflection at the level of the project team. The project-time pressures can inhibit learning processes. Besides project teams are temporary and therefore much learning may be lost when they disband (tendency to "reinvent the wheel", rather than learning from the experiences of previous projects);

- the trade-off between centralized vs decentralized approaches in knowledge creation, validation and dissemination processes. There is, in fact, the tendency to centralize learning (senior managers or specialized departments collect and validate the "lessons learned" elaborated by the team members) and to defer learning to future points in time (significant time passes among the identification of the possible improvements, their explicitation, their dissemination to the organization, the effective emergence of a similar problem, the idea of someone to reuse this knowledge);
- the reduced interactions with colleagues with similar competencies to exploit specialized knowledge domains. Besides, people are too engaged in their projects to share knowledge or help other people cope with similar problems.

These problems are manifested in attempts to reduce the learning of project teams to simple summaries and poorly maintained databases that few people have the time to use. From an ICT point of view the main challenge is to design KMS that make knowledge re-use in and across projects easier. From an organizational point of view the problems of managing connections among people with the same area of expertise and people with different area of expertise (generally collected around a project) are crucial (Migliarese and Verteramo, 2005).

According to McDermott (1999), this goal can be gained by adding a new "dimension" related to Communities of Practice (CoP) to the project-based organization. In the "Double-Knit Organizations" (DKO) Project Teams (focused on outputs) and CoPs (focused on learning) coexist.

The aim of the paper is to investigate the critical points (from both a theoretical point of view and by an in-depth empirical case study) in designing these innovative organizational solutions (e.g. group design, support mechanisms, formalization degree) that are difficult to manage and little investigated in the literature.

The paper has the following structure: in section 2 and 3 we underline the potential effectiveness of organizational solutions based on the crossing-approach and we present the open questions in regards to their design and management. In Section 4 we describe the analyzed case study (VP Tech) and the methodological approach used. The case study shows how a successful Italian consulting firm has crossed practices and projects (that is learning and efficiency). This organizational solution is considered a critical success factor. In the last section we draw the conclusion of the empirical research and the related lessons learned.

2. Crossing CoPs and Project Teams: an Organizational solution for improving KM in Project-Based Organization

Organizations are increasingly using project teams to accomplish specific tasks and to increase flexibility (Newell et al., 2006).

Depending on size and complexity, projects can be organized differently (Meredith and Mantel, 1995). A project, for instance, may be accommodated in a pure project organization, a self-contained section that is devoted exclusively to the project and will be disbanded when the project is completed.

This solution can show some limits. In particular, a pure project organizational structure can "lose" knowledge and learning opportunities: there is no "repository" or defined sub-structure aimed at collecting and developing functional and specialized knowledge. When team's members lose touch with their peers, they can have trouble keeping up with developments in their field (McDermott, 1999).

In addition to this, knowledge related to project output is captured, but there are several difficulties in acquiring knowledge related to process (how the project has been conducted and the knowledge generated during the project).

In this sense projects and project organizations require exceptionally efficient knowledge management, if they want to learn from their experiences (Kasvi et al., 2003).

A first solution to support learning processes and knowledge management is to enlarge existing specific jobs by knowledge related tasks (generally in the HRM function or Information System area) or to design new *ad hoc* roles. A second solution is to adopt two formal axes: projects and the functions (matrix organization). In both cases:

- there is the problem in balancing the formal power of the new or enlarged roles or functional departments with the formal power of project managers;
- the potentialities of informal professional social network are ignored along with the social dynamics that can be developed and turn out useful for competitive and strategic goals.

In this framework, the DKO (McDermott, 1999) that links project teams with CoPs seems to be an innovative organizational solution.

Communities of Practice have been described as a "privileged locus" for learning, creation and transferring knowledge – internally as well as externally – outside traditionally known organizational networks. The focus of the research about CoPs has moved, over time, from the study of small groups and of the learning processes which take place within them, to other subjects: organizational aspects (e.g. organizational mechanisms and managerial systems to support CoPs) and the innovative potential of CoPs (with special reference to the role of ICTs) (De Carolis and Corvello, 2006). The common element of these three subjects is the view of CoP as (1) a collection of people that engage in activities that encompass a common interest and ongoing learning through practice (a CoP is bound together by shared interest in a knowledge domain) and (2) a self-organizing system based on two elements: practice and identity (Lave and Wenger, 1991).

Members share interests, specific competencies, routines, formal and informal rules (Garrety et al., 2004). Generally, purpose and goals are formed around knowledge needs, are hazy (CoPs rarely have a specific result to deliver to the organization), and are medium-term.

Although they are typically self-organizing, CoPs benefit from organizational supports. They need "intentional" cultivation (Wenger et al., 2002), and people should have time and encouragement to participate. Managing a community means making and developing connections between members. Some coordination is needed. The community coordinator helps the community to focus on the knowledge domain, maintain relationships and develop its practice; he acts as a "contact maker" (Ruuska et al., 2005).

Even if size and membership are less defined and more dynamic if compared to project team, the community social structure represents a "home" for professional identity of members.

It is a social network which allows members to interact regularly with a selected professional environment and to learn through the dialogues, and, in case of geographically dispersed workers, without the support of a shared physical work space. In this sense, ICT systems play a relevant role to support distance interactions and discussions, norms and ground rules.

CoPs, operating within a project-based organization, allow for concentration of expertise (Garrety et al, 2004). They have flexible boundaries, no reporting relationships and are essentially self-managed and self-organizing. These are the main differences with the traditional "functions" in the matrix organization. In the same way as "functions", they represent a form of integration and development of specialized/technical competencies. In an original way they exploit the potentialities of informal professional social networks and are often the preferred way members can get feedback from knowledgeable peers.

Combining project teams and CoPs seems to be an effective way to make an organization simultaneously oriented to output and learning.

3. The open questions in crossing CoPs and Project Teams

From a theoretical point of view, the crossing-approach seem to be an effective solution for supporting knowledge and learning processes in a project-based organization.

How to implement this approach from a practical point of view seems less clear. This paper goes more deeply into emerging theoretical and practical issues in designing and managing a DKO, where CoPs and Project Teams are crossed. For example, it is difficult to balance the emergent and informal nature of CoPs with the managerial necessity for design and control. This problem can be related to the literature about "intentional cultivation" of CoPs, that is, their intentional promotion and support, and to the literature on groups design and effectiveness (Gladstein, 1984; Hackman, 1987). In order to identify the main open questions in implementing a DKO and considering CoPs as units of analysis, we have connected the two literature streams and identified the main design variables and factors that affect the effectiveness of CoPs. Moreover we have divided these elements in three classes:

- input variables: what organization "gives" to group;
- processes: how this group operates;
- output: what group gives to organization.

For each of the classes we have identified the following main open questions (summarized in table 1).

Table 1: Organizational variables and factors that affect the effectiveness of CoPs

Input (what organization "gives" to group)	Process (how this group operates)	Output (what group gives to organization)
Structure design: size, membership, competences needed, roles, hierarchy Design and formalization degree of tasks Resources: time, work space (physical or virtual) and financial resources HRM mechanisms	Coordination systems used Emerging roles Communication systems adopted Group culture Identity degree	Contribution to: Strategic goals – medium term Operational goals – short term

3.1. Input variable.

The main variables that organization can define to design and support CoPs are:

- Structure design: size, membership, competences needed, roles, hierarchy;
- Design and formalization degree of tasks;
- Resources: time devoted to group activities, work space (physical or virtual) and financial resources;

Balancing Learning and Efficiency Crossing Practices and Projects in Project-based Organisation.

- HRM mechanisms (in particular evaluation system, reward system, career development).

The "emergent" nature of CoPs and how to manage them is the first open question. Liedtka (1999) rejects the top-down approaches and the related traditional formal control systems. They would be inconsistent to the informal and voluntary dynamics that support knowledge sharing processes. Wenger et al. (2002) have a more barycentric position. They underline the possibility (1) to turn to informal control systems and a management that support the "natural" interactions performing a passive and external role (absence of interferences) or, on the other hand, (2) to turn to a strong sponsorship and to support the birth of what would arise spontaneously (identity as community member and natural knowledge flows). In this framework, it could be very useful to use planned meetings, social events, learning projects and/or the design of specific roles to carry out the knowledge management project. Scholars (McDermott 1999; Wenger et al., 2002) underline that it is possible to create "intentional" CoPs: these are intentional in their focus, start-up activities and support but, in order to develop the trust, connection and knowledge sharing it is necessary to support the natural process of Community development rather than impose an artificial one.

In all cases, the management should make explicit/visible the practices and single out the Communities.

This means to partially define the main tasks of CoPs and to give time and suitable spaces (physical or virtual) to employees in order to encourage and support trust based relationships and knowledge processes. Even when team members intend to share insight and information with other teams, team goals often pull so strongly on people's time that they simply cannot find the time to do it. CoPs inevitably compete with teams for people's time (McDermott, 1999).

The technological systems to support the remote interactions are different (synchronous communication systems, resource sharing systems, group processes support systems) and can have more or less effective results depending their real use in the community.

The level of involvement and the time spent in community activities should have an "organizational value", in terms of evaluation and reward systems and carrier plans. Deci and Ryan (1985), however, argue that extrinsic rewards (e.g. monetary rewards, tangible gifts) will have a negative impact on intrinsic motivation and hence performance. Another open question is, therefore, if and how to reward.

The main problems are (1) to balance formal organizational needs (control and supervision) and the natural organization of practice (knowledge developing processes) and (2) to give the adequate degree of organizational support. It seems to crop up the critical balance between formal and informal structure (Crozier and Friedberg, 1978). The level of organizational support is critical in two ways: on one hand Communities require recognition and support, but on the other hand, voluntary and informal aspects may lose their value if there is too much interference.

3.2.   Processes

To describe the real life of CoPs (how CoPs evolve, emerging dynamics etc.), we can observe the following elements:

- Coordination systems used (i.e. rules, planes, procedures, meetings);
- Emerging roles (coordinators, leaders);
- Communication systems adopted (face to face and/or virtual);
- Group culture (competitive/collaborative);
- Identity degree (awareness to be a member and level of real involvement).

It is a shared opinion that groups aimed at managing knowledge are self-organized and that members choose time and modalities of participation in the group life, respecting the boundaries outlined by formal design. Several studies show that sometimes it is ineffective (or counterproductive) to define, for example, roles and coordination systems that members of CoPs only partially accept or use. More often in CoPs some role is emergent (e.g.

leader, coordinator) and, in time, tacit and social behavior rules are established (e.g. when and who to contact, tools used). A first risk is that the management designs formal roles super-abounded or inconsistent with the modalities spontaneously activated by the members of a CoP. More generally, organizations have to refine their ability to perceive "organizational noise" (Ciborra et al, 1984) that is the low signals about the real dynamics among members. It could be necessary to identify the emerging roles, rules and systems adopted: sometimes it is better to "follow the crowd" rather than to persist in *ex-ante* designed solutions.

Typically CoP is a fragile structure that can quickly disappear when conflicts and disengagement undermine the mutual trust. These pathologies can depend both on contingent problems among members and on collaborative/competitive culture. It could be necessary (1) to pay attention to low signals of conflicts (2) to develop adequate conflict resolution mechanisms and (3) to promote a collaborative culture.

3.3. Output
We can value the contributions of CoPs to the organization in terms of:
- strategic goals –medium term (learning path, development of core competencies, innovation processes);
- operational goals – short term (training systems and solution of daily working problems).

When the activities/problems are ambiguous and not well defined it is difficult to define output levels, to plan activities and to define effective management control and evaluation systems. Moreover, an overly structured formal control and evaluation system can be seen as an "intrusion" and, therefore, negatively affect knowledge dynamics that are at the basis of CoPs.

CoPs are created in order to face poorly defined problems of learning and knowledge creation and sharing, where classic organizational forms can be weak.

In these situations, it seems to be more effective to value "contributions" of CoPs to solve new, contingent and unexpected strategic matters or operational problems, rather than to strive to design an effective *ex-ante* set of control variables. A CoP works well (it is vital) if it is effective in "case of emergency".

4. The Case history of VP Tech

4.1. Methodological approach

This paper has been developed within a FIRB research project regarding the role of KM for the competitive advantage of SME, started in 2005 in Italy and involving several important Italian Universities. Following the case-study methodology of research (Yin, 1994) the empirical work has been conducted during the last three years: three sessions of in-depth interviews have been conducted with VP Tech top management, some "Practice Group" (PG) leaders and members of PGs. Document acquisition was also carried out (Table 2).

Table 2: Plan of the conducted interviews

Number of inter-views	Phase	Timing
2x3	Organizational Analysis and study of the KM solutions adopted	2006
1x4	Analysis of Practice Group dynamics	2007
2x2	PGs effectiveness analysis	2008

The interviews, concerning the same key-points, were aimed at analysing the organizational and technological solutions adopted for KM, with particular reference to the PG's dynamics (questions about creation and development, emergent problems, reward systems effectiveness, communications tools used etc.) and their contribution to organizational performance. The findings of this analysis have been read and confirmed by the informants themselves.

4.2. IT security: the core business of VP Tech

VP Tech, established in Cosenza (South of Italy) at the beginning of 2001, operates in the IT consultancy sector. Its principal activities relate to the planning and integrated management of all that concerns IT security. VP Tech is a global partner for IT security, covering both the consultancy aspects of security organization and strategy and the realization and integration of technologies for the supply of turnkey solutions.

In the Table 3 the basic facts are given.

Table 3 – Basic information on VP Tech

Objective	To offer the market a group of Security services capable of combining the consultancy, technological and economic aspects in order to create value for its clients
Sectors catered for	Telecommunications, manufacturing, health and public administration, and presence in the financial market
Clients	Telecom Italia and TIM (telecommunications), San Paolo IMI and Intesa Sistemi e Servizi, Unicredito, Capitalia (financial institutions), Regione Lombardia – Progetto SISS (public administration), Pirelli (manufacturing)
Certifications	Certified in accordance with ISO 9001:2000 since 2003
Staff	Approximately 200 professionals distributed across the offices of Cosenza, Milan and Rome
Turnover	Approximately €20m (year 2006); €24m (year 2007); 28,5 €m (year 2008).
Market Share	Approximately 10% in "Italian Information Security Services" (2007 IDC data). It was 5% in 2003.
Principal collaborations	Close relations with universities and R&D centres and technological organizations at national and international level and access to European funding

Currently, VP Tech has a staff of 200 professionals distributed across the offices of Cosenza, Milan and Rome and a turnover principally deriving from the realization of projects for medium-large firms. Its turnover of €24m (2007) represents the 10% of the Italian market in IT security services (2007 ICD Data).

In this sector (ICT Security) the ability to innovate is a critical success factor. In fact technological development represents a driver for new forms of business in markets such as banking, telecommunications, health and public administration. These new forms of business (ICT based) require new ICT Security policies, both at the strategic and operational level.
VP Tech top management thinks that an effective knowledge management policy has a central role, both at the strategic level (support of innovation) and at the operational level (efficiency in projects and in solving customers problems). The rapid dimensional growth of the firm increased this need

(from 20 practitioners in 2002 to 200 in 2008). VP Tech in fact works by projects and it deals with the typical problems of project-based organizations. To face these problems, the VP Tech KM solution currently uses:

- technological levers based on a centralized information management system. This system collects the lessons learned and the contributions of the individuals. Access is managed via multiple levels differentiated by role;
- organizational levers based on the introduction of the Practice Groups (PG) in the organizational structure: this configuration (acknowledged by top management as a critical success factor) can be seen as a particular form of DKO.

4.3. Supporting KM in VP Tech: the introduction of Practice Groups

The design and implementation of a KM solution based on a centralized Information Management System was not a problem for an IT consulting firm used to producing and managing project documentation. Nevertheless, VP senior executives were conscious of the intrinsic limits of these solutions used to support learning and innovation. The main idea in VP has been to support the creation of groups specialized on topics relevant for the firm from a strategic point of view, where typical learning processes and dynamics of CoP develop.

To this end, VP senior executives decided to select the "practices", that is the main strategic expertise of the firms to be strengthened. Practices are topics transversal to the projects or market area: currently there are five workgroups (the Practice Groups, PG) covering different topics (three of them are explained in table 4).

The goals of these PGs are to consolidate and diffuse the knowledge developed during previous projects, to monitor the state of the art and to support the problem solving of people involved in the projects.

Each employee can join a practice, depending on his competencies or will to grow professionally. PG activities are mainly voluntary and they are developed as extra-time during the work within the projects.

Table 4– The Practice Groups in VP Tech (2008)

Practice Group	Focus	Members
Identity & User Management	Methodologies and Tools for IT users authentication and permission management.	40
Data privacy	Regulations and standards analysis, policy and procedures definition for secure personal data management.	15
Business Continuity	Methodologies and Tools for business continuity and for adverse events impact reduction.	15
Web application Security	Methodologies and Tools for IT security improvement in web-based applications.	15
Project Management	Methodologies and Tools for efficiency and efficacy improvement in project management.	15

People in PGs meet both physically (workshops, training courses) and virtually by means of forums, newsletters, and other collaborative ICT tools supporting dispersed workers (VP has three distinct offices and people often work at the customers).

The nature of practice groups has been partially modified during recent years following an interesting learning path.

At the beginning, these activities were absolutely informal and deliberately self-determined by the PG members: a practice leader was chosen by top management among the acknowledged experts in the practice theme, but its coordination role was soft and informal. Nevertheless, very soon this voluntary approach was not enough, due to the limited time people can spend. VP executives decided to make the PG activities more visible and formalized. Therefore, a few years later they decided to enlarge and enrich the tasks of PGs.

In particular, it was decided:
- to design a "coordination team" supporting the practice leader: owing to the high level of their competences, practice leaders are

nearly always busy and, so, they can spend little time in PG activities;

- to assign some formal tasks to the "PG coordination team" (for example they help the Human Resource Manager in evaluating the personal plan of technical training proposed by the employees, in supporting the professional entry in the organization, in organizing internal courses, or external learning experiences, and they can manage a training budget);
- to reward the efforts and the results reached by the coordination team, also linked to overall performance of the firm.

4.4.   The crossing-approach in VP Tech

The organizational structure in VP Tech can be considered as a form of "Double-Knit" Organization (McDermott,1999): the project-based structure has been enriched by the introduction of the internal Practice Groups. From an organizational point of view PGs are discontinuous (due to the periodicity of the work), permanent (due to the composition of the people involved) and homogeneous (due to the shared competencies of the members) groups of experts, specialized by themes and lines of service. The initial idea was to stimulate the creation of internal CoPs supporting learning and innovation. Nevertheless the real implementation has transformed the nature of PGs into something partially different from typical CoPs.

Using the schema proposed in section 3, we can describe the organizational variables and factors characterizing the implementation of PG.

4.4.1. Input

We can observe a medium level of formalization for each variable: the boundaries of the PG are defined by the top management: each member since the engagement is assigned to a specific PG, even if during his carrier, the employee can choose to become a member of other PG. The top management has chosen to limit the size of PG. At the same time each PG is composed by members working on different projects (market areas) and different offices. This heterogeneous membership enables the enrichment of the problem solving processes thanks to the multiple points of view around the PG topics.

New roles (the "practice leaders") aimed to coordinate the PG activities have been introduced. During the time the coordination has been reinforced with the "coordination team", previously described. It is important to underline that a new hierarchical relationship has not been introduced. The VP structure is not a matrix, but a project-based organization integrated by transversal groups with knowledge related tasks. These tasks are established by top-management and range from operational support in training activities to exploration of new business opportunities. The PG coordination team has a budget at its disposal to carry out its activities (150.000 Euros in 2007). With regard to HRM mechanisms, the evaluation system includes the assessment of the level and the quality of participation in PG and extrinsic rewards are provided.

Recently the company portal has been enriched with tools like discussion forum, blog and so on. Each PG has now a dedicated and organized virtual space that supports the knowledge flows. A large editorial-committee (the practice leaders are members too) manage the contents and participation levels are high.

4.4.2. Processes
The PGs processes are self-determined in terms of modalities of participation, communications systems used, and emerging roles. The management has adopted a medium formalization degree of the input variables (structure, tasks, etc) and several mechanisms to support PGs (reward systems, ICT tools, financial resources etc). At the same time VP tries to respect the informal and voluntary nature of these groups and it avoids affecting group processes.

The VP Tech management has demonstrated the capacity to be able "to perceive low signals". For example, the practice leaders are primarily chosen starting from their technical competencies, but due to the voluntary nature of activities their charisma and relational abilities are carefully considered in order to make the involvement of people easier.

Modalities of participation and activities are various and different among the PGs, but typically people feel free to propose new themes and to point out interesting news. Looking at the practices each employee has a map of what are the most valuable areas of interest, who and where are the experts, and how it is possible to contact them to ask for help in daily work or to improve their own competences. In the ICT sector the innovation rate is high, and the technical competences risk to be "perishable": the active participation in the practice group life is perceived as an opportunity to keep itself abreast of the technical developments rather than a top-down additional task.

4.4.3. Output
Over time PGs and their activities have taken on a central role for the firm's overall competitiveness. Virtuous dynamics have been produced: people actively and freely are participating in PG life, offering personal availability, and pointing out news useful for the community.

PGs have been able to both support the operational exigencies (in daily problem solving and in training needs) and to prove proactive and creative in exploring new technical solutions or business ideas. One of the most interesting results is that some order has been born from the new ideas that have emerged during the discussions inside the practice activities. In these cases VP, on its own initiative, has been able to propose solutions for emerging problems, anticipating client's requests.

PGs are seen as a strong element of identity both at the company and professional level. Practice leaders are often acknowledged as experts in their field outside the firm: they actively give some contribution in professional meetings, public conferences and professional or academic journals. Several common research projects are conducted with important Italian universities and research centers. In doing so, VP Tech is able to monitor the external state of the art and to strengthen its internal knowledge.

More generally, VP Tech considers PGs as their own way towards innovation and development of core competencies.

It is possible to state that PGs contribute:
- to the development of market insight capability: PGs represent the place in which to point out and to discuss innovation possibilities; this is a widespread and bottom-up process;

- to the evaluation of the gap between one's own competencies and the competitive needs. When a new competence has to be explored, a new practice group (or a sub-group) can be created by the top-level;
- to the acquisition of new technical competencies. The PGs manage the training programs in their own knowledge domain;
- to the development of the problem solving capabilities. Thanks to PGs it is possible to know "who knows what" (Cohen and Levinthal, 1990), where to search for information about how past and similar problems have been solved (best practice). All this following a faster process than into the past.

Through the Practice Groups in VP Tech a circular relation between projects and practices has been developed: the projects nourish the practices and vice versa. In the projects people acquire competencies, improving the practices through knowledge store and sharing (exploitation). In the practices new ideas are recognized and technical innovations are able to generate new projects (exploration).

5. Lessons learned and conclusions

Crossing Project Teams and CoPs (Double-Knit Organization, McDermott 1999) seems to be an effective way to make an organization simultaneously oriented to output and learning.

Referring both to group design literature and CoPs intentional cultivation literature, this paper analyzes the main open questions in implementing a DKO. We have identified three classes of variables/factors that affect CoPs effectiveness and are crucial in implementing DKO (see Table 1).

Following this scheme of analysis we have conducted an in depth case study in a successful Italian IT consulting firm. The introduction of PGs has transformed this project-based organization into a DKO. VP Tech executives acknowledge PGs as a critical key success factor. We have followed the implementation process during 3 years and we have analyzed the emerging problems and the adopted solutions. Referring to the proposed scheme, the implementing choices (previously described) have been the following:

- a medium level of formalization in input (what organization gives to PGs);
- self-determined group processes (how PGs work);
- operational and strategic contributions (what PGs give to organization).

Over time the PGs have became something partially different from traditional CoPs. These differences are summarized in table 5.

Table 5 - PGs compared to CoPs

Characteristics	CoPs	PGs
Support/design	Emerging from interactions. It be internal or inter-organizatio It can be identified and suppor (intentional cultivation)	Internal groups Medium level of formalization Hi level of support
Goals	Less defined, generic, longer term goals formed around kno edge needs	Strategic and operational goals (exploitation and exploration pro esses)
Size (numbers of members)	Not well defined	Small groups
Membership	Less stable, partially defined b top-management	Stable and partially defined by to management (in starting steps)

The choice to assign operational tasks (in addition to strategic medium term goals) stimulates the community to interact frequently and on actual problems, therefore, PG is constantly active. The groups' small size and their heterogeneous membership have been a relevant design solution. In small groups, the community dynamics (collaboration, control of disengagement, problem solving processes) are more simple and effective. Heterogeneous membership (members work on different projects and in different sites) supports knowledge sharing processes among projects. At the same time small groups make the design formal systems to evaluate groups' effectiveness less necessary.

PGs are considered effective if they are able to work well in "case of emergency" and if they are proactive in developing and exploring knowledge.

Therefore, this paper shows how:

- crossing "learning locus" and Project Teams can be an innovative solution in order to solve some typical problem of KM in project-based organizations;
- CoPs are an effective learning locus in project settings. Communities support knowledge exploration and exploitation processes from, across and between projects. They are a network in which specifically useful information can be found, in which professional competencies can be improved and a home for professional identity;
- CoPs need to be "cultivated": design efforts and various supports to CoPs are necessary particularly in the starting phases in order to comprehend the dynamics and to introduce some correction. The case study shows that the organizational top-down initiatives can partially change the informal nature of CoPs. PGs are, in fact, more structured, stable and formalized than traditional CoPs;
- PGs are an effective organizational solution for managing knowledge in project based organizations: the projects nourish the practices and vice versa. In the projects people acquire competencies, improving the practices through knowledge storage and sharing. In the practices new ideas and technical innovations able to generate new projects are recognized.

References

Alavi, M. (2000) "Managing organizational knowledge" in R. Zmud (ed.), *Framing the domains of IT management: Projecting the future through the past*, Cincinnati Ohio: Pinnaflex Educational Resources.

Bellini, E. and Canonico, P. (2008) "Knowing Communities in Project Driven Organizations: Analysing the Strategic Impact of Socially Constructed HRM Practices", *International Journal of Project Management* No.26, pp. 44–50.

Bresnen, M., Goussevskaia, A. and Swan, J. (2004) "Embedding new management knowledge in project-based organizations", *Organization Studies*, Vol. 25, No. 9, pp. 1535-1555.

Brown, J. and Duguid, P. (2001) "Knowledge and Organization: A Social-Practice Perspective" *Organization Science*, Vol. 12, No. 2, March-April, pp. 198-213.

Ciborra, C., Migliarese, P. and Romano, P. (1984) "A methodological inquiry of Organizational Noise in Socio-technical Systems", *Human Relations*, Vol. 37, No. 8.

Cohen, W.M. and Levinthal, D.A. (1990) "Absorptive capacity: a new perspective on learning and innovation", *Administrative Science Quarterly*, Vol. 35, No. 1, pp. 128-152.

Crozier, M. and Friedberg, E. (1978), *Actors and Systems*, University of Chicago Press, Chicago, IL.

De Carolis, M. and Corvello, V. (2006) "Multiple competences in distributed Communities of Practice: the case of a Community of financial advisors" in Fehér P. (eds) Proceedings of 7th *European Conference on Knowledge Management (ECKM)*, Budapest, Hungary, 4-5 September 2006 pp.116-125.

Deci, E. L. and Ryan, R. M. (1985). *Intrinsic motivation and self-determination in human behavior*. New York: Plenum.

Garrety, K., Robertson, P.L. and Badham, R. (2004) "Integrating Communities of Practice in Technology Development Projects", *International Journal of Project Management*, Vol. 22, No. 5, pp. 351-358.

Gladstein, D. L. (1984) "Groups in context: a model of task group effectiveness" *Administrative Science Quarterly*, No. 29, pp. 499-517.

Hackman, J.R. (1987) The design of work teams. In J. Lorsch (Ed.). *Handbook of organizational behavior*. Englewood Cliffs, NJ: Prentice-Hall, pp. 315-342.

Hansen, M.T., Nohria N. and Tierney T. (1999), "What's your strategy for knowledge management?", *Harvard Business Review*, Vol. 77, No 2, pp 106-116.

Kasvi, J.J.J., Vartiainen, M. and Hailikari, M. (2003) Managing knowledge and knowledge competences in projects and project organisations. *International Journal Project Management*. Vol. 21, No. 8, pp. 571–582.

Keegan, A. and Turner, J.R. (2001) "Quantity versus Quality in Project-Based Learning Practices" *Management Learning*, Vol. 32, No. 1, pp. 77-98

Lave, J. and Wenger, E. (1991) *Situated Learning: Legitimate Peripheral Participation*, Cambridge University Press.

Liedtka, J. (1999) "Linking competitive advantage with communities of practice" *Journal of Management Inquiry*, Vol. 8, No. 1, pp. 5-16.

McDermott, R. (1999) "Learning across teams: how to build communities of practice in team organizations", *Knowledge Management Journal*, No.8, May-June.

Meredith, J.R. and Mantel, S.J. (1995) *Project management–a managerial approach*. New York: John Wiley & Sons.

Balancing Learning and Efficiency Crossing Practices and Projects in Project-based Organisation.

Migliarese, P. and Verteramo, S. (2005) "Knowledge Creation and Sharing in a Project Team: An Organizational Analysis Based on the Concept of Organizational Relation", *Electronic Journal of Knowledge Management*, Vol. 3, No. 2, pp. 97 - 106

Newell, S., Bresnen, M., Edelman, L., Scabrough, H. and Swan, J. (2006), "Sharing Knowledge Across Project", *Management Learning,* Vol. 37, No. 2, pp. 167-185.

Swan, J.A., Newell, S., Scarbrough, H. and Hislop D. (1999) "Knowledge management and innovation: networks and networking" *Journal of Knowledge Management*; No. 3, pp. 262–75.

Wenger. E., McDermott R. and Snyder, W. (2002) *Cultivating Communities of Practice*, Harvard Business School Press, Cambridge, Mass.

Yin, R.K. (1994) *"Case study Research: Design and Methods"*, Thousands Oacks, CA, SAGE.

www.ingramcontent.com/pod-product-compliance
Lightning Source LLC
Chambersburg PA
CBHW061200220326
41599CB00025B/4554